PURPLE HOMICIDE

On the rise and rise of Neil Hamilton, one-time Minister for Corporate Probity:
'The higher the monkey climbs the tree, the more you can see its bottom'
Zairean proverb

On the terrors of Tatton:
'Bosnia was surely easier than this. Driving down the hill into Macclesfield with Nigel
Bateson, my cameraman there…we conclude it is much like driving down the Mount Igman
road into Sarajevo under fire. Much the same gradient but different dangers'
Martin Bell

On the BBC outside broadcast van erecting its aeriel in front of the Old Rectory, Nether Alderly:
'Get that bloody great penis away from my hedge.'
Christine Hamilton

On the 'homicidal purple' of Christine Hamilton's trousers:
'The idiot journalist from the OBSERVER…called them purple…
they're Thatcher blue. Anyone but an idiot knows that.'
Christine Hamilton, who made no objection to the word 'homicidal'

PURPLE HOMICIDE:
Fear and Loathing on Knutsford Heath

A pantomime by
John Sweeney

Foreword by David Soul
Illustrations by Martin Rowson
Research by Kate Edgley

BLOOMSBURY

To Molly

First published in Great Britain 1997
Bloomsbury Publishing Plc, 38 Soho Square, London W1V 5DF

Text copyright © 1997 by John Sweeney
Illustrations copyright © 1997 by Martin Rowson

The moral right of the author has been asserted

A CIP catalogue record for this book is available from the British Library

ISBN 0 7475 3775 5

10 9 8 7 6 5 4 3 2 1

Typeset by Hewer Text Composition Services, Edinburgh
Printed in Great Britain by Clays Ltd, St Ives Plc

CONTENTS

FOREWORD
by David Soul

I've always considered the relationship between playwright and actor to be mysteriously symbiotic; the writer contributing theme, dialogue and structure and the actor breathing life and personality into the written word. And so I was delighted when John Sweeney asked me to contribute the foreword to the published version of his new play (albeit a pantomime).

But, as you will discover when you relive it, the Tatton campaign of 1997 and the characters who drive the action combine to create something so surreal as to make ridiculous the notion that an American actor and former pop star, celebrity and ex-TV cop could contribute anything more than perhaps the purchase price of the book. And yet, I was there, with John Sweeney (or 'Starsky' as he likes to be called) to participate in one of the strangest – and yet most rewarding – moments of my adult life.

You see, neither Sweeney, the journalist who has 'seen it all', nor myself, the actor who's spent thirty years working in a virtual world of commercial television, could possibly have imagined or fictionalised what was presented to us on Knutsford Heath. In fact, it was the real people in *Purple Homicide* themselves who handed to us one of the most implausibly wonderful scenarios either one of us could have created, alone or together.

Arriving late at the Alderly Edge Meeting Hall, my palms were damp, my stomach churned. I've never felt particularly comfortable walking into an enemy's camp. But I had accompanied the press corps, including John Sweeney, to see for myself what the 'other side' was all about. Our group paused briefly at the door. It flashed through my mind that at a previous such public meeting John's journalistic fervour had bordered on belligerence and he was asked to leave. I hoped he wouldn't cause a scene tonight.

The meeting was already in session. Having just left the happy, high-energy confusion of the Bell headquarters, where it was impossible to tell who was actually running the show, the mummy-like attention of the assembled faithful gave little doubt as to who was in charge at Alderly Edge. The pall was palpable: more like a funeral service than a public forum. And the drone of the Conservative candidate's un-miked voice – a certain cure for insomnia, I thought – intensified my already queasy feeling of self-consciousness.

It was bad enough that I was an outsider and a Yank to boot, but the fact that I was also the 'token celebrity' from the other camp who had made known his intention to confront the candidate about his views on the 'public trust' (sleaze is sleaze, no matter which side of the Atlantic you come from) meant that I'd managed to work myself up into quite a state. The lifeless atmosphere didn't help matters.

Of course, I was wearing cowboy boots. All Americans do. Praying I wouldn't clump too hard on the wooden floors or trip on or over anybody, I separated myself from the journos and tiptoed off to find a seat closer to the front of the auditorium. Respectfully skirting the perimeter of the room, I passed an imposing blonde woman sitting in the back row of folding chairs. Was this the famed Lady Macbeth? I certainly didn't want to be noticed by her. I'd seen her in action on TV. I quickly looked away and my stomach turned over again.

I think the candidate was in the midst of not answering someone's question or eulogising himself (I'm not sure which) as I gingerly slipped across the plastic-covered seat of a booth halfway into the auditorium. I wanted to avoid the whoopee cushion effect. Oops! Too late. Every head, it seemed, turned to the sound of the intruder. The candidate paused. A quick glance. Stop time. It was apparent that the comment had not been appreciated. Heads leaned into each other. 'Isn't that Hutch?' I pretended it wasn't me.

So why *would* an American actor, only temporarily living in London, end up stumping the Tatton constituency with Martin Bell looking for votes? Well, it certainly wasn't because we'd both had careers on TV, although if I hadn't been flipping through

channels one summer night in 1996, I would never have encoun-
tered 'the Man in the White Suit'. He was appearing on *Newsnight*
(Neil Hamilton's favourite programme) discussing his favourite
topic: principled journalism. I lingered long enough to get hooked.

At the time, I didn't know Martin Bell. I had no idea who he
was. I didn't realise, for example, that for thirty-five years he'd been
one of the BBC's most respected international correspondents, or
that he'd been awarded an OBE. I was fascinated only with what he
was talking about and mesmerised by the way he said it. Martin Bell
exuded integrity. He spoke clearly and simply. He was unequivocal
and yet humble in manner; so self-deprecating, in fact, as to border
on arrogance. But then, in today's world of unbridled self-service,
perhaps real humility is the height of arrogance. By the time the
programme was over, I had decided to call him.

Coincidentally, I'd also been developing a television series
based on a character not too dissimilar from the man I'd seen on
Newsnight. Perhaps Mr Bell, with his understanding of TV
journalism, could help me focus the predicament of my central
character – a TV-newsman torn between the business of the news
and his own conscience. I called the BBC Foreign Desk and left a
message, counting on the curiosity of the journalist for a call back.
He called. 'This is Martin Bell. What can I do for you?'

I met Martin for the first time at his favourite hang-out, La
Gaffe, a delightful Italian restaurant in Hampstead (where,
incidentally, the first discussions regarding his candidacy were
to take place). Meeting him in person only strengthened my
initial feelings about the man, and my girlfriend, Alexa Hamilton
(no relation to Neil), was totally charmed. Martin does know how
to treat a lady. I gave him the proposal for my television series,
asked him to read it and suggested we might get together again to
discuss it. He subsequently invited us to his home; and then we
returned the invitation. We were to become friends.

Cut to mid-March of 1997. Alexa and I are preparing David
Mamet's *Speed-the-Plow* for a run at the Theatre Royal in Lincoln.
When an actor rehearses a play, he goes into ostrich mode: he

loses touch with what's happening in the world outside. But I was at least paying enough attention to be aware that the campaign was heating up. Opinion polls indicated that the Labour Party was doing pretty well and that there was talk of corruption in the Tory camp – talk which involved Neil Hamilton, MP for Tatton.

One day after rehearsal, and quite out of the blue, I heard that Martin Bell had announced his intention to stand against Mr Hamilton for the Tatton constituency, the fifth safest Conservative seat in England. I was as dumb-struck as everyone else. What the hell had happened? Only a week before, Martin had been putting the finishing touches on a documentary he'd made about the new Secretary General of the United Nations, Kofi Annan. In fact, in conversation with Martin only a few days earlier I'd made arrangements to meet with him and a writer to begin development of my new series. Martin was to function as my consultant. He'd certainly said nothing to indicate he was contemplating anything as dramatic as standing for Parliament.

I grabbed the telephone and finally located him in his Knutsford office, the basement bar of the Longview Hotel.

'Good on ya,' I said, not really knowing why I would say a stupid thing like that.

'You think so?' he asked.

'Absolutely,' I bluffed. But, I continued, if there was anything I could do to help him in the campaign, he could certainly call on me.

Typically, Martin had little to say, but he appreciated the offer despite the fact that what he expected would be the shortest-lived political career in history. The next forty-eight hours would tell the story, and if Neil Hamilton did not step down Martin would stand against him. He said simply that the people of Tatton deserved better than what they had.

Because I'd come to know the man and to respect his integrity, I didn't question him further about the sanity of what he was considering. I could only support him. Sometimes one person can make a difference.

A few weeks later, someone from Martin's office called to

inquire if I'd come up for a photo-op the following Monday. As my play closed on Saturday, I said, 'Yes, of course.' I went for the day . . . but then they couldn't get rid of me. Something important was in the air and I wanted to be there.

I settled back to listen to what this guy, Neil Hamilton, had to say. Many of the constituents I'd met on the streets campaigning with Martin had said they'd never once even seen the fourteen-year veteran of Parliament. I felt rather privileged. I also wanted to hear how he would deal with the allegations that he'd taken 'cash for questions'. Funny how much we rely on the media for our opinions about people; but then, I've been dealing with that problem my whole career.

I was not unimpressed by his smoothness. Pretty slick, I thought, though not much in the way of substance; except in his categoric denial of the 'sleaze' charges that had been levied against him. Innocent until proven guilty, he kept saying. Why, then, was he making such an effort to defend himself? The old saying, 'Where there's smoke, there's fire', flashed through my mind. Hamilton finished his comments and turned immediately to his glass of water, maybe to put out the fire.

Time for questions. I rephrased mine in my head and wished that someone would pay me to ask it. But that apparently only happens in Parliament. I decided to hold back for a while and let the constituents have their go. As a genuine outsider, I didn't want to appear too eager. I wondered what the reaction would be to my American accent. In the States, outsiders like me are called 'ringers' and are not generally appreciated.

A couple of questions about local issues were asked. Someone asked Hamilton about his position on the issue of European currency, to which he gave a surprisingly interesting answer, and then a reporter from the Evening Standard, I think, asked something about tax, and then . . .

Like a bullhorn from the back of the room, it came. There was no mistaking that voice. It was John Sweeney. Uh-Oh! Here we go. 'In his report . . .' Then there was something about money and lies, as I recall. Actually it sounded more like an indictment than a question, but despite the volume and the insistency of tone, the question was clear and well documented and deserved, I thought, a clear answer.

When the groans and epithets from the Hamilton camp finally tailed off and Lady Macbeth had pulled her laser-like glare off Sweeney, all eyes and ears shifted back to the front. It was not an easy thing for Hamilton to hide his loathing of John Sweeney. His answer, as I recall, went something like this: 'I've experienced these vicious attacks by this man from the Observer *before, and this is precisely the kind of unwarranted charge and distortion of the truth that is typical of this newspaper's attempt to discredit me and obfuscate the real issues of this campaign.' I now understood what was meant when folks talked about the 'hate–hate relationship' between John Sweeney and the Hamiltons. My thunder stolen, I decided not to ask my question. In fact, I chickened out.*

The meeting ended and Hamilton's supporters gathered round him to bolster and commiserate. I was going to leave, but then my unfinished business drew me back. Before I could leave, I decided, I had to talk to the man. Finally, when he'd greeted the last of a group of about ten, I moved in and offered my hand.

'Hi, my name's David Soul,' I said.

'I know,' he said.

'And I'm supporting Martin Bell.'

'I know.' He smiled wanly.

'Something's troubling me and I'd like to get your opinion on it.' He smiled patronisingly but said nothing.

'What is your definition of the public trust?'

Hamilton paused for a moment and then, in those sincere and measured tones peculiar to the practised politician, he launched once more into the press for having taken a lot of unsubstantiated charges and manipulated them against him. This, he emphasised, was a dangerous thing for democracy. He never answered the question, but that was all right because, in keeping him occupied for ten minutes, I discouraged about a dozen people from sticking around to say hello. We were even.

The place was all but empty when I walked out. I hoped I still had a ride. I bumped into a group of friendly Conservative supporters lingering in the foyer.

'How's Starsky?' one of them asked.

What an original question, I thought.

'Fine,' I said.

'*You still friends?*'
'*Absolutely.*'
'*Where is he?*'
I almost said, '*I hope he hasn't left yet, I need a ride,*' but I caught myself and said '*Los Angeles*' instead. I went out to look for Sweeney.

Remember that great line from Peter Finch in Paddy Chayevsky's *Network*, 'I'm mad as hell and I'm not going to take it any more'? The campaign was, first, a demand by the people for an end to corrupt practices in the halls of government. There is a standard of public conduct to which officials must conform. And where the people's trust is concerned, there is a 'behaviour becoming' the mandate given to their representatives. At the same time that Bell's campaign sought to unseat Hamilton, it was also a call to renew those basic principles of decency and integrity so very crucial to the spirit and legacy of the democratic process. In this sense, Martin Bell proved to be more conservative than his opponent.

Secondly, the campaign was about 'the art of the possible', which, ironically, is also the classic definition of politics. In early April, Martin Bell was one man alone with his phone in the Longview Hotel facing an overwhelming Neil Hamilton majority. On the morning of 2 May, he walked into the count to a standing ovation and an overwhelming victory. Not since the early 1960s, when John Kennedy captured the imagination of my generation and gave us the leadership we longed for, have I been part of a grass-roots movement which inspired so many to commit so much.

Against seemingly impossible odds, stretching minimal resources to the limit, this campaign 'contraption', as Martin liked to call it, canvassed the neighbourhoods of Hamilton's constituency, listening to and talking with thousands of people who had never ever seen a candidate, much less their own Westminster representative. The excitement spread like wildfire through the people of Tatton. It began to matter that Martin Bell won, and it mattered to people that they were involved. And always at the lead was the Man in the

White Suit, quietly reminding everyone, supporter and opponent alike, 'You can make a difference.' He did, and they did.

It was about 1 a.m., two days before the election, when we finally got back to the Longview Hotel, the early site of Martin's headquarters. Despite a gruelling day of canvassing, nobody was ready for bed; it was like coming down from a performance in the theatre – it takes a while for the adrenalin to wear off. We gathered together in the bar, journalists and campaigners, for a late drink and to talk about – what else? The campaign. Gradually, people started drifting away and John Sweeney and I were the only ones left. Suddenly it was quiet. We were in our own thoughts. Then John looked over at me. Through the tough veneer of this often cryptic journalist, I saw in his misty eyes what this campaign really meant to him.

'What if Martin doesn't win?' he said quietly.

In *Purple Homicide*, John Sweeney has captured the intensity, the pathos, the heart, the humour, the crisis, the climax and finally the triumph of the people. He didn't need actors to tell the story. He had the real thing. The story of Tatton will remain with us as an extraordinary experience – and with our children as a perfect example of democracy in action; a moment when good men did something.

Officially, *Purple Homicide* is about the campaign for a seat in Parliament between the Conservative incumbent, Neil Hamilton, and the Independent, former BBC War Correspondent, Martin Bell. Unofficially, it's about Good triumphing over Bad. And it's a story filled with the most wonderful collection of characters you will ever meet.

DRAMATIS PERSONAE

The House of Hamilton

Macbeth	Mostyn Neil Hamilton
Lady Macbeth	Christine Hamilton
General Wojciech Jaruszelski	Peter McDowell, the Tatton Tories' election agent
Panda Bear	Alan Barnes, chairman of Tatton Conservative Constituency Association
Squirrel Nutsford	Councillor Derek Squirrel, Deputy Mayor of Knutsford
Mr Heavy the Bouncer	The Hamiltons' minder
Interesting Druid	William Roache
Blonde Groupie	Pauline Breland, Hamilton acolyte
Grey Bun	Tory supporter
Crusty Majors	Tory supporters
The Brick Red Lubyanka	The Tory campaign headquarters

The House of Bell

The Man in the White Suit	Martin Bell, OBE
Catherine Deneuve	Melissa Bell
The Clean Machine/The Contraption	The Bell election team
The Women's Battalion of Death/ Bell's Belles	Antonia and Sophie Harrison, Sophie Solomon
Disciple of Sir Karl Popper	Oliver Kamm

K1	Kate Jones, Bell's election agent
K2	Kate Edgley, Bell's press officer
Table Mountain	Nigel Bateson, Bell's minder
Hutch	David Soul
Former Deputy Chief Constable	John Stalker
Obi Wan Kenobi	Sir Alec Guinness
Spy	John Le Carré
The Old Electricity Showroom	The Bell campaign headquarters
Man with Beard	David Geen

Lords, gentlemen, officers, soldiers, murderers, attendants and messengers. The ghost of Banquo and other Apparitions

Hecate	Press Association
The Three Witches	Press, TV and Radio
Banquo's Ghost	Ian Greer
Godot	Sir Gordon Downey
Vladimir and Estragon	The House of Commons Select Committee on Standards
Miss Moneypenny	Burnel Penhaul, BSc (Chem. Eng.) Hons, first-class
Man in Leotard	Tommy Sex
Lord Byro	David Bishop
The Alien	Michael Paul Kennedy
The Alien Abductee	Ralf Nicholas
Mr Eerily Normal	John Muir
Man on Coach	John Major
Bovver	Man in fear of Inland Revenue Special Compliance Unit
Julia Heartless-Bastard	Julia Hartley-Brewer
Teabag	Simon Sebag-Montefiore
First Murderer	Lynda Lee-Potter
Second Murderer	Nigel Dempster
Third Murderer	Paul Eastham
Fool	John Sweeney

PROLOGUE

This is not a serious work of political philosophy, a Lichtenbergian doctrine, arguing the case for the principle of democracy.

Oh, yes, it is.

This is not a factual history of the Tatton by-election.

Oh, yes, it is.

This is a pantomime script.

Oh, no, it's not.

The battle for the Tatton constituency in the 1997 general election was the strangest, most peculiar, most absurd, most hilarious political contest fought in a generation. It was also, in an odd way, the most important. Those of us who were there spent some of our time, as the English do in times of trouble, mugging up on half-forgotten Shakespeare. In the pubs and stews of Knutsford *Macbeth* was obviously the most quoted play, but *King Lear, Much Ado About Nothing* and *Henry V* got a look in. King Harry's speech had a special resonance for those of us who were there during the battle for Tatton:

> And gentlemen in England now a-bed
> Shall think themselves accurs'd they were not here,
> And hold their manhoods cheap while any speaks
> That fought with us upon Saint Crispin's day.

This script attempts to catch some of the flavour of that battle.

This pantomime would not have been written had my expenses in Knutsford been reasonable. They were not. I would like to thank the exasperated executive of the *Observer* who, boiling with rage, threw my expenses claim back at me and said: 'Sweeney, you have spent more money in Knutsford than we plan to spend on our entire budget for the Hong Kong handover. Get out of my sight.'

So I had to write a book.

That said, I would very much like to thank the editor of the *Observer*, Will Hutton, and his deputies, Jocelyn Targett and Paul Webster, for their forbearance. The *Guardian*'s editors, ancient and modern, Peter Preston and Alan Rusbridger, led the fight against Hamilton from day one. Their best tribute is their newspaper. There were many times when the *Observer* wanted me to leave Tatton and work on other stories, but I demurred. I and others felt that the election there symbolised the struggle for democratic accountability which was being fought across the nation, and today continues across the world.

The champion of that cause in Tatton was, of course, Martin Bell.

Bell believed that somehow his campaign caught fire, caught a public mood. Likewise, if *Purple Homicide* works as a pantomime, it is only because it bottles the spirit of the battle for Tatton.

One person who did more than anyone else in capturing that spirit was the book's researcher, Kate Edgley. She was indefatigable in tracking down people, transcripts, tape recordings, notebooks, memories, recollections, jokes and anecdotes. She read the drafts, added sense and cut out nonsense.

Bell's team was known as the Clean Machine. Every single member of the Clean Machine served that cause; and my only worry is that in writing about the celebrated few I have omitted to acknowledge the hard work of hundreds. For those who are not specifically mentioned in this book, my apologies.

My thanks go to Bell's daughter Melissa, his election agent and publisher Kate Jones, his driver-*cum*-minder Nigel Bateson, his famous Belles, Antonia Harrison, Sophie Harrison and Sophie Solomon; and his not-so-famous Bags.

Also to Sue Addison, Peter Bracken, Bill Le Breton, Laura

Gillan, Edward Gilsenan, Alan Olive, Geoff Pullar, the Rev. Pauline Pullen, Michael Solomon and Julie Tempest.

A number of workers on the Clean Machine made available their diaries to me.

In particular, I would like to thank Sebastian Doggart for his waspish reflections on the Clean Machine.

Many thanks as well to Oliver Kamm for his notes on policy and the Natural Law Party, and Mark Whittle for his campaign diary.

It has been said of the Clean Machine that it was not so much a political campaign as a pub crawl with attitude. Readers must make up their own minds.

I wish to thank : (in Knutsford) Steve and Pauline West of the Longview Hotel, Alan and Kathryn Stimpson of the Freemasons' Arms – and all the Most Worshipful Drinkers within – and my hosts and the regulars of the Cross Keys, the Angel, the Builders' Arms, the Red Cow, Cafe Rouge, Est Est Est, the Knutsford Wine Bar, the Lord Eldon, and the White Bear; (in Alderley Edge) the Brookfield Arms, and the de Trafford Arms; (in Chelford) the Dixon Arms; (in Wilmslow) the Blue Lamp, the Boddington Arms, the Carters' Arms, the Farmers' Arms, the Nose Wine Bar, the Horse and Jockey, and the Falconbearer; (in Peover) the Bells of Peover; (in Handsworth) the Wilmslow Flyer; (in Mobberley) the Bull's Head, the Roebuck, the Bird in Hand, the Railway Inn; (in Great Budsworth) the George and Dragon.

Some kind of debt is also due to Neil and Christine Hamilton, their agent, Peter McDowell, the chairman of the Tatton Conservative Constituency Association, Alan Barnes, their friend William Roache, and their muscle, whose name I never knew but is called in the book Mr Heavy the Bouncer.

Thanks, too, to the Voices of *What the Papers Say*, a programme which should be on all the year round: Delia Corrie, David Mahlowe and Peter Wheeler.

Thanks to Jon Kelly of Tatton Labour Party, to Roger Barlow

of the Tatton Liberal Party, and to Richard Cussons, Robin Estridge and Michael Field and all the other Tories who saw through Hamilton from the word go.

Thanks to Miss Moneypenny and her supporters, Lord Byro, in whose lists I was honoured to serve on election night, and the other candidates who so enlivened the battle for Tatton.

Outside of Tatton I would like to thank Roger Absalom, Demitri Argyropulo, Martin Brandon-Bravo, Julia Hartley-Brewer of the *Evening Standard*, Gary Calton of the *Observer*, Michael Cockerell, who first suggested I write a book on the battle for Tatton, Jez Coulson, Derek Deep-Throat, Peter Edwards, Channel Five News, Kate Flett, who housed Mistah Kuvtz, John Foot of University College, London, Jonathan Gebbie, Sir Alec Guinness, Thomas Hickson, Graham Hinde of the *Evening Standard*, Ian Hislop and the team at *Have I Got News for You*, Martha Kearney of the BBC and the Tunnel Club, John Le Carré, David Leigh of the *Observer*, Ann Leslie of the *Daily Mail*, Peter Macdiarmid of the *Independent*, Lawrence Matheson of the *Knutsford Express Advertiser*, Clarence Mitchell of the BBC, Jojo Moyes of the *Independent,* the staff at the National Foundation for the Care and Treatment of Victims of Torture, Alex and Anna Patel, Henry Patterson, Phil Pedley, Thomas Reeves, Toby Sculthorpe, John Stalker, Robin Stummer of the *Independent on Sunday*, Barbara Sweeney, Leonard Sweeney, Molly Sweeney, Sam Sweeney, Ed Vulliamy of the *Guardian*, and Andreas Whittam Smith.

Thanks to the Resources Module Podule of what used to be called the Observer/Guardian Library. Whatever it is called, the Info-Nodes who work for it are rather wonderful.

Special thanks to Peter Sharratt, the producer and cameraman of BBC's excellent fly-on-the-wall documentary, *Mr Bell Goes to Westminster*, for all his help and assistance, also to Louise Osmond, Jim Nally and all at ITN who worked on Channel Five's excellent fly-on-the-wall documentary. Thanks also to everyone at CBS for their help and cooperation.

I would like to thank my friend Andrew Billen for his constant help and unstinting encouragement.

An extra special thanks to my new friend David Soul, who kindly took time out to write the foreword to this book. He is the only Hollywood star ever to have played the Knutsford Drop-In Centre, and he played it magically.

Martin Rowson was not at Tatton, but his brilliant cartoons are as pin-sharp as photographs. They capture the changing mood of the election as battle raged. Thanks also to him for drawing illustrations to 'Stodge and Pig go to the Museum' before our starters had arrived.

Thanks to anyone else I may have forgotten due to exhaustion.

Thanks to all at Bloomsbury, in particular David Reynolds for seeing the possibility of *Purple Homicide*, Esther Jagger for matchless copy-editing, and Monica Macdonald and Helena Drakakis for their wonderful enthusiasm.

To the memory of two wonderful people who would have loved Tatton, had they been alive: Paul Jenks, murdered in Osijek in January 1992, and Seàn Devereux, murdered in Kismayo in January 1993.

To Anne Patterson, whose fine novel *In the Absence of Peter*, about the mystery disappearance of a war reporter, should be published soon.

To my son, Sam.

This book is dedicated to my daughter, Molly, and everyone else who will one day grow up and have the vote. Let her, and them, never forget that it is precious and should never be thrown away.

ACT ONE

By the pricking of my thumbs,
Something wicked this way comes.

Scene I: Knutsford Heath

Dead coypus levitate as the witches come to Knutsford Heath to watch the murder of a day-old politician called Martin Bell. The witches coil and slither, muttering dark spells into their mobile phones.

Enter a smoothie-chops in a check suit with the good looks of a knitting pattern magazine mannequin, Mostyn Neil Hamilton, the former Minister for Corporate Probity, sitting member for Tatton in the Conservative interest and a fighter who gives no quarter. And his *belle dame*, Christine Hamilton, a force of nature with the poise of a tigress beginning to take notice. Her eyes glitter with flecks of granite.

The scene that day, Tuesday, 8 April on the heath: green scrubby grass, a line of bare trees, grey sky. The witchcraft of around twenty-five journalists gathers in a huddle, hubbling, bubbling, troubling. A few people mill around the edges, including the statutory Englishwoman with dog, presumably a watcher from MI5. A photographer in a red jacket scurries from one side to the other with his small stepladder, trying to find the best position. A man weighed down with a TV camera on his shoulder hurries to the scene. Above the huddle the dead coypus

float, the long whips of their tails running into the headphones of
the TV soundmen. The three witches – Press, TV and Radio –
are ready.

Enter Martin Bell, a man in an off-white suit with a grumpy
face. He takes in the media witches and scowls like Badger in *The
Wind in the Willows*: 'Uh, company'. He limps to the centre of the
hacks. Hamilton and Christine make their way, as if they are made
of air, through the huddle. Bell faces Hamilton and Christine,
who are side by side. The three of them are tightly packed,
with not much breathing space between them and the
hacks. Cameras and microphones point expectantly;
the whir ring and clicking which continues
throughout the scene has already begun; faces
watch. All eyes and lenses are on Bell;
throughout, they barely seem to
move towards Hamilton or
Christine except during her
first question. With that one
question Martin is put on
the back foot; every time
she repeats the question,
it's not only her
granite eyes
which burn
into him; the
eyes of the press
also demand
a response.

Bell mumbles a greeting, but his words are over-ridden by Christine, bright and garish in a red, blue and green jumper and chunky necklace of white beads. She opens her mouth. Her tone is author-itative, the timbre of her voice almost metallic,

the woman who must be obeyed – Mrs Thatcher's 'No, no, no'
meets Dr Who's adversary, Davros, King of the Daleks: 'We shall
exterminate!'

Christine: 'Do you accept that a man is innocent unless proved
guilty?'

Bell looks a worried man, with reason. He gives the impression
of someone who feels that he is improperly dressed, that he would
have rather gone home and changed his off-white suit, white shirt
and red and yellow tie of the Cheshire Regiment for a flak jacket.
He studies Christine quietly, his head on one side: 'Yes, of course
I do . . .'

A mystery blonde, from her body language a friend of the
Hamiltons, wearing a mauve top and black jacket and standing
next to Christine, nods in time with her, her eyes fixed on Bell.

He continues: '. . . but that's not—'

Christine cuts in, no lessening of the 'we shall exterminate'
tone, long deliberate nod of the head, riding over the top of Bell
saying '. . . that's not an issue—'

'So you accept that my husband is innocent.'

Bell tries to reply, his voice reasonable yet cowed: 'I think
there's a lot—'

Christine, raising her voice to 'EXTERMINATE THEM' pitch: 'Do
you accept that my husband is innocent?'

The whirring and clicking of cameras intensifies. Bell looks
away, blinking. His face is a picture of resignation to the fact that
being pleasant and gentlemanly isn't working. He looks down at
the ground. Later, Bell whispers to a friend: 'To compare
Christine Hamilton to Lady Macbeth is unfair. On Lady Macbeth.'

Gently, he gesticulates: 'Look, I'm not going to be facing an
ambush here.'

Bell looks up at Hamilton, raises his voice a little, makes a
firmer gesture with his hand, nods his head in motion with the
words to assert some small degree of authority.

'Let's just see, let's just see, let's just see what comes out.'

Hamilton, exuding the air of a country gentleman in his check suit, blinks in sequence with every nod of Bell's head as Bell struggles to find common ground: 'I . . . I don't know.'

Three words no politician should ever utter.

The mystery blonde gasps, then looks down and shakes her head.

Bell repeats the forbidden words. 'I don't know. I'm standing here—'

Christine cuts in again, imperious: '—because you're not prepared to wait for Gordon Downey?' – a reference to the parliamentary inquiry into allegations that Hamilton took *baksheesh*, money and favours such as a stay in the Paris Ritz Hotel, from the Egyptian proprietor of Harrods, Mohammed Al Fayed, once described by an enemy as the 'phoney pharaoh', in return for questions asked in the House of Commons.

Bell continues: '. . . because a lot of local people have asked me to stand here. The impetus comes from local people. And let them just choose between us.'

Christine's eyebrows vault skywards: 'I thought it came from a dinner party. In London.'

Now Hamilton interjects for the first time, talking over Christine, his pudding face a mask of quiet reason: 'I . . . I . . . I would just like to say, then' – his voice gaining poise, authority – 'that you are prepared to give me the benefit of the doubt on the allegations that have been made against me?'

Bell nods his head, firmly: 'Absolutely. Absolutely.'

Hamilton gives an affirmative nod, then turns his head away slightly to signify an end to the conversation: 'Good.'

It was a deadly moment. The spell was cast.

Scene II: The Old Rectory, Nether Alderley

I arrived, thanks to whatever they call British Rail these days, too bloody late, bumping into Hamilton and Christine gaily strolling back towards the gloomy red-brick citadel of the Tatton Conservative Constituency Association headquarters. They were hand in hand in the fashion of lovers, smiles of satisfaction in place.

'How's the campaign going, Mr Hamilton?'

'Where are you from?' cut in Granite Eyes, minerally.

'The *Observer*.'

'We don't talk to the *Observer*,' she said. It wasn't quite a threat, more a declaration of war. They were smiling because they had won.

It wasn't the first time that I had met Christine. How could I ever forget our first meeting? A week before the Battle of Knutsford Heath, before Bell had announced his candidature, the prospect offered to the eye by the green fields running up to the Old Rectory, Nether Alderley, was delightful. Daffodils danced in the breeze; the weathercock on the church roof crowed a westerly and the grass flattened as the clouds scudded over the flat pancake of the Cheshire plain towards the sandstone knife of Alderley Edge.

The Hamiltons' Rectory is a dream of Englishness in brick, cheek by jowl with a fine church where the tombstones silently shouted the human defence for Piers Merchant, the married Tory MP who was in dire trouble at the start of the election campaign:

> The grave's a fine and private place,
> But none I think do there embrace.

Merchant had been snapped snogging a bimbo by the *Sun*, but was to brazen it out without even quoting Marvell to his constituents.

Through a fine sash window in the Old Rectory one could see an oil of a mutton-chopped Victorian paterfamilias scowl at the tombstones; the tombstones scowled back.

Even before Bell had announced, the only interesting question in the election thus far had nothing to do with all the boring twaddle which engaged the policy wonks. It was: would

Hamilton step down? I had been sent by the *Observer* to Tatton to find an answer to that very question. Tourist sight-seeing over, it was time to pop the question. A short walk past the nod-nodding daffodils took me in front of the kitchen window. There, no sign of Hamilton but I was clocked by the Tigress of Tatton. Over the portal of the Rectory was a Latin tag: '*Deus nobis haec otia fecit*': 'These hours of ease are God-given.' No one had told Christine. She opened the door inwards as I was about to knock, leaving me, as it were, treading on a step that wasn't there.

'You are wasting your time. He has no statement to make. He is not making any statement.'

Christine was beautifully frightening – Tory Wife meets Vlad the Impaler. Fearing that we might not hit if off at first, I had brought her a gift, a copy of *Sleaze* by my colleagues David Leigh and Ed Vulliamy. Would she mind autographing my copy? (An autographed book always boosts the resale value at secondhand bookshops.)

By way of response, I got a perfectly articulated Pandora Maxwell 'Piss off!' and she slammed the door, but not before our eyes met and she gave me a look of . . . what? Loathing? Yes, but was there also, amidst the hate, a flicker of something else?

'He's not going to go, you know. He's going to tough it out.' This was the wisdom of a dyed-in-the-wool local Tory called Michael Field, who had resigned his membership. Field, a cravatted retired former managing director who stood his round in the pub in Alderley Edge like a true English gentleman, was not a Hamilton supporter: 'I feel tired and sick about the whole thing. This business that people feel "they're all at it" – it's very bad for public confidence. All along, I've never said that he's right or wrong, just that he ought to go because his honour has been questioned.'

No one from the constituency association would talk to me. But Field reckoned that Hamilton had the full support of the constituency officers, and that because Tatton was one of the safest Tory seats in the country he would get re-elected, even though his vote would fall.

The ferocity of the look Christine gave me stirred a memory. The last time someone had looked at me like that had been three weeks before in a town called Fier in Albania. The other person was a member of the Shik, President Sali Berisha's secret police, who had motioned as if to reach for his gun in a concealed shoulder holster. Of the two, Christine Hamilton was the more chilling.

Back at the battlefield of Knutsford Heath, I watched Hamilton, Christine and their mystery blonde friend walk off. Bell had lost. He looked as sad as, in Georg Christoph Lichtenberg's phrase, 'a dead bird's birdbath'. The gloom in his soul was written on his crumpled face. I have rarely seen Bell so downcast, even in Bosnia where I have seen him angry and depressed. Bell is not an easy man to read or to get to know. He is the very opposite of 'Hail, fellow, well met'. His small talk is negligible, his manner sometimes off-putting, while his face seems permanently set in a worried frown. But then, you could say, he has had reason to look worried.

The consensus of the hacks was that Bell's political career was over before it had begun. One BBC reporter said later that day: 'Bell's finished. He just looked like a bumbling old fool. Not a serious player. Hamilton will walk it.'

The Battle of Knutsford Heath was a brilliant ambush, a reward for the political daring of the Hamiltons. It was supposed to have been Bell's first press conference in Knutsford, held on the heath just outside his then campaign headquarters, the Longview Hotel.

With Hamilton had been not one devotee, but two. The mystery blonde standing next to Christine and sharing in the Hamiltons' nods, adding to the pressure on Bell, turned out to be Pauline Breland, a doggedly loyal member of the Tatton Conservative Association, so much so that she could be described as the Blonde Groupie. Had Bell known who she was, had he registered anger at the ambush rather than mumbling his dismay, he might have won some sympathy from the secret, black and midnight hacks. But he had not. The ambush was, of course, not very fair. But as Benjamin Disraeli once observed: 'In politics, nothing is contemptible.'

The newspapers the next morning and in the days following read like obituaries of Bell's career. Carole Malone in the *Sunday Mirror* is a real-life version of *Private Eye*'s mind-shrinking female columnist Glenda Slagg. The verdict on Bell's performance from the woman who 'tells it the way it is . . .' told it the way it was:

> There's something a bit iffy about blokes who wear white suits. If you met one in a disco, your first thought would be John Travolta. Your second thought would be 'prat'. Which is why I'm not sure about Martin Bell. The man reputed to have the highest dry cleaning bill in the BBC [not true – Bell was not a presenter of daytime television] reckons he wears the white suit in war zones because it's lucky, which is nonsense because he got shot [he was shelled] a couple of years ago.
>
> I suspect Martin's reason for wearing the suit has nothing to do with luck and everything to do with vanity, the same vice which convinced him he could make the switch from war reporter to politician. He can't, of course. Proven by his head to head with Christine Hamilton on Knutsford Heath which reduced him to a gibbering wreck.
>
> Martin should have stuck to the day job. You know where you are with the Serbs. The Tories are a whole different ballgame.

It was the same verdict in nearly all the other papers, though most of them said so in less lurid terms than the woman who 'tells it . . .' blah, blah.

The fatal admission that Bell was prepared to give Hamilton the benefit of the doubt – 'Absolutely. Absolutely.' – meant that the anti-Hamilton campaign had been mauled badly in its cradle. Worse, far worse, was the effect of the respective performances of

Bell and Hamilton – leaving aside Christine. Bell came across as someone unsure of his ground, hesitant, shy almost to the point of being incapable of articulating his mind. Hamilton was sure-tongued, smooth, self-assured. Just before Hamilton and Christine left the heath, the two men had a final exchange:

Hamilton: 'I don't want to hijack the whole campaign.'

Bell: 'Well, you haven't done badly.'

Hamilton, looking back in an interview with the BBC, was certain he had been the victor: 'I think we contestably won round one; he was put immediately on the back foot. It was very productive because it exposed the true nature of his campaign. He said one thing on the heath, he did another in the campaign. I had anticipated that we could set the ground rules of the election campaign in that encounter. I wanted to establish what it was he was going to accuse me of. He said he was going to accuse me of nothing. In fact, he spent the whole campaign accusing me of things I had denied. So his whole campaign was a fraud.'

Bell himself agonised over his failure at Knutsford Heath. Later, he reflected: 'I'm not the kind of chap who goes up to people he's never met before and says, "You, sir, are a liar and a scoundrel." It's not who I am. So I treated it much as I would have treated a Serbian road block: "Look, there's trouble there. I will placate and conciliate and live to deal with it another day." '

Put that way, Bell's dismal performance at the Battle of Knutsford Heath is more understandable. The rest of the world saw an arrogant man in a check suit and a haughty Englishwoman. Martin Bell saw a troop of cut-throat Chetniks, high on slivovitz, sharp knives in their belts. The *Guardian*'s Ian Traynor once witnessed what Bell had to contend with at the hands of the Serbs at a road block in Bosnia:

'The Serbian commando, armed to the teeth, found what he seemed to be looking for – the BBC cuddly toy. As Martin Bell, his BBC crew, and a host of Western reporters looked on nervously, the commando drew his knife, up-ended the teddy, inserted the blade at the crotch, and gutted it.'

If that was the film running inside his head on Knutsford Heath,

no wonder Bell appeared hesitant. But the Serbian road block
metaphor came later, and from a surprising source. At the time, he
had just mumbled everything the Hamiltons had wanted to hear.
His irritation with himself was deep: 'Afterwards I thought of all
the smart things I should have said and how I should have made
the distinction between what he was charged with but was not
proven, and the admitted wrongdoing out there. I failed to make
that distinction which was a political mistake but I was, then
especially, a political amateur.'

It had all started so sweetly, so smoothly. Hamilton had seemed
easy meat. He was mired in allegations of sleaze, sourced by Al
Fayed and written up by the *Guardian* and the *Observer* newspapers to the point of boring their readers silly. When Hamilton
decided to pull back from a libel case against the *Guardian* for its
cash-for-questions story, on 1 October 1996, the newspaper had
clobbered the Tory MP with a headline that seemingly spelt the
end of his political career: 'A liar and a cheat.'

But Hamilton had an inexhaustible supply of chutzpah, and
powerful friends. After the collapse of the libel trial everybody
waited for Godot. That was the name that we gave Sir Gordon
Downey, whose report was always promised but hadn't turned up
yet. Waiting for Godot: they were all doing it – Bell, the
Hamiltons, the hacks, and Vladimir and Estragon on the House
of Commons Select Committee on Standards. He had been
charged with investigating the allegations that a number of Tory
MPs, but most spectacularly Hamilton, had taken money and
favours from Al Fayed, the lobbyist Ian Greer and/or others in
return for asking questions in Parliament. But just before the
report was due to be published, Tory Prime Minister John Major
prorogued Parliament and called the election. The effect was
simple: the Godot Report could not be published until the
election battle was lost and won. It let all the Tories under
investigation by Godot off the hook until after the voters had
deliberated.

And it gave Major an escape clause every time he was asked

about the 's'-word, sleaze. On BBC1's *Breakfast with Frost* on Sunday, 6 April, Major was pressed about how he would like the Tatton association to vote: 'I've not interfered . . . they know their Member of Parliament, they know he vigorously protests that the main charges against him are untrue and that the matter is being investigated.' The beauty of his reply lies in the tense of the verb. That the matter 'is being investigated' meant that Major could not possibly prejudice the report's findings. That the report had been completed and was only a few days from being made public before Major pulled the plug on Parliament was purely a coincidence.

Frost hit Major with a jewel of a quote from Alan Clark, the saucy diarist and Tory candidate for what *Private Eye* for some reason calls the seat of Kensington and Legover: 'You must separate bonking, which everybody does, from taking bribes.' Major blinked and replied: 'Alan puts it in his own colourful way but I agree with his remarks . . . If Sir Gordon Downey reports that people have behaved very badly, if they have behaved well below the standards required of a Member of Parliament, then Parliament has very draconian powers.'

Major's 'if . . .' trick worked – or, at least, it appeared to work – beautifully. But, infuriated by Major's cunning plan, the Labour and Liberal Democrat parties made noises that they would stand down in Tatton if an anti-corruption candidate would step forward.

But who would risk taking on Hamilton, the proprietor of 32,000 Tory votes in the fifth safest Conservative seat in the country? Anyone who stepped forward as Mr Clean would be picked to pieces by the Tory rottweiler newspapers, in particular the *Daily Mail* and the *Mail on Sunday*. One possible candidate was Andreas Whittam Smith, the founder of the *Independent* news-paper and a Cheshire lad. He thought about taking up the challenge, then demurred. Other possibilities who had been mentioned in the newspapers were Richard Branson, the Virgin entrepreneur and hot-air balloonist; Frances Lawrence, the widow of a headmaster murdered outside a London school; Judge Stephen Tumim, the former inspector of prisons; and Terry Waite, the Beirut hostage. But no one had come forward.

Scene III: The edge of madness, London

The election campaign, the longest in living memory, droned on, all liveliness and electricity suppressed by the spin doctors and media managers of the big three parties. That all changed, thanks to the Bosnia connection. On Thursday, 3 April, five nights before the Battle of Knutsford Heath, Bell had gone to the edge of madness and beyond. *The Edge of Madness* was, in fact, not a description of Bell's state of mind but an exhibition of photographs of Sarajevo taken by Tom Stoddart – who had been injured in Sarajevo in 1992 – at the Royal Festival Hall. The images were unutterably bleak black and white photographs of the Bosnian capital under siege. The two men were, of course, old friends, brought together by a common empathy for the people of the city and despair at Western apathy, which let the murder continue for so long.

Bell had provided the foreword for Stoddart's book of photographs, a moving and beautifully written few hundred words in his trademark clipped and measured style. Stoddart's partner is Kate Hoey, the Labour MP for Vauxhall and a well-respected politician. Stoddart was also the photographer chosen by the Labour Party to portray Tony Blair in its manifesto – a fact which Hamilton was to play up again and again in his demonisation of Bell as 'a Labour stooge'. The group of old Bosnian hands went upstairs for dinner in the People's Palace restaurant after the formal opening of the exhibition.

The conversation took an odd lurch.

'You're what we're looking for,' said Stoddart.

'I'm what?' said Bell.

Bell was so astonished that he scarcely offered an answer. He

wrote in his election diary: 'Tom takes my silence as acquies-
cence. I go home rather troubled and sleep badly.'

The next day conveyed something of his agony in his diary:

> It is a day of great uncertainty and reflection. Perhaps the best
> result will be that nothing will come of the conversation. But, if
> called, what do I say? There are legions of reasons to decline. I am
> happy in my work and have never been happier in my private
> life. Against that, there may come a time in a man's life, perhaps
> once or twice, when he is challenged to take a stand and make a
> difference. It will always be easier to refuse. This could be such a
> time. And I am a hostage to my history. I have spoken
> extensively about the need for a principled journalism and a
> principled diplomacy. Why not a principled politics? Against all
> my instincts of self-preservation, I am minded to accept if asked.

After the People's Palace dinner Stoddart phoned Alistair Campbell, Tony Blair's bagpipe-playing press officer and a political fixer
of low cunning and high octane. Campbell contacted the Liberal
Democrats about the suitability of Bell. For the Liberals, Bell was
sweet. He was a household name, admired for his evident courage
and decency. He was also respectable, with the refined tones of an
earlier generation, seemingly ideal for a Tory seat. Bell, who had
been a Liberal at Cambridge, had come to admire and respect
Paddy Ashdown's stance on Bosnia. At Bell's home in Hampstead
Garden Suburb the phone started to ring: Campbell, then Dick
Newby, one of the back room boys in the Liberal machine, then
Ashdown himself.

But for Bell's candidature to go ahead, a fix was needed. The
local Labour and Liberal parties in Tatton needed to be persuaded
that their own candidates should stand down: not so easy, because
Hamilton's track record made him look potentially vulnerable.
And why should local Tatton people stand down for some TV
johnny who knows more about a psychopathic psychiatrist called
Karadzic than a town called Knutsford?

On Sunday Bell was driven up to Tatton where he was passed from Liberals to Labour, in the manner of 'some character in an old spy movie, transferred like a parcel between men in suits at secret meetings in car parks'.

While waiting for the executive committee of the Tatton Labour Party to figure out what to do, Bell sat downstairs in the bar of the White Bear in Knutsford, just on the other side of the roundabout from the Conservative constituency office, to the puzzlement of the pub-goers.

'I suppose,' one of them asked conspiratorially, 'that you are on some kind of secret assignment?'

'Why, yeah,' answered Bell. 'Actually, I am.'

The Liberals were the hardest to convince. They voted by the slimmest of margins, six votes to five, for their candidate, Roger Barlow, to step down. The Labour people in Tatton saw the appeal of an independent candidate immediately, but were unhappy about losing the chance of unhorsing Hamilton for themselves. For Jon Kelly, Hamilton's runner-up last time, it was a bitter-sweet decision to make way for Bell. Kelly said later: 'There was a great deal of resistance in Tatton Labour Party to the idea of me standing down. People do expect to have their own candidate wherever they live.'

But Barlow and Kelly saw the greater good, and agreed to bow out. Everything had to be ratified by full meetings of both the Liberal and Labour parties in Tatton. With those qualifications entered, the fix was in. Bell was going to go for it, standing as an independent, anti-corruption candidate.

On Monday, 7 April, Bell called a press conference in a Westminster hall, formally announcing in person that he was going to stand. His decision electrified a very boring election campaign.

To the job lot of political hacks who sprinkle cynicism on their Frosties every morning, Bell was the candidate from another planet. His manner was strange, his answers honest, his unease at being on the wrong – probed, rather than probing – side of the

TV cameras evident. At one point Bell admitted: 'I'm scared to death. I would rather run the trench-lines of Dobrinja,' – the most dangerous and exposed salient in Sarajevo – 'run Sniper Alley in my armoured car, Miss Piggy, than do this. This is one of the strangest things that has ever happened to me.'

This wasn't an exaggeration. Bell wrote in his moving book on Bosnia, *In Harm's Way: Reflections of a War Zone Thug*, 'Professionally I see myself as a footnote.' He belongs to an earlier generation of TV and radio reporters, accustomed to telling stories, to letting the images tell their own story with only a few sharply honed words of commentary, not to vapid self-advertisement posing as 'analysis'. He has a disdain for what he calls 'Well, Trevor's, the absurdist exchanges between the reporter in the field and the anchorman in the studio, now common in British television but originated by ITN's Trevor MacDonald:

'What is the mood like at the Commons tonight, Michael?'
'Well, Trevor . . .'

Despite the instant demonisation of Bell as the media candidate, this kind of forceful self-projection was alien to his character. The press conference would have been a doddle for a whole slew of smoothly fluent broadcasters – Nick Ross, Martyn Lewis, a Dimbleby, Major or Minor – but it really was hell for Bell.

The hacks were uneasy with Bell because he was a species of category mistake. Reporters, even high-profile TV reporters, scoffed at politicians; they did not do politics. Here was one of them, albeit someone who had spent seventeen of the last twenty years in places where you could not get canapés for love nor money, talking with passion about morality. The *Guardian*'s Simon Hoggart caught the palpable unease at the press conference: 'His voice was dark, full of foreboding, and his expression ran the gamut from anguished to despairing. He kept rubbing his face, as if wiping away the sins of the world, or possibly the remains of lunch.'

Bell told those gathered for the press conference at the Institute of Civil Engineers: 'I believe, and the opinion polls reinforce this, that there is deep disquiet in the public at large about our standards of conduct in public life. And it's just a few, but it contaminates, affects the reputation of the many. And it's in everybody's interests that we sort this out and I think the British people want this.'

Like a pack of curious velociraptors from *Jurassic Park*, the hacks started to monster their prey. The hall had been booked and paid for by the Labour Party to the tune of £375. What did he make of that?

'I will happily deliver a cheque for £375, tonight!'

More, he said that the press could see his tax returns and he disclosed how little he had in his bank account. Had he ever fiddled his expenses? After all, foreign correspondents and television reporters were famous for their creative accounting. He acknowledged that some had made large sums through sharp practices: 'But those days are gone forever. As it happens I did live through them, without making material advantage of them. It seemed a sad obsession.'

Tory Central Office would be looking through his past, searching for skeletons. 'I have looked at my cupboard and I can't think of a damn thing.' He added: 'I have never even had expenses queried until last November when my taxi driver in Delhi was illiterate and I didn't get a receipt. The BBC queried that.'

Could Bell be this pure?

Matthew Parris, the *Times* columnist, former Tory MP and easily the most elegantly readable torch-carrier for John Major – if not Neil Hamilton – in Fleet Street, was pessimistic. He wrote the next day: 'I'd give Martin Bell a week until his character is torn to shreds. This is not because there is any defect in Mr Bell's character but because no reputation, however untarnished, is untarnishable. If St Francis of Assisi were to stand for Tatton, he would find himself under press suspicion within days.' (One could speculate on the *Sun* headline if the creeping things that creepeth

on the face of the earth went to town on St Francis: 'I WAS SAINT'S
SEX SLAVE ZOMBIE – SHEEP'.)

Parris went on, ominously for Bell:

> Is there nobody in Mr Bell's valiant career who is prepared to
> speak ill of him? If there is, the press and the Tories will seek
> them out. After sustained media attention, Snow White's
> reputation would drift – why, after all, the uncharacteristic
> spring in Grumpy's step? Put Max Clifford on the case of Big
> Ears, and bang go Noddy's chances of political stardom. Every
> Batman has a Robin in his closet.

Parris, who is openly gay, probably knew that Bell is hetero-
sexual and the Batman and Robin crack was several billion miles
off the mark. But as Anatole France once wrote: 'Of all sexual
perversions, chastity is the most peculiar.' The hint was plain: if
the hacks looked for dirt, they would find some. The *Times*
columnist went on, raising a more philosophical objection to
Bell's candidature:

> Whatever interest this candidate may arouse, Britain's media
> professionals will not quite, in their hearts, approve. Some will
> be a little jealous, others, more old-fashioned, may think it
> unprofessional to step over the unstated line between reporting
> the news and making it. Most, I suspect, will derive schoolboy
> glee from watching a candidate whose whole platform must
> consist in an implicit claim to personal virtue, stumble. As for
> the voters of Tatton (mostly Tory) many will see a BBC
> candidate as being not above politics, but of the covert Left.
> I'd place a small bet on Hamilton winning.

More right-wing pundits opened up in the next few days. Fleet
Street's Lord Snooty, Charles Moore, the editor of the *Daily
Telegraph*, pooh-poohed Bell's candidature on the airwaves, in his
newspaper and in an article in the *Guardian*. There he wrote:

It seemed self-evident to many in the media that Mr Bell was
the right man to be an anti-corruption candidate, simply
because he is a good journalist. They did not see the arrogance
of that assumption, its woeful distance from the views of the
public, who think that journalists are at least as despicable as
politicians. . . . I cannot get over my amazement at the
readiness of Labour and the Liberal Democrats to play along
with this journalistic triumphalism and stand down in Mr Bell's
favour. The message they are sending out is that no politician
can be trusted to oppose corruption. If Neil Hamilton is
corrupt, surely all the more reason for the voters of Tatton
to be offered the chance to put in a man from another national
party? Why, one asks Tony Blair and Paddy Ashdown, is
Martin Bell better than their parties' candidates?

Janet Daley, the right-wing *penseuse*, rubbished the mountain
of evidence against Hamilton as 'media self-indulgence . . . the
esoterica of newspaper gamesmanship'.

The all-comers' prize for the most vigorous machine-gunning
of Bell thus far went to Fleet Street's Mr Angry, Paul Johnson,
who swept the trenches from his nest in the *Daily Telegraph*:

The voters must realise that if they vote for Mr Bell, they will
be voting not just for a reporter with a famous face, but for the
media as a whole. . . . They will be voting for the *Sun* and the
News of the World, for their hidden cameras and their wired-up
character assassins. They will be voting for Rupert Murdoch
and everything he stands for. They will be voting for television
– with its endless sex and violence – and for Channel Four and
its boss, Michael Grade – Britain's pornographer-in-chief.

On and on went Johnson, as if – we'll change up a metaphor
now – spitting chunks of Axminster from his foam-flecked mouth
in the general direction of a man who has never worked for
Murdoch or the *Sun* or the *News of the World* or Channel Four.

Nor was Bell, for that matter, a lesbian – it had been a programme about lesbionism which had occasioned the *Mail*'s stigmatisation of Grade as the arch-pornographer. Johnson's molars ground on: Bell was a 'self-righteous carpet-bagger . . . who admires Paddy Ashdown's views on Bosnia and, if elected, would press for a large military presence in the Balkans. . . . Tatton electors must weigh carefully the Balkans factor.' Hamilton, on the other hand, 'may not be perfect. But at least he stands for the constitutional process as opposed to media tyranny.'

The bookies agreed with the pundits. Ladbroke's made Hamilton the 5–1 odds on favourite, with Bell at 3–1 against.

Back in Tatton the Hamiltons, though confident of victory, were not best pleased that Bell had had the effrontery to stand as an independent 'anti-corruption' candidate at all. Christine shrieked: 'It's a flaming cheek. He's got, as far as I'm aware, absolutely nothing to do with Cheshire, and even less to do with Tatton.'

Bell was beginning to sense that the Hamiltons were the kind of people who, faced with a teddy bear, got out not a picnic hamper but a disembowelling knife: 'When Mrs Hamilton said I had a flaming cheek to stand, first of all I realised I had made my first tactical miscalculation by not bringing my flak jacket with me, and then I thought well I'm sorry it's my democratic right to stand. I could stand for the Hebrides if I wanted to.'

The Hebrides would have been easier.

On Tuesday his campaign opened and (it seemed to many) closed with the Battle of Knutsford Heath.

After the calamity, his luck continued bad. The first Bell campaign office was – appropriately, some might think, for an ex-journalist – a dive bar, the cellar of the Longview Hotel. The Longview has little in common with the Paris Ritz, but the pleasant hilarity of the staff and an oddly tall moustachioed proprietor (though one called Steve, not Basil), together with a small but terrifying proprietress (though one called Pauline, not Sybil), suggested another, fictional, hotel: Fawlty Towers.

Within the dive-bar-*cum*-campaign-HQ the chaos that first
Tuesday was unimaginable. The one phone rang constantly. The
telephonist doubled as the candidate. Seedy types drifted in and
out, listening to snatches of conversation, spinning a yarn, taking
down the odd note. Hacks. A man in a suit who might be
described as a thinking woman's bank manager drank in the
scene. He turned out to be ITN's political editor, Michael
Brunson. He talked about the Battle in reverential tones: 'That
was my favourite political moment since Thatcher came down
the steps of the Paris embassy and grabbed the microphone to
announce: "I fight on, I fight to win." ' She lost.

Over in the corner was a large florid hack with a face the colour
of a bruised tomato. 'It's Nigel Dempster,' said a woman
volunteer who had come in to help, believing she had recognised the *Daily Mail*'s gossip columnist and the Man Who Knows
the Royals. Nearly right: it was the *Daily Mirror*'s James Whitaker,
the Man Who Really Knows the Royals. Brunson is normally to
be found in the stews of Westminster, hunting down nuances
from the Cabinet. Whitaker is normally to be found crawling
through the heather near Balmoral, playing peeping tom with the
nice but dim types in the Royal Family. That Brunson had been
choppered up to Tatton by his organisation and Whitaker had
been pulled out of the glens was evidence that the national
campaign was incredibly boring. And what was going on in this
part of Cheshire had, in some strange way, gripped the imagination of the entire nation. It must have done, if Tatton was a bigger
story than the bonking habits of the Royal Family.

In the dive bar the Bell team started to take shape. Melissa Bell,
his daughter – of whom it cannot be said that she is hideously
deformed – manned the fax machine. In Brussels, where she had
been working in the marketing department of Reuters, she had
seen her father being monstered by the hacks on Monday. Could
she take unpaid leave? she asked her boss. He said no. She quit.
Catherine Deneuve was to become the face that launched a
thousand tons of slobber and drool from Fleet Street's finest.

Colonel Bob Stewart, Bell's old friend from the time the Cheshire Regiment served in Bosnia, looked on, with martial bearing, bursting with praise for Bell: 'He's a friend, he's a very intelligent man. He's a very decent man. He's someone that cares a lot about people.'

If there was anyone who needed to be flattened by a tank, the Colonel would give the order. He is a brave and decent ex-soldier, one loved by his troops, but a man with a disturbing streak of naïveté when it comes to speaking his mind in front of hacks. While serving in Bosnia, he had an affair with an aid worker and, subsequently, left his wife. 'They call me "Bonking Bob", you know,' he told the hacks in the dive bar. It was a joke against himself, told ruefully. The next day this admission appeared in the *Times*. The newspaper made no mention of the fact that under Colonel Stewart's leadership of the Cheshires every single aid convoy got through to the hungry, an achievement not matched by later (and posher) regiments. But 'the dirt' on the Colonel was on the record and, the next day, 'Bonking Bob' beat a retreat to London, where he stayed for almost the entire campaign. So at the very start Bell lost the only connection he had had with Cheshire. The media witches were to make it much, much worse.

In the dive bar there was a man with a beard fluttering around.

'Could I have a gin and tonic, please?' I asked Man with Beard. He looked at me as if I had asked him for a bowl of cat sick. Suspecting he might be a deaf barman – anything was possible in the Longview Hotel – I repeated my order for a gin and tonic, clear and loud.

His face contorted into a new rictus of horror.

'A gin and t—'

He cut in, brusquely, and introduced himself as David Geen, a former BBC producer who was helping Martin with the campaign.

'Sorry,' I said.

Bell was on the phone, an almost empty glass of red wine on

the table: '. . . you see I haven't even got a typewriter. It's just me and Melissa and an ex-BBC producer, Dave.'

Melissa: 'We need a plan and we need professionals, we need an office.'

Geen: 'Well, we're not sweating. I mean. . . .'

Melissa: 'Well, perhaps a computer or something, or even a typewriter. . . .'

Brunson (helpfully, but not ever so very helpfully): 'Well, you can get a mobile phone. There's a mobile phone shop in town.'

Bell (on the phone): 'I'll send the other half of the campaign staff up to receive your fax.' (Off the phone): 'We need an office, I need a phone. Find me an office, find me an office.' (On the phone): 'I don't really have a proper campaign, it's just me and my daughter and she's standing up by the fax machine, but I've got nothing. . . .'

A fax came through from Campbell, Blair's press officer. Bell read it, then slipped it into his pocket. He was an independent candidate and it would be politically embarrassing in Britain's fifth safest Tory seat for Bell to be seen receiving help from the Labour or Liberal Democrat machines. The right-wing newspapers would make mincemeat of him if they found out. But without professional help, the Hamiltons would make mincemeat of him anyway.

On the other side of the road and along a few hundred yards from the Longview stood the Brick Red Lubyanka. Within the Tatton Conservative Constituency Association headquarters the Hamilton war machine was in battle mode. The Hamilton posters were ready to be printed, the Hamilton placards had been planted in the fields and hedgerows and Hamilton's 32,000 votes looked impregnable. The Hamiltons' loyal agent, Peter McDowell, was in place, plotting. McDowell exuded a slightly sinister presence, despite his wry sense of humour. A small, dark, still man, he has bad knees and often sports dark, anti-glare spectacles of the kind made fashionable by General Wojciech Jaruszelski, the enforcer of martial law in Poland. General Jaruszelski and a host of Tory ladies speaking in accents with which you could cut tungsten ensured that no hacks made it past the front door of the Hamilton machine.

That evening the focus of the war switched to the Dixon Arms in Chelford, where the Tatton Conservative Constituency Association was due to choose its candidate to run for Parliament. There was only one candidate: Neil Hamilton. In past elections it had always been a mere formality, but some suspected it might be different in 1997. A few local Tories had popped their heads over the parapet to say that Hamilton should step down 'in the interests of the party'. Some, like my friend Michael Field, had resigned. But the majority of constituency officers were paid-up members of the Neil Hamilton fan club. The *Times* that morning had treated its readers to declarations of support from the Tatton Tory officers which would not have seemed out of place in Kim Jong Il's North Korea. Under the headline: 'Media "dirty tricks" strengthen resolve of Hamilton supporters', the newspaper found that only one out of ten constituency officers had reservations about their MP. From their standpoint, they were sick of being told by the media what to think.

Jan Verney, the president of the Constituency Association, who was due to chair the selection meeting that evening, told the *Times*: 'Neil Hamilton should fight on. The man is innocent. . . . I suspect that somebody will call for a secret ballot at the meeting. I suppose Martin Bell will get a few votes but it's a bit rich, isn't it? We know basically this is a battle between the media and Neil Hamilton and one of you puts up.'

Alan Barnes, the chairman of the Constituency Association and a former boxer with the look of a panda down to his last bamboo shoot, was more derisory: 'I support Neil Hamilton. . . . Martin Bell is just a media hack.'

Blonde Groupie – also known as Pauline Breland, the Hamilton loyalist who had turned up at the Battle of Knutsford Heath – repeated the Tory mantra, one that turned the former minister from someone who was the author of his own disgrace into someone entitled to a fair hearing: 'Neil Hamilton is innocent until proven guilty. I will vote for him. Martin Bell's involvement is further evidence of media dirty tricks. I don't care whether it is a secret ballot.'

Heather Craig, a Knutsford town councillor, said: 'We are 110 per cent behind Neil. . . . These people who are calling for a secret ballot are chicken-livered. They should stand up and be counted. I have my own feelings about Martin Bell. They are private.'

The question of a secret ballot at the selection meeting was not academic. Quite a few Tories, privately, had expressed their reservations about Hamilton, but many were uneasy about doing so in an open meeting. Tony Martin, the constituency treasurer, who looks a little like Frank Cannon, the affable but well-built Californian TV detective – as such, the first of many real or imagined TV cops who were to litter Tatton by the end of the campaign – was opposed to the MP standing again: 'Neil Hamilton shouldn't fight on. He has lost the confidence of the electorate.' But, crucially, the arrival of Bell in the race had firmed up the loyalty of many doubting Tories. Martin said: 'Martin Bell is seen as a Lib–Lab candidate. There is a siege mentality inside the association and this considerably strengthens their resolve. I have had twenty phone calls this morning from people who were prepared to support me but are not going to now. If we are going to move it at all, a secret ballot is the only way we will.'

While a bowls match continued on a green at the back of the pub, Tatton's Tories formed a long and exquisitely ordered crocodile, showing their credentials at the door to the hall at the back of the pub. Miscreants, hacks pretending to be Tories and those who were behind with their membership dues were not allowed in.

The gatekeeper, controlling the selection of the Elect and the Damned, was hidden from view. Tony Martin bounded up to the door, only to be blocked. He was against Hamilton. He was one of the Damned.

Martin leaned against the closed doors and made beseeching noises through the crack: 'Peter, would you kindly open the door, please?'

The doors remained shut. He turned to the hacks, agog: 'I think this is a wonderful example of the attitude of the arrogant, pompous bunch who run this Conservative party.'

Watching this scene, Charles Lamb's 'Lines Written during the Time of the Spy System' came to mind.

> . . . Worms of all monstrous size
> Crawled round; and one, uncoiled, that never coils.
> A dismal bell, inculcating despair,
> Was always ringing in the heavy air:
> And all about that detestable pit
> Strange headless ghosts, and quarter'd forms did flit . . .

Martin flitted into the meeting, eventually.

The selection meeting became more surreal when a black Range Rover purred through the car park, in it one of the most famous faces in Britain, a loyal Hamiltonian and 'serial adulterer'. Children bowed before the Range Rover in mock adoration. The man in the all-terrain motoring accessory was famous for being, in the words of Richard Ingrams, 'a randy schoolteacher who sired a love child by the local hairdresser, Denise, and most recently caused a minor scandal when he jumped into bed with his headmistress'. Ingrams was, of course, writing about the fictional Ken Barlow, of Granada TV's *Coronation Street*. The actor who plays the libidinous Barlow, William Roache, is a man of fine and upstanding character, a Tatton Tory and the Hamiltons' most famous supporter. He is the only man in England who has brought a libel action for being called boring. He won. Roache is also a druid, worships the summer solstice and has taken part in an Old Religion festival at Stonehenge. With Roache backing him, Hamilton had Tatton's interesting druid vote sewn up.

'Look,' cried one of the snappers as Roache's Range Rover

pressed slowly through the huddle of hacks. 'Look at the bag in the back.'

It was a green bag with one word on it: Harrods. The shop owned by Al Fayed, the man who said that you could hire a Tory MP just like a London taxi.

And then came the Hamiltons. There is no question that, like Lady Thatcher, Christine has got balls. On their way into the Dixon Arms there was a mad scramble as the media spasm of dead coypus, camera batteries, ack-acking photographers and world-weary scribblers pressed against the Tatton Two.

'No placards,' she announced in the same imperious tone as Lewis Carroll's Red Queen cried 'Off with his head!' Someone had placed a bizarre banner calling for better television pro-grammes for pensioners in her way. She walloped it and moved on, her husband bobbing along gently in the wake of her trail of devastation.

ITN's Michael Brunson fed her a line: 'So, facing the music, eh?'

She turned and gave him that look – and I may have been mistaken – charged with the eroticism of power: 'Face the music . . .' she said, then flicked her head back in the style of the Allied Dunbar ad, '. . . and dance.'

They went in, faced the music and blasted the opposition orchestra off the face of the earth. It is the normal practice at selection meetings for the candidate not to be present while the local party deliberates. At Tatton on the night of the Battle of Knutsford, Hamilton and Christine were treated to a standing ovation when they entered the hall and stayed throughout, listening carefully to each contribution.

Only three dissidents were called to speak. They were Richard Cussons, a Knutsford stationer, Tony Martin and Derek Squirrel, a well-known local Tory. Martin was first to speak. He told the meeting that the executive should resign and that it was a disgrace that Hamilton was still standing. He was greeted with boos and cries of 'Shame!'

When Cussons was called to speak, one cry went up: 'He's just a friend of Martin.' Cussons started off by saying that this was not so. He quoted two leader articles in the *Daily Mail* and the *Times* which censured Hamilton and called for him to stand down for the good of the party. 'This is not a personal thing. This is about the good of this constituency, and the party nationally. We need to consider the party first.'

Finally, Squirrel spoke against Hamilton. In mid-flow Blonde Groupie relieved him of the microphone, saying: 'You've had your five minutes, you've had your five minutes.' Her cry was taken up and echoed around the hall.

Squirrel looked a dazed and confused squirrel. He was the deputy mayor of Knutsford and was due to become the next mayor of Knutsford, all things being well. The Conservatives have a majority on Knutsford Town Council.

'You've had your five minutes!'

Squirrel Nutsford sat down, his bushy tail between his legs.

Nearly all the Tories who spoke lambasted the media witch-hunt. Critical to Hamilton's plea of innocence was his argument that the case against the *Guardian* had collapsed not because of him but because his co-plaintiff, the lobbyist Ian Greer, had pulled out and let him down at the last moment. This line had been reinforced a few weeks earlier when Greer's former managing director, Andrew Smith, had addressed the annual general meeting of the Constituency Association, supporting Hamilton against Greer.

Enter Banquo's ghost.

A few days after the selection meeting the terrifying spectre that haunted Hamilton – Ian Greer – flitted into Tatton, albeit only in print. Greer, touting his own slim volume about the affair, *One Man's Word*, complained bitterly to the *Knutsford Express*: 'It would appear that Tatton Conservative Association has been told half-truths by Andrew Smith to ensure Neil Hamilton's re-selection. I am shocked that Andrew Smith, who is on the threshold of his own political career, has allowed himself to be used in this way. I do not know whether he was coached or not. It would appear that his memory is very selective.'

Ho hum. Opinion in the milk bars of Fleet Street see-sawed on this one. Some said that Hamilton had blinked first in pulling out of the libel action against the *Guardian*; other Milky Bar Kids agreed with Smith and thought that Greer had backed down first.

But to loyal Tories at the meeting, it would have appeared that Hamilton had been a wronged man. The friends of the Hamiltons made a consistent and well-rehearsed argument; more, they appealed to 'fair play'. This argument still works in Middle England.

Well before the adoption meeting was over, an outraged Cussons walked out and gave his account to the slithering of hacks. Cussons is a loyal Conservative who believed that Hamilton should have stood down for the good of the party. The meeting had been stacked in favour of Hamilton supporters, he said. 'After I spoke, a councillor said that what I was doing was not Christian. I am a Christian.' He was aghast, stunned at the intensity of the hate.

Another Tory whispered: 'People are afraid. They are afraid, not of him, but of her.'

The Hamiltons had wanted an open ballot; their opponents

within the Constituency Association had not. As usual, the Hamiltons had had their way.

I nipped inside the pub, now crowded with bowls players, to watch the Battle of Knutsford Heath on the BBC1 *Nine O'Clock News*; in my utter uselessness as a reporter I had missed the real thing, but a TV or the notebooks or tape recorders of colleagues can make up for a whale of journalistic incompetence. It was all there in bitter technicolour, the Hamiltons fluent in their attack, Bell defensive, uneasy in his defence. The bowls players looked away, bored and uninterested in Bell's catastrophe, and relived the highlights of their game in a way which brought to mind W.H. Auden's 'Musée des Beaux Arts':

About suffering they were never wrong,
The Old Masters: how well they understood
Its human position; how it takes place
While someone else is eating or opening a window
　　or just walking dully along . . .

Watching the battle on the television with the bowlers was like watching the first reel of a James Stewart movie, where the bad guys are walking all over the stammering good guy: an English version of *Mr Smith Goes to Washington*. You could call it *Mr Bell Goes to Westminster*. Only, on the strength of what I had just seen and the indifference of the bowlers, Mr Bell Would Not Go to Westminster.

Also watching the *Nine O'Clock News* was the man who had so often been its star reporter, not now in a trench in Bosnia but in a dive bar in Knutsford. Bell had said that, if Hamilton was dropped, he would disappear from the race and it would return to the usual three-cornered fight. If Hamilton was selected, then the pressure on Bell would really bite.

The anchorman, Peter Sissons, shone with excitement: 'Since we've been on the air, Neil Hamilton has been adopted as Conservative candidate for Tatton. We are joined, again in Tatton, by our political correspondent Nicholas Jones. Nick, remind us of how the meeting divided?'

Jones: 'There were 282 party members at this meeting and 182 voted for Neil Hamilton, for his reselection. He failed to get the support of 100 of the members who were here and 35 of them actually voted against Mr Hamilton. The other 65 abstained. So you can see it was a resounding victory for Neil Hamilton. He is safely reselected as the candidate.'

Bell protested grumpily to the television set in the dive bar: 'What do you mean? It doesn't sound resounding to me.' The set ignored him.

Jones carried on: 'As for Martin Bell himself, he's making it very clear this evening that he feels fired up now by the decision of this local party tonight, and Mr Bell has even gone as far as to say he thinks he could actually win this seat and become the MP here for the next three or four years.'

Moments later, we hacks were allowed into the sepulchral hall at the back of the pub for the Hamiltons' first press conference of their campaign proper.

First, the snappers took their snaps. Hamilton and Christine stood on stage, lit up by the cameras flashing. They were arm in arm, with Christine raising the thumb of her free left hand. She was in a Caledonian number, less garish than usual but still from the Tory wives' club wardrobe, with a broad, full smile splitting her moonface. Hamilton's smile was more restrained, his suit a darker grey than his hair, his eyes blinking constantly. Christine wrapped her free arm around him, closed her eyes and rested her head on his shoulder. He hugged her tightly. It was a deeply moving show of affection, if you like that sort of thing.

Hamilton began to mumble smoothly into the microphone, his reedy voice lost in the machine-gunfire of camera shutters. He was politely advised to use the microphone.

'. . . and Bell has accepted my bona fides. . . .'

Bona fides.

Scene IV: The edge of madness, Sarajevo

Something rang untrue. In Sarajevo in the bad times there was not much to do in the evenings. At dusk we gathered in the BBC office, sipped slivovitz – it tastes like tank anti-freeze mixed with prune juice – and looked out of the window at the city burning. And we talked. About love, the Bosnian story, sex, where Maggie O'Kane had got to now, the madness of UNPROFOR press officers, the poetry of Radovan Karadzic – 'Farewell, Sarajevo: your aortas will gush without me' – and, in his absence, the prose style of Martin Bell.

He doesn't say much, but what he does say is in beautifully transparent English. He likes Shakespeare, but not the comedies. Once he covered a royal tour in Canada entirely in rhyming couplets. During a visit to Charlottetown, the capital of Prince Edward Island, he reported:

> The climax of the tour and not a fun day
> If this is Charlottetown, it must be Sunday.

No one at the BBC noticed.

Allan Little, one of the other BBC correspondents who knocks around the bad places in the world, is a superb mimic and has the memory of an elephant with added Pentium chip. As the shells crashed down on the big city he used to retell, with awe in his voice, some of Bell's commentary lines. During the Gulf War, President Bush descended from a chopper and raced across the lawn of the White House as Bell intoned: 'Grimmer than before, but no less determined. . . .'

Little used to go on and on – you must understand, there was nothing else to do, no one else to talk to – about Bell's prose style. 'When UNPROFOR went into Slovenia, he did one minute ten [seconds] without a verb. . . .' From memory, Little banged on in Bell's clipped telegraphese: 'Through the rolling countryside of Slovenia, far from the war zone – for now – but not for long. Not by military convoy but by commandeered civilian bus. The French enthusiastically, the British less so. . . .'

I had to listen to hours of this. So I know how Bell uses the English language, his love of cadence and paradox, his taste for clarity and simplicity. He doesn't use Latinisms like *bona fides*. He doesn't like foreign languages. He never learnt even a few snatches of Serbo-Croat. I remember sitting in the BBC's beloved armoured car, Miss Piggy, in Bosnia and listening to Bell say 'Good morning, good morning' in reply to some Bosnian Croat grunts on a checkpoint.

'Why don't you say "*Bok*" or "*Dubar dan?*", Martin?' I asked him.

'Only ever speak in English. They get a "Good morning" from me, that's all.'

Something rang very untrue. I had just watched the televised humiliation of Bell by the Hamiltons on Knutsford Heath, and now his tormentor was putting *bona fides* into Bell's mouth.

In late August 1992 I was standing on the marble floor of the entrance lobby of the Hotel Esplanade in Zagreb – it was the Gestapo HQ during World War II: they always picked the best hotels – drinking in the scene, the self-important flurry of hacks scurrying in and out, a TV crew checking in their monstrous boxes of techno-junk. I was poised to return to Sarajevo for the *Observer*. I recognised one of the TV crew, a likeable chap, but I couldn't remember his name. He worked for the BBC and his face was white.

'Haven't you heard? Martin's been hit.'

'What? When?'

'This morning.'

He explained that Bell had been hit in the groin by incoming artillery. He was going to be all right and was being medi-vacced out of the Big City. This was terrible news. Bell was as near as any journalist could be to being invincible. He was our rock, steady, trustworthy, a man who would look after, not just his crew, but the whole British press corps, if need be. If Bell could get hurt in the Big City, then no one was safe. . . .

We all got on the phone to our newspapers to buy 'Martin Bell' groin flaps for our flak jackets. The *Daily Star* called him: 'Lead Belly Martin'.

I had first met Lead Belly Bell in the flesh earlier that terrible summer in Sarajevo, when the Bosnian Serb murder machine was at full power and they were hitting the city with up to three thousand shells a day. The BBC office was then based at Sarajevo's concrete telephone exchange building, the PTT. We had started talking because of Bell's family connection with the *Observer*. His grandfather, Robert Bell, had been its managing editor and Martin always took an interest in the latest atrocities going on in my office back in London. His father, Adrian Bell, was a farmer and novelist who compiled the first *Times* crossword in 1930 – not that that mattered a bean in Sarajevo.

I remember him pounding a table in despair at the feebleness of the United Nations in the face of the suffering of Sarajevo. It was rare to meet a journalist, in particular a TV reporter, not overcome by cynicism. It wasn't a scene for the cameras, but he showed a powerful and almost frightening anger that the world could be so cruel. He is a still, calm man most of the time, but he runs deep.

I had an appointment at the Presidency to interview the beleaguered Bosnian President, Alija Izetbegovic. Bell said: 'Some might say he is their Churchill.' That day the shells rained down. I had arranged with Keith Bernstein, a British photographer, for him to pick me up at the Presidency in his car and run me back to the Holiday Inn, but he never came. His friend, photographer Tom Stoddart, had broken his leg while running from sniper fire and Bernstein had raced him to hospital. Five years later Stoddart launched Bell's political career.

Repaired and patched up – though he still suffers pangs from his wound – Bell returned to Bosnia. He now positively clinked with good luck charms. For someone who appears to be rational, cool-headed and reserved by temperament, Bell is amazingly superstitious. He only ever entered the Holiday Inn in Sarajevo through a hole in a shell-blasted window, not through the door, on the west side of the gruyèred lobby. (This was eminently sensible. The main door of the hotel was in full view of the Serb anti-aircraft guns, targeted at us.) Less sensible was his habit of always going clockwise around the corridor. The trademark white suit was well known; less famous were the green socks. No other colour need apply. He listened to *The Love Songs of Willie Nelson*, both sides, every day. He carried with him a silver dollar, a four-leafed and a five-leafed clover, a fragment of water-snake skin in an envelope, a brass pixie of execrable taste, countless silver crosses and St Christophers. Thus far, they have worked a treat.

In the spring of 1993 the focus of the British media corps had moved to the central Bosnian town of Vitez, where the Cheshire Regiment was posted. The massacre of Ahmici had shocked the world; shocked even us. Its epicentre was the basement of a house where seven charred bodies – what had been women and children – lay. The victims, as usual in Bosnia, were Muslim civilians; the killers this time Bosnian Croat extremists. Bell broadcast the story with a cold fury at the inhumanity of it which became etched into the minds of millions at home and abroad.

A few days later the Cheshire Regiment took us on a sortie into the hills above Bosnia. The convoy consisted of two UN Warriors and Miss Piggy, driven by Bell. At one point the Warriors left us on an exposed bluff to do a recce in the valley below. They disappeared over a hill. We waited for our escort to return. And waited. The pock-pock of crossfire between the Croats and the Muslims grew more intense. What had started out as a bit of random shooting was fast becoming a small battle. A mortar shell whizzed overhead. What was hard to bear was the pointlessness of our position. We were exposed but could see precious little. There was nothing to report other than our own fear. Where were the Warriors?

A few villagers found us on our bluff. One was a dark-haired old lady, literally gibbering with terror. Her fear was infectious. I could feel myself slipping into a panic.

Bell came over, stern-faced: 'Sweeney, what are you doing here?'

It was like a slap in the face. I got a grip on my nerves, went over to a rabbit hutch and conducted a mock-interview with the bunnies about the hopes for peace in former Yugoslavia, their views on the international mediator, stigmatised by Denis Healey as Lord Owen of Split, and their faith in Bosnian ceasefires. The rabbits twitched their noses by way of reply. It was as sensible a reaction as any in Bosnia at that dark time. A few of my colleagues provided some laughter, probably out of charity. But I had got my courage back. I had been on the point of looking like a coward in front of them and the intervention of one man had prevented that.

That day Bell did not save my life – that hadn't been at risk – but he did something very important for me: he saved my dignity.

Now Hamilton was robbing Bell of his. Reporters are supposed to be models of impartiality, to be objective, neutral, passionless. But that's not good enough. How could one be neutral that September day in 1939, as the Wehrmacht tanks rolled over the Polish border? 'For their part, German sources said. . . .' How could one report the Romanian revolution? Impartially? I had been in Bucharest, that Christmas Day of 1989. Did I report that on the one hand defenceless students fought to overthrow a tyrant, on the other hand the forces of the Securitate loyal to the government tried to restore law and order? No, I did not. I had printed what I saw with my own eyes, what I believed to be true, what moved me. Wrong, yes, dead wrong, to assert things for which you have no evidence, but it is right and proper for reporters to take sides. We are people too.

Bell himself is the dean of the school which argues that the journalism of neutrality is dangerous and deceiving. Shaken by the murder in former Yugoslavia – and by the apathy of Western governments who looked the other way – Bell came to believe that the 'dispassionate' reporting on which the BBC so prides itself was wrong-headed. 'I do not believe we should stand neutrally between good and evil. You cannot report the Ahmici massacre or the flight of refugees or for that matter Dunblane in the same language that you'd use for an exchange of parliamentary insults. Reporters can be human too, and should be. We are not desiccated chronicling machines. We are not apart from the world, we are part of it, and we are responsible for what we do. My answer is what I call the journalism of attachment, journalism which knows as well as cares.'

Bona fides.

And it is always our right, too, to challenge what might be false or misleading evidence.

So I stood on a chair at the back of the hall behind the Dixon Arms in Chelford and spoke up: 'Did Martin say *bona fides*?'

Hamilton: '. . . and Mr Bell has accepted my bona fides. . . .'

Hamilton had the use of a microphone and two powerful

public address speakers. But. . . . When I was ten my parents moved from Altrincham, just up the road from Knutsford, to Chandlers Ford in Hampshire, and I was bullied at school because I had a northern accent. To get rid of the flat vowels, my parents sent me to elocution lessons. They made no difference to my accent, but my teacher, Derek Saunders, made me do lung and voice projection exercises which meant that I learnt to shout extremely loudly. For this reason, *Private Eye* calls me 'Fog-Horn Voiced John Sweeney'.

Sweeney (foghorn switched on): 'Did Martin say *bona fides?*'

Hamilton: '. . . accepted my bona. . . .'

Sweeney (incredibly, ear-shatteringly, Concorde-taking-off-with-a-full-fuel-load-just-next-to-your-ear-loud): 'Did Martin say *bona fides?*'

Hamilton: '. . . oh, it was a paraphrase. . . .'

Got him. A victory, of sorts. The Tory hacks didn't like it. Paul Eastham from the *Daily Mail* hissed something nasty at me. Still, the *Daily Mail*'s proprietor had thought Herr Hitler a good thing in the thirties. My father, a nineteen-year-old shipyard worker at Cammell Laird in Birkenhead at the time, had not. Not agreeing with the proprietor of the *Daily Mail* and his acolytes was in my genes.

But Eastham's swipe had derailed my attack train. Hamilton had recovered himself and he was abusing Bell, his voice super-smooth, as if rolling around the room on castors. He got a hug from Christine, sporting a blue rosette the size of a small radio telescope dish. It was that picture of togetherness that made the front pages the next day.

Back at the Longview, Channel Five's camera crew door-stepped Bell for his 'on the record' response to Hamilton's victorious reselection. Bell looked utterly exhausted as he stood in the doorway of the hotel, his head tilted downwards, lifting it occasionally to show raisin gingerbread-man eyes rolling and twitching in distress.

'My reaction to the result is that I thought I was in for a short

campaign. Now I know I'm in for . . .' – he stopped, angst
twisting his face, as if he's about to say 'I'm going to withdraw' –
'a long campaign and it's going to take me' – his head down,
speaking to the ground – 'to the House of Commons. I am
interested in the campaign, what happened in the voting. I appeal
now to the hundred Conservatives in that meeting who did not
vote for Mr Hamilton to contact me and we're going to get
something going here.'

It didn't sound as if he meant it.

Just before he went to bed Bell reflected: 'It isn't easy, it was
never going to be easy. It's going to go the whole way and I hope
it's not going to get as nasty as I think it's going to get.'

It did.

Scene V: The edge of madness, Tatton

The next morning at the Longview Bell had breakfast with Nick
Jones, the BBC's political correspondent and an old colleague.

Bell: 'Off the record, have you had any special instructions at
all?'

Jones: 'A certain sort of BBC thing that we mustn't get too
close.'

Later, Bell expressed irritation with the way in which the BBC
was fast distancing itself from its former employee: 'The BBC
went into one of its reflexive modes in which it denied that I had
ever worked for it. They stopped referring to me as the former
BBC reporter. The BBC was taken out of it. I became a former
TV reporter. As if I had never done anything for the BBC.' He
quoted Sir Thomas Wyatt: 'They flee from me they that some-
time did me seek. . . .' The next line continues, rather more
erotically: 'With naked foot, stalking in my chamber. . . .'

Jones defended the corporation's cold shoulder: 'You crossed
the line into politics. You could have crossed the line into public
relations, but you crossed the line from us as journalists so. . . .'

Bell: 'And I should pay for that, should I?'

Jones: 'No, no, no. There's that mental barrier between us, that suddenly emerges when you take the sort of action like you did.'

Bell: 'But I regard you all as my mates. . . .'

Jones: '. . . we all regard everybody as our mates, but we watch what the official position is.'

The official position was that Bell was trouble; worse: he was, given the BBC's corporate goal of not annoying the Conservative Party, an embarrassment. To erase that embarrassment, the BBC began to apply a little low cunning.

On Wednesday morning the Bell campaign team – such as it was – travelled from Knutsford, a nice, olde-worlde place full of alleys and pubs – to Wilmslow town centre, a soulless pedestrian precinct, crawling with urban anomie and chain store outlets.

Despite the encouraging presence of Melissa, Bell's patter on the streets for his first proper walkabout was not very fluent. Robin Stummer of the *Independent on Sunday*, not exactly an enthusiast for the Conservative Party, described the scene: 'Melissa has been there when Bell has been at his most dazed, wandering the streets like an unguided, low-velocity missile, one hand fumbling in jacket pocket, the other hanging expectantly in mid-air, always vaguely embarrassed by the reporters and camera crews.'

Vote Vague Embarrassment Against Corruption would have neatly summed up the Clean Machine's candidate that day. Melissa told Stummer: 'He's not a politician and doesn't want to be a politician in the sense that people understand.' Stummer continued with finely poised irony: 'And in the sense that people understand, Bell has so far not been a politican.'

Still, there were quite a lot of shoppers who smiled sweetly at him and wished him good luck. Were they serious? Or were they just Tories who smiled at someone they recognised from the flickering blue god in the living room, but were going to vote Conservative as usual? It was impossible to call. He treated one man in a dark suit with the following opening gambit:

'This is my second day as a politician.'

'Why don't you stick to reporting? You're very good at that. I mean, did you feel you'd been set up by the other parties?'

The tone of his voice was hostile. Bell had just bumped into the Wilmslow equivalent of a Bosnian Serb Chetnik. Only, this difficult man hadn't been on the slivovitz all night.

Bell: 'No, I don't. I felt that there was a demand from inside the constituency or I wouldn't have come.'

Difficult Man: 'Do you have any fundamental beliefs?'

Bell: 'Yes. I do. . . .'

Difficult Man: 'What are they?'

Bell: 'I'm going to talk about the other issues after nomination.'

Difficult Man: 'Such as?'

Bell: 'I'm going to talk about education. . . .'

Difficult Man: 'What do you know about education? What experience have you had?'

Bell: 'Well, what about having two children . . . ?'

Difficult Man: 'Yes, but I mean in terms of being a politician what experience have you had? I mean surely the electors of Tatton want a professional politician representing their interests.'

Bell: 'I think there's an upside and a downside.'

Difficult Man: 'What about late payment of debt? What about uniform business rate? What about the impact of Europe? The social chapter? The minimum wage? Who's going to discuss these with us?'

Walkabout over, Bell had gone back to the Longview for a break from his first day's campaigning. He entered the side door of the hotel, not the front – an echo of his mode of entering the Holiday Inn in Sarajevo. This was probably unnecessary. Say what you like about the Longview, it is unlikely that a Yugoslav People's Army mortar shell will crash into the hotel lobby.

Bell watched the *One O'Clock News* back in the hotel, conscious that many more Tatton electors would see him on television than meet him on the street.

The bulletin reported: 'Martin Bell took his campaign to the

streets of Wilmslow this morning with a walkabout in the town
centre, giving the voters the chance to take him to task.'

And up popped the Difficult Man: 'Surely the electors of
Tatton want a professional politician representing their interests?'

They had broadcast this, the second humiliation of Bell in two
days, without mercy or regard to fairness. None of the nice smiley
ladies saying nice smiley things made the bulletin.

He was so aghast at what the BBC had done to him that he
picked up the phone and started to dial the corporation.

Bell: 'I'm going to complain to the BBC now.' To the phone:
'Is that the *One O'Clock News*? This is Martin Bell. . . . Cathy,
this is a call I never thought I was going to make. . . . You're
bloody right, it is. I do my first walkabout in Wilmslow, I have
twenty-five in favour, I have three against and you give me just
one of the three against. What kind of journalism is that? How can
you defend it? . . . OK. . . . Will you send my protests to the
non-journalist involved? I'm going to denounce you in forty-five
minutes. I really am. I'm resigning from the BBC and if that's the
BBC's journalism, well, f*** 'em.'

He put the phone down and said: 'Bastards! Bastards!'

The bastards' corporate goal was beginning to grind him down.

He walked over to Knutsford's Little Theatre and made public
his resignation from the BBC at his first press conference not to be
hijacked by the Hamiltons. And then he went on to say that the
moment he quit, standards collapsed. After a bubble of laughter
died, he went on:

'It has become quite obvious to me in these past days, especially
now we're in for the long haul, that I couldn't remain even
theoretically and technically a BBC reporter. It was easier for
them and easier for me to resign. I'm not going back. I expect to
be the next Member of Parliament for this constituency so I have
necessarily burned my bridges behind me. They took this quite
well. In fact, I would say with a certain degree of relief.'

We hacks reacted to this announcement by shuffling our
bottoms in our seats. Had we been decent human life, the

movement might have been mistaken for a small gesture of respect for a man who had worked for the BBC for so long, and who had served the principle of honourable journalism with such dignity.

Then Eastham, the man from the *Mail*, opened up on Bell. He was aggressive, clever, tough, giving Bell no let-up, asking questions about local issues which he could not possibly expect him to know the answers to. He was much better at monstering Bell than I had been at monstering Hamilton. I had crudely shouted Hamilton down, but Eastham's technique was detailed, forensic, exposing Bell's weaknesses to the neutral hacks. I watched him work with rapt attention and thought to myself: 'I could do that.'

On and on Eastham went. Bell cut in: 'You seem very vexed.' It wasn't much, but it was possible to sense a small stirring. The political toddler was beginning to stick up for himself in the playgroup. But still, he was only a baby who could fall over at any moment and scrape his knees, while the big boys nicked his sweets.

Outside, a man wearing milk bottle glasses, red and white bathing cap and star-spangled leotard, surrounded by two ill-clad women, soaked in the sun. 'I could do with some sleaze this afternoon,' he confided, wistfully.

The setbacks continued. Even political geography was against Bell. The constituency was vast, a Rorschach Test ink-blob thrown at the map of the Cheshire countryside which forms the underbelly of the Manchester conurbation. Tatton was the place to move to once you had made it. It is an ugly name for a pretty, leafy constituency, one caused by the truncation of a fine country estate, next to Knutsford, called Tatton Park. Just opposite the Brick Red Lubyanka in Knutsford was a gleaming showroom of chrome and leather gas-guzzlers, soft-top BMWs and hideously expensive Rolls Royces: a neat symbol of why Hamilton enjoyed a 22,000 majority.

To punch through to the people of this natural Tory constituency, Bell had to meet them. But there was no geographical centre to the seat. Both headquarters were based in Knutsford – theoretically, where King Canute of holding-back-the-sea fame had forded a river – but that was dwarfed in population terms by the suburban sprawl of Wilmslow. To the west there was rolling farmland, dotted with the blue standard of the Hamilton posters, and on the extremity of the constituency the working-class village of Barnton, serving a ghost of British industrial might, an all but derelict ICI plant. They were Labour voters, but many of them hadn't bothered to go to the polling station in years. And, besides, why should they turn out for a southern ponce in a fancy suit who probably thought mushy peas was avocado guacamole?

Over on the far east of the constituency was Alderley Edge, a village which boasts psychoneurotic pretensions of grandeur, a hint of witchcraft – followers of the Pagan religion reportedly prance naked on the Edge under moonlight – and the highest number of bottles of champagne bought per capita in the United Kingdom. This is partly because Mancunians leave their grisly, rain-sodden metropolis by the banks of the ship canal and go south when they have anything to celebrate; but also because the population of Alderley Edge is extremely rich. One psephological twist was that Alderley Edge had been part of the neighbouring constituency of Macclesfield and some of the Tories, loyal to their old, independently minded MP, Nicholas Winterton, were not best pleased to find themselves in Hamilton land. Just up the road from Alderley Edge was Nether Alderley and the Old Rectory. Of all the areas in the constituency, it was Alderley Edge that was of the deepest blue.

And that was where the Bell campaign headed to meet disaffected Tories. One, Patricia Field, is bluer than blue, the chairwoman of the Alderley Edge Tory branch and the wife of my friend Michael Field, who had quit the Tatton Tories in dismay. Patricia had not been allowed to speak at Tuesday's adoption meeting. No woman from the floor had. She told Bell: 'The meeting was a disgrace.' Finally, a result for Bell?

As Mrs Field was speaking, her words were interrupted by two yobs crawling by in a black Ferrari. The passenger leaned out and bawled through a megaphone made from a rolled-up newspaper: 'Bell-Pillock!' The engine revved: 'Bell-Pillock!'

To paraphrase Pope: 'We may see the small value God has for black Ferraris by the people he gives them to.' With a throaty roar the four-wheeled phallus moved on, it is hoped to an appointment with a 20-ton cement-mixer with dodgy brakes on a blind bend.

Bell walked on to be met by a furious man who started shouting that he had nothing to do with Tatton and knew nothing of the constituency.

Furious Man: 'Neil Hamilton has done a damn good job for his constituency and that is what his constituents want. They want somebody that will look after them. . . .'

Bell: '. . . at the end of this, if people want him as their MP, that's fine. . . .'

Furious Man: 'I heard you on the radio this morning. "I will get him out, I will get him out" – that's what you said. It's got nothing to do with politics.'

He walked off, blinded for some reason to Bell's decency. Bell stood there, blinking, a frown of puzzlement on his face, his hand raised in the air as if to shake the hand of an imaginary friend. It was a hateful moment, one that typified the bitterness of the fight. I wanted to go up to the Furious Man and shout: 'What do you mean "It's got nothing to do with politics"? This is a democracy. It's precious and we must care for it. Hamilton has allowed himself to be bought by the favours of rich men. He has cheapened our democracy. This is absolutely about politics, it's why people fought for the vote in the first place, it's . . . it's. . . .'

But that would have been the end of my role as an observer. And anyway we would probably have got into a fight.

Later that day, Bell phoned the one political leader who had shared Bell's outrage about what was happening in Bosnia in the last decade of the twentieth century, Paddy Ashdown.

Bell: 'Well, I'm feeling a bit lonely at the moment. I'm going to see the Labour Party this evening. I think that's all right. But I'm absolutely desperate to get a professional organisation in place. . . . I need professional organisers. I'm hoping by tomorrow to have a prominent local Tory on board. But it's difficult for them. I've got to have a Tory. Although lots of Tories are pledging their support, I need somebody prominent. . . . Thank you very much indeed, Paddy, I appreciate it. Well, it's hard work and it's a steep learning curve but I'm going to get there. Thanks, Paddy, thanks, bye.'

The members of Tatton's Labour Party met at a school in Knutsford to ratify – or not – the decision of the executive committee to withdraw Jon Kelly in favour of Bell. The party's deputy leader, John Prescott, had arrived to square the local members. Almost everyone at the meeting was aware that, if Labour and the Liberals fought it out, the opposition would be cruelly split and Hamilton would coast home on the back of their divisions. Hacks were strictly banned from entering the meeting. But it would have been fun to listen to Prescott. I walked around the back of the school looking for an open door or an inviting window, to be met by a couple of other hacks similarly engaged. There was no way in.

New Labour, new locks.

At the end of the meeting, Prescott emerged to tell an alfresco press conference: 'The meeting tonight of the Tatton constituency Labour Party overwhelmingly endorsed the withdrawal of Jon Kelly as the Labour candidate on the condition that the Liberal Democrats confirm their intention to support the candidature of Martin Bell.'

I had missed Prescott going into the meeting because I had had a quick drink beforehand in the pub. I missed Prescott going out of the meeting because, bored with waiting for the outcome, I had gone to another pub for a natter with some of the other hacks. Their names are legion. Thus far, I had a not-ever-so-enviable strike rate of missing every single important event in the campaign. But when Bell and Melissa emerged I bummed a lift from them back to the Longview.

Melissa: 'So, good results, eh?'

Bell, at the wheel, the candidate as chauffeur: 'Good result.'

Sweeney: 'Wonderful. Well done.'

Melissa: 'Prescott was amazing.'

Sweeney: 'He's a star.'

This was a bit rich, considering I had not clapped eyes on him, either entering or leaving the hall.

Melissa: 'The speech went really well. He's' – she indicated her father – 'becoming—'

Sweeney: '. . . great. You're getting better—'

Melissa: '. . . every minute.'

Bell (gloomy as ever): 'I need minding. I need people who can get me in and out of cars and so on.'

Sweeney: 'Not that way, Martin – you're going the wrong way.'

Melissa: 'We got completely lost on the way, actually.'

Back in the Longview's dive bar, Bell was playing campaign receptionist again.

Bell: 'I've just got in from my Labour Party meeting, which seems to have gone well. . . . Thank you, I think I'm going to need it. This man' – Hamilton – 'is a rottweiler. I'm personally motivated to get this bastard out.'

Hamilton was altogether smoother. On the night he had been selected as the Conservative candidate he had rubbished Bell: 'He seems like a nice guy, totally unsuited for politics.'

Given the chaos, the want of organisation, the lack of experience, the admission that Hamilton was innocent until proven guilty, the hostility of the BBC, the failure at Knutsford Heath, Hamilton's crack sounded, then, like the epitaph of Bell's political career.

Bell was Pop-Eye, without the spinach.

And that was before Hamilton sent in the lawyers.

ACT TWO

... Light thickens, and the crow
Makes wing to the rooky wood.

Scene I: The Old Rectory, Nether Alderley

To understand the enemy, you have to wander inside their minds. Christine Hamilton is, on the face of it, far easier to read than her husband. What you see is what you get: a pocket-sized Mrs Thatcher, so ferociously loyal to her man as to make a Japanese attack dog appear a chihuahua decked out in pink booties. But she is, at least, uncomplicatedly loyal. She is driven by the single precept: 'Stand by your man.' It may have led her to some strange and odd positions, but it is a code not without honour.

And there is a mocking self-awareness that she is, in some way, a player in the pantomime of British national life. The crowd may boo her and throw custard pies, but there she is, on the stage, taking it on the chin. 'Don't say I'm not a sport,' you can almost hear her challenge as the custard pies land home.

Her vulgarity to the press fits neatly into this psychological view of her. She gave good doorstep. There was an earthiness about her language which was rather appealing. 'Piss off' became the routine form of verbal heavy artillery that rained down on hacks – 'snakes' – who knocked on the front door of the Old Rectory. 'Get those reptiles off my daffodils' was another refrain. The choicest abuse of all was directed at a BBC outside broadcast van with a telescopic radio aerial which raised itself above the Old Rectory hedge: 'Get that bloody great penis away from my hedge.'

We did love it when she talked dirty.

For us, Hamilton was always called Hamilton, but Christine was Christine.

Like dozens of other hacks, Robin Stummer of the *Independent on Sunday* had fun with her: 'That evening, there were stirrings at the Old Rectory. A rigid blonde mane appeared over the holly hedge, followed swiftly by a large, pale face. "Are you press?" she asked. "Oh, you are – just please bugger orf, will you? I mean in the politest possible terms." '

Coming from the Independent Group of newspapers, Stummer wasn't touched with the sign of the Devil as I was, working for the *Observer*, part of the Evil Empire that is the Guardian Newspaper

Group. Stummer does a nice line in hangdog politeness on doorsteps –  'Sorry to trouble you . . .' – and could make a good living selling life insurance policies. His hangdoggery worked, and he was allowed an audience with the nation's most wanted couple.

Stummer reported Christine as saying: ' "You can come out, Neil, I think he's tame." Hamilton then appeared over the holly. His wife did the talking. When would they start going on walkabouts? "Next week, I suppose," answered Mrs Hamilton. "But we don't want a media circus. People round here of the Conservative mind know the BBC as metropolitan southerners, but we don't want to be told what to do by outsiders. Look, I'm sorry I told you to bugger orf. . . ."

"And what, Neil, would you do if you lost your seat?"

"I'm sure there would be a job for me at the BBC. Or I could emigrate to Bosnia." '

BBC

O.B. UNIT

This exchange captures the Hamiltons as, presumably, they would wish to be seen. Their motto is 'We Do Things Together' – WDTT – and it is clear from their behaviour in front of Stummer that there is a fair bit of truth in their aphorism. What is odd, very odd, is that Hamilton, despite being under threat from the man in the white suit, allowed Christine to appear to dominate him so in public, in front of a reporter.

Watching them perform together, it was hard to think of a former minister of the crown and his loyal Tory wife. They conjured up an altogether different picture, that of a comedian and his straight man plugging a panto, working the audience like the late Eric Morecambe and his partner Ernie Wise, say, doing *Puss in Boots* at Scarborough. Originally, Eric was the straight man and Ernie the wit. But over the years their two roles crossed over, with Ernie becoming boring and predictable and the audience looking to Eric to supply the real laughs with his surreal humour. Likewise with Christine and Hamilton. He is, theoretically, the famous wit, but as the years have gone by the roles have been reversed.

From the Battle of Knutsford Heath on, Christine became the Hamilton for the killer quote, the truly amazing piece of effrontery, the bish-bosh of attack. 'If Martin Bell thinks shrapnel is bad, wait till he's dealt with me,' she told the *Sun*'s Woman Editor, Jane Moore. That's a perfect soundbite for a tabloid like the *Sun* and Christine supplied them, day in, day out, with the relentlessness of a Gatling gun mowing down the fuzzy-wuzzies at the Battle of Omdurman. Not very fair on the opposition, but in politics, as in war, only one thing matters: winning.

Soundbites don't come that easy. They have to be planned, rehearsed, thought through, the bad ones rejected, the good ones played up, repeated until they sink into the national conscious-ness. In the critical first week of the campaign, Bell, who has a feeling for the beauty of the English language, did not come up with one crisp soundbite. The Hamiltons, in particular Christine, had produced dozens. They were winning, and he was losing, the battle of words.

There was also something about her attack, the gusto and bravura with which she defended her man, which was attractive. It is odd and probably wrong-headed to describe Christine as enticing, but, as Henry Kissinger said, 'Power is the greatest aphrodisiac.' It was frightening the way her love of power drew her on, but it did have a certain magnetic quality. Once abused by Christine, one couldn't get enough.

And then there is the Christine Hamilton Look. Baudelaire, not one of life's natural Conservatives, described the Christine Hamilton Look in his poem 'Le Chat', translated by Joanna Richardson:

> . . . Her glance,
> Like yours, endearing beast,
> Cold, searching, cuts and shivers like a lance. . . .

It didn't take long before some of the other hacks got to say that 'Sweeney had a thing about Christine.'

Maybe.

She was born forty-seven years ago, her full name Mary Christine Holman, the daughter of a general practitioner in Ringwood, Hampshire. She had an idyllic childhood, with a boat on the Solent and ponies galore. 'I was always in the saddle,' she said once.

Christine was educated at Wentworth School in Bournemouth which, according to Lynda Lee-Potter of the *Daily Mail*, in one article in early 1997, 'teaches middle-class girls not to blub, complain or let the side down'. Lee-Potter went on: 'She truly does have the kind of strength that makes one wonder how the British lost India.' One could say that it was because the Indians were fed up of being bossed around by memsahibs, but that would be ungallant. In another piece a few months later Lee-Potter tweaked her metaphor: 'Christine Hamilton has the valour

of the early Christian martyrs and truly does make one wonder
how the British ever lost the Empire.' The answer from the
Indians would probably be the same.

Christine did reasonably well at school and read sociology and
politics at York University. There, she got to know two young
men who would become right-wing Tory MPs and, subsequently, were outed as homosexuals. They were Michael Brown
and Harvey Proctor. The Hamiltons, Brown and Proctor became
loyal friends. All four have left their droppings in the national
safari park.

Christine first met Hamilton in the late sixties at a conference of
the Federation of Conservative Students. 'It sounds absurd, but
our eyes met across a crowded room,' she has said. 'He had great
big Victorian sideburns and was already going grey. It was love at
first sight for both of us.'

But she hesitated before taking on Hamilton. Despite fancying
him, she did not vote for her future husband in a ballot for the
chairmanship of the FCS but instead plumped for Andrew Neil,
the squaloid Scot who went on to become an ornament of
Tramps nightclub and the editor of the *Sunday Times*, where
his philosophy was described as: 'If you can't fuck it or plug it in,
Andrew isn't interested.'

After three years courting Hamilton, she dumped him when
she got her first post in the Commons as secretary to a Tory MP.
'Poor Neil was a perpetual student. He didn't want to go out into
the big wide world, so he spent about eight years at university,'
she later said. 'I just realised that I had to make a break. It was
awful, a bit like kicking a dog.'

She kicked the dog anyway, and started to work for a Tory
backbencher with a fantastic name, Wilfred Proudfoot. She
moved two years later, for the inducement of an extra £20 a
week, to work for another MP who had spotted her efficiency
and attack. Sir Gerald Nabarro was a man with even more facial
hair than the sideburned Hamilton. He was, at the time, the man
with the most celebrated moustache in England: his whiskers

were like the handlebars on a Harley Davidson made hirsute. His career was equally curly. He was a wealthy man, with four Rolls Royces, each with a personalised numberplate: NAB1, NAB2, NAB3 AND NAB4.

Nabarro was the motorist's champion who came up in court on charges of having driven around a roundabout the wrong way. Christine sat in the gallery every day, clutching a piece of lucky white heather for him. The first trial was aborted. At the end of the second, Nabarro was acquitted. She was photographed hugging him. She was younger then, and, according to a don, then a student journalist, who met her at Cambridge around that time, 'a very attractive woman'. The dry academic continued, deploying non-academic terminology: 'She was a real stunner.'

One photograph catches a look in her eye, as she gleams at Nabarro, which is adoring, delighted and erotically charged. He rewarded her loyalty with a new Mini.

After Nabarro's death in 1973 she moved to MP number three, spending ten years as secretary to Michael Grylls, a silver-haired Tory nabob, who was later to become implicated in the cash-for-questions affair. It was while she was working for Grylls that she fell, once more, under Hamilton's spell.

She told Lee-Potter: 'We always exchanged Christmas cards and then, when he was in London once, he rang me up. I invited him to dinner and as soon as I opened the door and saw him, I thought: "Christine, you were a fool to let him go." He arrived on February 17, 1978, and never went home again.'

Christine married Neil on 4 June 1983 in a pretty little church on a beach in Cornwall, near her parents' then home. 'We didn't have a honeymoon, because it turned out to be the Saturday before the general election.' Five days later, Hamilton entered Parliament.

Their partnership would be, for others, claustrophobically intense. Politicians usually walk the lobby of the House of Commons, where political journalists and MPs meet, on their own. 'Not Hamilton,' one MP told my colleague Jay Rayner. 'He would almost never be seen in the lobby by himself. Christine was always there by his side to make sure he didn't say the wrong thing.'

'In many ways,' she has said, 'we lead an intensely incestuous life. I know everything that he is doing. I read his letters, answer his phone, organise his diary. I know this arrangement sounds like a recipe for divorce but it works for us.'

Is it possible that she keeps close to him for fear of what he might get up to in her absence? a reporter once asked. 'Utter rubbish. Basically, all either of us wants out of life is what the other wants.' What neither seemed to want was children. 'We didn't make this decision because we thought they would be incompatible with a successful career but because we simply didn't want them.'

Throughout her time in Parliament, Christine was an extremely hard-working servant of the constituents. She attacked their difficulties with the same gung-ho as she attacked everything else in life. And, it is true to say, she attacked life's pleasures for Hamilton and herself in exactly the same way.

Ian Greer, the parliamentary lobbyist who helped to tarnish Hamilton's reputation, was introduced to her husband by Christine. He was yet another gay man in her circle. It was Greer who caused Hamilton his greatest misfortune when in 1996 he pulled out of the joint libel action against the *Guardian*, leaving Hamilton in a jam and allowing the paper its 'A Liar and a Cheat' headline. In his somewhat self-serving autobiography, Greer addresses himself to Christine's way of doing things and her willingness to call in favours. Back in 1988, her husband was booked on a trip to the United States which she could not afford to take without a little help. She placed four calls to Greer asking for a free ticket, then for an upgrade, then for help when her flight was merged with another and she was going to lose her upgrade. 'To keep her happy,' wrote Greer, 'I arranged for a car to pick her up from Newark and drive her into New York.' Finally, she called a fourth time and asked for all the flights to be rearranged again, to fit a change in her plans.

In the eighties, when Mrs Thatcher reigned supreme and the Labour Party looked set for permanent opposition, free trips seemed something of a cult in Christine's circle of friends. If you look at the Hamiltons' trips, together with those of Michael Brown and some of the other big trippers in their circle, you might almost be forgiven for wondering whether there was something of a competition, a game going on: who freebies furthest freebies best.

Brown, then MP for Scunthorpe, did very well for himself. According to *Roth's Parliamentary Profiles*, the indispensable guide to these freebies, Brown went to Taiwan as a guest of the Anti-Communist League for World Freedom Day in 1984; to Namibia at the expense of its then South African-sponsored regime in January 1985; to Northern Cyprus as a guest of President Denktash in March 1985; to the USA as a guest of the US Foreign Policy Council in April 1985; to Israel as a guest of the Conservative Friends of Israel in January 1986; to South Africa as a guest of the South African government in April 1986; to Iceland as a guest of Fylkir Ltd and Grimsby Town Football Club in August 1986; to the USA as a guest of US Tobacco Inc. in September 1986; and to Bophuthatswana – a curious black homeland 'state' with a white South African Defence Minister – as a guest of its President, Lucas Mangope, in September 1987. . . . The list goes on and on. He even went to Iraq, as a guest of an Arab council friendly to Saddam Hussein, though this was before the Gulf War, when the Father of the Iraqi Nation was a loyal friend of the West, even if he had used chemical weapons against the Kurds. What of five thousand gassed Kurds at Halabja, if a free trip was on offer?

The Hamiltons' stay in the Ritz is well known, though the MP did not record it at the time in the *Register of Members' Interests*. But Hamilton was often travelling for free, so much so that two things mark out his early parliamentary career: his enthusiasm for the death penalty and his love of free trips. *Roth's Parliamentary Profiles* records the freebies Hamilton owned up to: in March 1985 he

visited Hong Kong as a guest of its Government Office; two
months later he visited Ankara as the guest of the Turkish
Parliament, and in September that year visited the USA as a
guest of the government. In February 1987 he visited South
Africa as a guest of its government, and again a year later, this time
as a guest of its Chamber of Mines. A month later, in March 1988,
he was in New Zealand as a guest of its government, and in May
1988 he was the guest of the Czech Communist regime which at
the time was harassing a playwright called Vaclav Havel.

Bell went to Czechoslovakia in 1969. The BBC paid. He was
asked to leave by the Czech Communist government. I went in
1988. The *Observer* paid. After a week I made my excuses and left.

One of the great heroes in my life is a Czech, or rather
Moravian, writer called Ludvik Vaculik. His book *A Cup of
Coffee with My Interrogator* is a beautiful expression of resistance to
brute power. With his friend Havel he was a founder member of
Charter 77, penalised, humiliated and monstered by the Czech
secret police, the StB, throughout the seventies and eighties, until
the Velvet Revolution.

Vaculik was a victim.

They would arrest him for no reason. Because he was a writer
they didn't beat him up but just subjected him to hours and hours
of pointless questioning, 'applying logic as round as a shaven
skull'.

He mocked his tormentors with gentle irony:

A crisp winter afternoon was advancing behind the bars from
the White Mountain towards the darkness. My Lieutenant-
Colonel was standing by the window, his hands behind his
back. From the courtyard came the sound of women's voices as
female prisoners took their exercise.

'Look, Mr Vaculik,' he said with a smile I could not see from
where I was sitting, 'I know you'll put all this into one of your
articles . . .'

'I expect so, if I'm given half a chance.'

He was silent for a while. Then:

'And you'll call it: "A cup of coffee with the interrogator".'

I almost fell of my chair. It was no use – they knew everything.

While they played with Vaculik, Hamilton had been their guest.

Unlike Hamilton, whose wit and aggression in Parliament marked him out as a favourite of Mrs Thatcher, Brown never slithered very far up the political greasy pole. During the last Parliament he was exposed as a homosexual by the *News of the World* and lost his seat in the Labour landslide of 1 May.

Christine's other great friend from York University is Harvey Proctor. He is less well known for his tripping than for his public enthusiasm for the repatriation of black and brown people from Britain and a more private enthusiasm for spanking the bottoms of male prostitutes, known in that pretty grim trade as 'rent boys'. For this reason he enjoyed the soubriquet in the House of Commons of Harvey 'Whacko' Proctor. His first reaction to newspaper allegations was: 'I am entirely innocent.' Later, in 1987, charged with four counts of gross indecency, this was amended in court to just four words: 'Guilty, guilty, guilty, guilty.' He was forced to quit Parliament.

One could say that Christine has been a trifle unfortunate with her men friends. You can fault her luck but not her pluck. After Proctor's embarrassing exit from the political demi-monde, a number of friends 'rallied round' – a favourite phrase in Tory circles – and stumped up the cash for him to buy a shirt business in Richmond. Fifteen Tories invested in Proctor's shirt shop, including Michael Heseltine, Tristan Garel-Jones and Jeffrey Archer, to the tune of £5000. Archer told the *People*: 'I don't think the best thing to do when someone is down is to kick them. Perhaps there is decency left in some people.' To this noble sentiment, he added: 'And anyway, there are tax advantages in investing in this.'

One day, according to Christine, two gay-bashers turned up

and thumped two men inside the shop, Proctor and Hamilton, breaking the latter's nose. While the two men nursed their wounds, Christine leapt out of the shop and ran after the thugs.

There does seem to be a streak of physical aggression in her nature. More recently, when Alan Rusbridger, the languid editor of the *Guardian*, went against Hamilton in a mud-slinging contest on *Newsnight* over 'cash-for-questions', he was advised by BBC staff not to leave via the green room, the hospitality suite. There, Christine was lying in wait: 'She is offering to plant one on your nose.'

The downside, the despair, the misery, she only admitted to in what must have been an unguarded moment with the friendly Lee-Potter, whose article appeared in the *Mail* two days after the Battle of Knutsford Heath: 'I'm full of all the human frailties. Basically I'm as soft as anything. I can't bear being out of sorts with people. I suppose, in a way, I'm a typical Tory wife and this whole thing has been terribly wounding. I just take Temazepam every night. I don't think about whether I should or shouldn't. I just do it because I never sleep.'

But, despite the pressure, she never cracked in public. It is hard not to have sympathy for the Tory Wife on Temazepam. And yet. . . . She is not the angel she does not look like. It was Christine who introduced her husband to Ian Greer. It was her signature which appeared on the receipt from Peter Jones department store for a set of expensive garden furniture for which Ian Greer paid. It was she who booked the room at the Paris Ritz, the stay at which made concrete in the public mind the host of sleaze allegations against Hamilton. She and Hamilton charged everything – even postage stamps – to their room, and ate every meal in the hotel's most expensive restaurant, running up a total of £2500 in extras. And Hamilton could not have cleaned out the mock marble mini-bar in Room 356 alone.

When the couple asked if they could stay again and were told by Al Fayed's office that the hotel was full, it was she who phoned to check and discovered to her humiliation that there were many rooms available. She had been greedy, or allowed herself to go along with her husband's greed. Yet that was not enough to condemn her in our eyes. There are plenty of greedy people in this world, many of whom work in the newspaper business.

Her energy and attack were impressive, even admirable, but the questions which troubled the other hacks and me were simple ones. To whom is Christine harnessed? Who benefits from her energy? She is a great fighter, but what, exactly, is she fighting for?

The answers are her husband; her husband; and her husband.

Scene II: Fascist Italy, 1943

Open the door and walk inside the mind of Mostyn Neil Hamilton. It's a strange, eerie world, full of shadows and echoes of those who, in T.S. Eliot's phrase, 'march in step'.

If you study Hamilton carefully, a puzzle emerges. He is greedy, a self-confessed assiduous free-tripper, hungry for the appurtenances of power. But time and again, he appears to gamble everything he has. He feasts with panthers. For him, risk, danger, playing it to the edge: that's how he gets his kicks. A more cautious, more prudent man would never have got into so much trouble. There is a romantic love of the gesture, the stance, the pose.

Consider the Ginger Biscuit which was proffered to the television cameras after news of the stay at the Ritz, paid for by its owner, Al Fayed, broke in the *Guardian* in 1994. He held up the biscuit, his fingers trembling, daring the enemy to do its worst.

Consider the Battle of Knutsford Heath, a deliberately engineered scene of political melodrama.

Consider the Hamiltons' appearance on *Have I Got News for You*, after the fall. There is an element in Hamilton's character that does not seem so very different from Piglet in the Winnie-the-Pooh stories. Piglet bobs up and down in the river, having fallen in while playing pooh-sticks, declaring while drowning: 'Look at

me, I'm swimming.' There is no doubting Hamilton's showman-
ship, nor his daring. He is more exhibitionist than calculator.
Michael Portillo once, reportedly, said of David Mellor: 'I cannot
understand how that man has let his lust govern his ambition.'
The same criticism, that Hamilton has let his lust for danger over-
ride his ambition, could be made of the former Minister for
Corporate Affairs.

And then there is his strain of greed, the hunger for the brown
envelopes. This can be explained by a lust for a lifestyle that he
could not easily afford. But that is too simple for Hamilton. With
a little trimming here and there he might perhaps have done
without so much money, so many free trips, so much '*baksheesh,
baksheesh!*' from Al Fayed. Any conventionally ambitious Conservative politician would have called a halt at some stage, would
have reined in his appetite, but for Hamilton there was, it seems, a
psychological urge to push it to the limit, to empty the Ritz mini-
bar, to rack up the biggest bill in the shortest possible time. It is the
dare and not the money that turns him on. There is something
almost sexual in his hunger for money.

And there is yet another, darker strain. All his political life he
has flirted with the Neo-Fascist fruitcakes of the far Right,
dressing up, strutting their stuff, posing here as Mussolini, there
as Hitler. In Britain, even half a century after the end of World
War II, this is politically suicidal. And yet it is as if he cannot stop
himself from having a bite from the Neo-Fascist apple. The
danger of the politics that cannot speak its name has an appeal for
him which is irresistible.

During the campaign Hamilton played cod psychiatrist, ana-
lysing Martin Bell, giving a mock diagnosis that he was going
through a 'mid-life crisis'. But Hamilton himself appears to have
suffered a 'through-life crisis'. He is an exhibitionist and a
masochist, one who is tempted by dark desires. Not quite the
stuff of 'Back to Basics' as set out by John Major, but then the
Conservative Party has always been the broadest of churches.

His early life is unexceptional on paper. He was born on 9

March 1949 in Fleur-de-Lys, Monmouthshire, the grandson of Welsh miners. His father was a chartered engineer in the mining industry, a boss rather than a collier. He was brought up not in the red valleys like the Rhondda, the engine room of British socialism, but on the softer edges of the South Wales minefield. He went to the local grammar school in Amman Valley and from there to Aberystwyth College, then a far-flung satellite of the University of Wales. Aberystwyth is not exactly the first grove of academe. Its only serious claim to fame in the furniture of the British mind is a modern myth, no doubt utterly apocryphal, that a President of the Students' Union, wearing only a pair of green wellington boots, once pleasured a sheep on the steps of the college. It is safe to say that Hamilton's alma mater boasts more sheep-shaggers than Nobel laureates.

After Wales he studied law at Corpus Christi, Cambridge and became a barrister at the Middle Temple. He earned his living as a tax lawyer and made two unsuccessful attempts at getting into Parliament. In March 1983 he beat local Cheshire MPs Mark Carlisle and Jock Bruce-Gardyne for the nomination to the new, rock-solid Tory safe seat of Tatton. In the wake of the Falklands War, the 1983 election was a shoo-in for the Tories. He had a job for life, or so he and his new wife must have thought.

It was at Aberystwyth in the late sixties that Hamilton first showed his love of playing Fascists. For the student elections he staged a pocket-sized Nuremberg rally. It was a joke, of course, but one so elaborate and studied that it gives rise for unease. He turned up surrounded by several 'bodyguards', one sporting Ton-Ton Macoute dark glasses and toting a gun (albeit a toy) to the sound of Richard Strauss's 'Thus Spake Zarathustra' – music full of Nazi echoes. The Strauss piece is no tum-tee-tum-tum, but a musical expression of the Superman myth set out in Nietzsche's famous essay. Hitler and his chums took up the 'Superman' stuff and added their own notion of *Untermenschen* – 'sub-humans': Jews, Slavs, gypsies and so on – with grisly results.

Hamilton marched into a single spotlight, wearing a black

cloak, black trousers with riding boots and a white jacket crossed with a red sash and large medallion.

Full-blown Fascism is not on in Britain. The suggestion was there, but what Hamilton actually presented to his student electors was a species of panto Fascist: 'I'm the Leader' – 'Oh, no, he's not.' But at least one of those present found it offensive. A woman fellow student was so disgusted by Hamilton's performance that she was moved to write a letter to the *Guardian* about it almost thirty years later. 'It was Nuremberg in Wales,' she recalled. 'Being the daughter of a Holocaust survivor, I found his delivery in particularly bad taste. There was no doubt in my mind that given power Hamilton could be dangerous. His craving for attention was quite evident then – this is a man who has an enormous ego.'

Hamilton's political prospectus for the student elections was plainly a joke, albeit pathetic and unfunny. Yet again the labour behind the joke puzzles. He knocked out a manifesto which read: 'The constitutional pedants, the ledgerbook minds will be resolutely crushed beneath the iron heel of a victorious people marching on the road to destiny.'

Hamilton had an endorsement, from the 'Maharaja of Jaipur (who is alive and well and living in Bradford): "I am most happy to

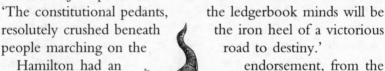

be commending Neil Hamilton for the post of Supreme Autocrat. Long Live King Victoria! Move right down de bus please. Hold tight." '

Clearly, the man who was to become the *Spectator*'s Parliamentary Wit of the Year in 1989 had to start somewhere. And where better than a fresh-faced Welsh version of Bernard Manning?

Hamilton came nowhere in the elections, but he did get his hands on the student newspaper. He changed its name from the *Courier* – boring – to *Feudal Times and Reactionary Herald*, and decked it out with a logo identical to the imperial eagle of the Kaiser's Germany. You get some flavour of the cast of Hamilton's mind from his first editorial: 'The transformation is now complete! We have ascended from the pit of barbarianism and Leftist semi-intellectual filth, which was neither clever nor pleasing, to what, I trust, will be recognised as literate and stimulating.' He went on: 'We welcome all but the rag-and-bone brigade, the spiritual heirs of the Vandals, who have no right to be in a place of learning. He who has no standard of cleanliness and personal appearance is hardly likely to have any other appendage of civilisation attached to him.'

The paper sent along a reporter to interview Lord Hamilton at his self-styled headquarters, Reaction House. His despatch: 'I felt once again that inner glow which told me that the great days of Britain's history were not past, that there would be one more name: HAMILTON, inscribed alongside the heroes of old – Lord Eldon, Horatio Bottomley, King Richard II. . . .'

Consider Hamilton's heroes of old.

Lord Eldon (1751–1838) was a bitter enemy of democracy, reform and religious liberty throughout his period of office as Chancellor from 1801 to 1827. He opposed the emancipation of Catholics – why should my forbearers be denied the vote? – the abolition of the slave trade and the reform of the House of Commons.

Horatio Bottomley (1860–1933) was a loathsome 'yellow'

paper journalist who fuelled anti-German hate during World War I, though he did not himself fight in the trenches. In 1891 and 1901 he was charged with fraud and acquitted. Between 1901 and 1905 he had sixty-seven bankruptcy petitions and writs filed against him. In 1922 he was imprisoned for fraud.

Richard II (1367–1400) was the inventor of the poll tax, a levy so hated that the men of Essex and Kent, a hundred thousand strong, rose and marched on London: the Peasants' Revolt led by Wat Tyler. Richard publicly conceded to the requests of the leaders, then cheated on his word and had Tyler beheaded. Later, he had the Duke of Arundel beheaded and the Duke of Gloucester done to death. His reign came to a sticky end in Pontefract Castle in 1400, when he himself was murdered.

Hamilton's heroes are, then, a racist, democracy-hating bigot, a xenophobic fraudster and a cheating, murdering monarch. Perhaps Hamilton's sense of history was askew; perhaps not. Martin Bell's heroes are Sir Thomas Moore, William Gladstone and Winston Churchill.

While Hamilton was knocking out this stuff for the *Feudal Times and Reactionary Herald*, Bell was also working as a journalist, though not making up rubbish about himself or eulogising scum. He was reporting the Tet Offensive in Vietnam.

It did not take that long for Hamilton to move from panto Fascism to taste the real thing. But to understand the company Hamilton was to keep, it is necessary to know something about the nature and history of Italian Fascism. Compared to Nazi Germany, Mussolini's Italy has always enjoyed a comic-book reputation: the pomp was sillier, the tortures less cruel, the killing less methodical. All true, but if you were unlucky enough to get on the wrong side of the Fascists things were not so funny.

Readers should be aware that during the campaign in Tatton, I became utterly obsessed with Hamilton's flirtation with Neo-Fascism in Italy and his later mimicry of Adolf Hitler in Germany. I remember that the boss class at the Evil Empire (the *Observer*) once tried to get me away from Tatton. The ruse they thought of was for me to follow the Prime Minister around the north-west. When the Major bandwagon, such as it was, stopped for a brief spell I rushed over to a phone and started calling professors of Italian politics and history who were meeting at a conference in Glasgow, hitting them with abstruse questions such as what exactly Giorgio Almirante had got up to in the Salò Republic. At the end of one long phone call I saw a slurry of hacks scurry for the bus. I caught up with them to discover that Major had just given a very important press conference. I had missed it, as usual.

'What did he say?' I asked one of the big political hitters of the Westminster lobby.

'Usual boring rubbish,' said the politico and mounted the bus.

What follows, then, represents the fruits of completely ignoring a Prime Minister.

The sea-change in the history of Italian Fascism came on 8 September 1943, when King Vittorio Emanuele III staged a coup against Mussolini, the whole country revolted and fifty thousand Allied prisoners of war escaped into the countryside. In the south the Allies were able to protect the gains, helped by thousands of Italian partisans. But in the north the Nazis acted swiftly. They liberated Mussolini, rounded up as many prisoners of war as they could find and cracked down on the partisans without mercy. They did this under the name of Mussolini's reborn Fascist Italian Social Republic state, named the Salò Republic after a spa town in the north of the country. The film-maker Pier Paolo Pasolini paid homage to the nastiness of the republic in his coprophagous epic *Salò, or the 120 Days of Sodom*, completed just before he was brutally murdered.

Theoretically Mussolini was still in power, but in practice Italy was under Nazi rule. The chief function of Mussolini's Fascists was to provide propaganda cover for the Nazis' oppression of the partisans and to take part in the manhunt for the escaped prisoners of war.

'Nazi oppression' is just a phrase. Here is one example of what it meant. That autumn an Italian peasant called Alcide Cervi and

his seven sons sheltered two British prisoners of war from Fascist
patrols. Someone informed on them, and on 25 November 1943
Cervi and his sons were arrested and taken to prison. Just after
Christmas all seven sons were shot dead; their mother died of
grief. Cervi himself escaped when the RAF bombed the prison in
which he was being held, though the misery of his life with his
wife dead and his sons executed can only be imagined.

Complicit in war crimes such as these was Giorgio Almirante,
the chef de cabinet of the Salò Republic's propaganda ministry.
Before the war he had been a Fascist journalist on the paper *Il
Tevere*, which started a violent anti-semitic campaign in 1934.
Then he was promoted to be secretary to the editor of *La Difesa
della Razza* (*The Defence of the Race*), a vicious organ of the Fascist
Party. Around 140,000 copies of *La Difesa della Razza* were
printed and distributed in 1938, coinciding with the enactment of
the Racial Laws which forced all Jews in Italy to register with the
authorities and banned them from public employment, schools
and the dignity of ordinary life.

Almirante's stuff was high-octane hate. For example, on 5 May
1942 he wrote in an article in *La Difesa della Razza*: 'Our racism
must be of the blood, which flows in my veins, which I feel inside
me, which I can see, analyse and confront with the blood of
others. Our racism must be that of meat and muscles.'

Under the Salò Republic, Almirante had a 'primary role in the
direction of war and racist propaganda'. In May 1944 he drew up
a plan for 'racial propaganda', which called for the 'elimination
from national life of Jews and citizens of foreign blood'. Paul
Ginsborg, the expert on Fascist Italy, gave Almirante short shrift
when he tried to moderate his image after the war: Almirante
'later tried to hide his racist and violent past behind a mantle of
respectability'.

After the war was over the Fascist Party was banned, but in
1946 Almirante smoothly created a new party called the Movi-
mento Sociale Italiano (MSI), its name a direct and obvious
reference to Mussolini's Fascist Italian Socialist Republic. The

Neo-Fascist MSI got nastier and nastier and in the late sixties was linked to a chain of terrorist atrocities in Italy, including bomb outrages. Almirante played up to his reputation as someone who had cheered on cold-blooded murder by entitling his autobiography *Diary of an Executioner.*

It was Almirante's MSI which invited three young Britons, if not to bear the Fascist yoke, then at least to be their guests in 1972. And one of the three who turned up for the congress of the MSI's youth wing – the Fronta della Gioventù – was Neil Hamilton. At twenty-three he was a mature postgraduate, and had already held the post of National Vice-Chairman of the Federation of Conservative Students with special responsibility for foreign affairs.

Hamilton travelled to Pescara on the Adriatic where he relaxed among the Neo-Fascists, street fighters and suspected terrorists at the four-star Grand Hotel Adriatico, feasting on 'the racism of meat and muscles'. Almirante was there, according to reports in Italian newspapers.

At the end of the week-long MSI congress in 1972 – by which time an intelligent student activist like Hamilton would have worked out what Almirante and company believed in – it was time for the speeches of thanks. Hamilton scribbled down a speech on Hotel Adriatico notepaper, learnt it and then declared to the young Neo-Fascists: 'I would like to say in the name of the British delegation how happy we are to be here. We thank you for the kind hospitality which we have sincerely received since our arrival in Italy. We hope to be able to receive you in the best possible way in England when we reciprocate your hospitality.'

Hamilton has always made a joke of the trip and said he only attended as an observer. The fact that he made a speech, condemned at the time by one Italian newspaper, sits oddly with his claim that he was simply an observer. Another newspaper, *Roma Flash*, reported on 15 September 1972: 'Delegates of the Monday Club, Neil Hamilton and Michael Pearl, which adheres to the Conservative Party, spoke in succession. They both

illustrated the methods of fighting and the aim of their organisation.'

Hamilton claims he made 'a light-hearted, meaningless speech'.
After his opening courtesies to Almirante's young thugs, he said:
'Europe is sick. Where there is chaos, there must be order. And
where there is weakness, there must be strength.' This is
Mussolinispeak. He went on: 'We are the guardians of the
future, we cannot afford to fail. Long live you of the Right.
Long live anti-Communist Italy. Long live the British Empire!'

'Some circumstantial evidence is very strong,' wrote Thoreau,
'as when you find a trout in the milk.'

On 8 October 1972 the *Sunday Telegraph* devoted three
paragraphs to the trip under an admirably succinct heading:
'Tory trio visit fascists'. The paper reported: 'One of those
who went, Mr Neil Hamilton, 23, until recently vice-chairman
of the Federation of Conservative Students, said last night: "We
went to find out what went on in Italy, but were not representing
the Monday Club in any way. We go to great lengths to say we
are not a Fascist organisation." ' To add to the impression that
Hamilton had not attended as a Monday Club member, he wrote
down 'Feudalist' on his MSI identity card.

Hamilton changed his story eleven years later. In a letter to
Searchlight magazine, published in October 1983, he wrote: 'Over
10 years ago I was a student member of the Monday Club. In
1972 the MSI held a Youth Congress in Italy and invited the
Monday Club to send three observers to it. The Monday Club
invited me to be one of these observers. . . .'

All this ancient history would never have come to public
attention had not the BBC's flagship programme, *Panorama*,
become interested in the right wing of the Conservative Party
and broadcast *Maggie's Militant Tendency* in January 1984.

The programme, produced by James Hogan, introduced by
Fred Emery and reported by Michael Cockerell, aired evidence
that Hamilton was a Neo-Fascist sympathiser, on the books of a
virulently racist and anti-semitic outfit called Tory Action.

Hamilton's trip to the Neo-Fascist rally was also featured on the programme, which was not entirely flattering about the sitting member for Tatton. *Panorama* used footage of an open-air rally held by MSI to illustrate what Italian Neo-Fascists look like. But Hamilton had spoken at an indoor meeting, and he made much of this minor discrepancy in the subsequent attack on *Panorama*.

Along with his fellow Tory MP Gerald Howarth, he sued for libel. The BBC said it stood by its journalism. Hamilton had been on the brink of settling the case, with the BBC paying him no damages, when an unexpected benefactor had emerged. The late billionaire nationalist Sir James Goldsmith, obsessed with what he saw as the communist domination of the media, offered to pay all Hamilton's legal costs. With nothing to lose financially in taking the case to court, Hamilton now broke off the secret talks he had been having with the BBC about a settlement. The case came to court in 1986 and after only four days the BBC caved in, before a single word of its own evidence against Hamilton had been heard. It was to prove one of the pivotal libel actions of the 1980s, providing the Conservatives with much ammunition against the BBC. The corporation apologised to Hamilton and Howarth, paying them their costs and £20,000 damages each.

The *Panorama* team of Cockerell, Hogan and Emery put out a statement disassociating themselves from the settlement and regretting that the jury had not been given the opportunity to reach a verdict on the basis of *Panorama*'s thousand pages of evidence and thirty witnesses.

The defeat over the programme was to affect the cultural history of Great Britain. *Maggie's Militant Tendency* was the latest in a series of programmes – including *Real Lives* featuring Sinn Fein's Martin McGuinness – that had enraged Mrs Thatcher and the Tory government. Now the BBC Board of Governers – which had been increasingly politicised by Mrs Thatcher, with her insistence that the criterion for new appointees was whether they were what she called 'one of us' – turned against the old ideals of public service broadcasting.

The BBC's old guard was crucified, its Director-General
Alastair Milne sacked, journalists responsible for *Maggie's Militant
Tendency* and others in sympathy with its thrust were purged, and
a new broom was brought in to reformulate the BBC's mission
and message.

Enter John Birt.

After the programme was aired Hamilton said that he had been
damned by guilt by association. 'I claim that the programme,
taken as a whole, conveyed the impression that I am a virulent
racist, anti-semite, Nazi and Fascist who opposes democracy and
believes in incitement to violence and racial hatred to achieve
political ends.'

Now that we know that Hamilton lied to the Deputy Prime
Minister, Michael Heseltine, over the £10,000 he got for cash for
questions from lobbyist Ian Greer, his old victory against the BBC
can be seen in a different, darker light.

Back in 1986, Hamilton looked like a wronged man. Immediately after the settlement he wrote a long piece for the
Sunday Times of 26 October 1986, crowing over his victory. In
the Murdoch weekly he set out his version of why he took
Almirante's hospitality:

> While I was at Aberystwyth I did go to the Young MSI
> conference in Italy. But the MSI is a perfectly legal constitu-
> tional party. Indeed, it is a criminal offence in Italy to attempt to
> resurrect fascism and, if there was any connection, MSI would
> be suppressed and its leaders jailed. . . . At the time I was living
> on social security of £6 a week because I had no grant. I was
> editor of the student newspaper and I was sleeping on a bedroll
> on the floor of the office. A free week on the Adriatic in
> September was hard to turn down. At the end of the week the
> foreign observers were asked to make a thank-you speech. I
> thought it would be amusing to make a speech in Italian and do
> a send-up. Although it was not humorous in content, I would
> do it in such a way as to make fun of the Italian histrionics.

Whatever gloss one chooses to put on Hamilton's words, the fact remains that as a twenty-three-year-old student, newspaper editor and astute student politician he travelled across Europe to give succour to a political party whose members believe that the wrong side won World War II. And then he thanked them.

But there was more. *Panorama* had also looked at the sinister far-right political groupuscule known as Tory Action. Headed by the celebrated reactionary ex-spy, George Kennedy Young, a former deputy director of MI6, Tory Action indulged in deeply unpleasant abuse of black and Asian people and Jews. It published a regular round robin, offerings in which included a diatribe against 'Lithuanian Leon' – the then Home Secretary Leon Brittan, who is Jewish – and 'Latvian Lawson' – the then Chancellor Nigel Lawson, who is also Jewish. Hamilton and his fellow MPs and friends, Gerald Howarth, Harvey Proctor and Warren Hawksley, were all 'correspondents' – on an internal Tory Action mailing list. Exactly who was doing what within the inner circle of Tory Action remains muddy, but one thing remains clear – they weren't making jam to raise funds for the church roof. *Panorama*'s report was subsequently rubbished in a classic *Daily Mail* headline, 'Lies, Damned Lies and *Panorama*', but its evidence on Hamilton's queasy long-term association with the far Right was substantial and well detailed. The programme had carried out its own investigations and had come to the same conclusions as a secret Young Conservatives report on right wing extremist infiltration into the party which has never been published. The six-person YC inquiry team included four parliamentary candidates and a barrister and, after nine months, had come up with a great deal of disturbing evidence of extremist infiltration.

The most dramatic instance had come during the 1983 general election, when it was revealed that the Tory Parliamentary candidate for Stockton North, Thomas Finnegan, had stood for Parliament only nine years earlier for the National Front. Both *Panorama* and the YCs had found many other instances of similar infiltration of the Tory party by racialist groups and individuals.

The then Conservative Party chairman, John Selwyn Gummer – now plain old John Gummer – found the whole subject so uninteresting that he dealt with its publication in an unusual way. In a press release on 28 January 1984, the day the report was delivered to him, he said, 'The YCs have written to me' to present a number of concerns about infiltration. He made no mention of the 200-paragraph report. Gummer's press release was not sent to newspapers or the Press Association but placed in the Commons press gallery at 5.45 on Saturday afternoon. His ploy worked beautifully: there was hardly any newspaper coverage until *Panorama* went on air with a special programme timed to coincide with the delivery of the report.

Panorama treated viewers to a reprise of Hamilton's performance at Aberystwyth, his enthusiasm for comic-book Fascism, his trip to the Neo-Fascist congress in Italy and his links with Tory Action.

Being on the internal mailing list of G.K. Young's Tory Action bulletins cannot be passed off as a youthful joke. The group claimed not to have members as such but merely contributors and sympathisers, even though some of them refused to acknowledge any such link. Tory Action also had a much wider mailing list for its literature, but *Panorama* believed it was significant that Hamilton's name was listed in the much smaller and more select list of 'correspondents'.

One bulletin, dated Autumn 1982, carried this commentary from its northern correspondent about a disappointing by-election in Moss Side, an inner city area of Manchester with a large West Indian community:

> The result was pretty dismal but, there again, with the extraordinary concentration of coons, and the proletariat, life's failures and human seconds, little else could be expected. I went and had a look at some of the coon-infested

areas and it was quite appalling. I felt like taking over a loud-speaking van and simply going round saying: 'Get out of my country.'

Another bulletin from Tory Action attacked the Queen for consorting with non-whites: 'On every occasion the monarch has to be photographed beaming at a piccaninny while Prince Philip and Prince Charles caper about in yarmulkas,' referring to the skullcap worn by Orthodox Jews.

In the *Sunday Times* article on 26 October 1986, Hamilton wrote of his first meeting with G.K. Young through the Monday Club in the late sixties: 'With his distinguished war record and service to his country he was an impressive figure to a young student.'

Hamilton was on Tory Action's 'correspondents' mailing list for a number of years. He hosted a reception at the House of Commons for the organisation. He could have demanded that his name be taken off the mailing list. He could have exposed G.K. Young's bulletins for the sick, paranoid rubbish they were by bringing them to the attention of the newspapers when he first received a copy. He could have denounced Tory Action in Parliament. He chose not to do so.

Scene III: The Reichstag, 1983

Once in Parliament that summer of 1983, Hamilton started free-tripping. The first big one, the one that was to get him into almost as much trouble as the Ritz, occurred right at the start. It was to Germany, and Hamilton was a member of a delegation of Tory MPs and Tory parliamentary candidates who visited Berlin from 31 July to 6 August. One delegate was Tony Kerpel, who wrote to the BBC in April 1984, when he was Leader of the Conservative Opposition on Camden Council:

As I also wrote to the Party chairman 'I do recall seeing Neil
Hamilton give Hitler impersonations, including one occasion

during a visit to the Reichstag building.' This impersonation was not a full blown salute, but consisted of Mr Hamilton walking with his right forearm held upright, palm bent back, and left across the body. On the occasion of the Reichstag visit, and Mr Hamilton's Hitler impressions, one member of the group observed that Mr Hamilton must have felt he was in his spiritual home.

Kerpel added for the record that this was 'not the sort of conduct which one would expect' from an MP.

Faced with the charge that he had given a Nazi salute in Berlin, Hamilton wrote to the then Tory Party chairman, John Gummer, on 30 January 1984: 'I make it absolutely clear that, whilst in Berlin, I did not do any goose-stepping nor did I at any time give Nazi salutes. Indeed, I have always thought that the latter was a criminal offence in the Federal Republic.'

Hamilton changed his story when he wrote his account of his libel victory in the *Sunday Times* of 26 October 1986: 'When we visited the Reichstag I made a short speech of welcome in German. Before I went out on to the balcony and out of sight of our hosts I gave a salute with two fingers to my nose to give an impression of a toothbrush moustache. Somebody on the trip clearly did not have a sense of humour.'

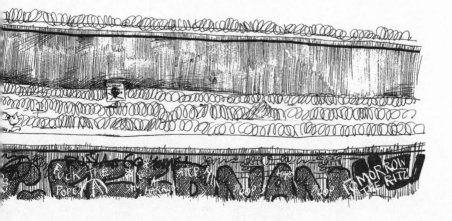

Christine has boasted of her husband's ability as Hitler's mimic: 'All he has to do is pull down his fringe a little, blacken a cork with a candle and paint a moustache and he looks like Hitler.'

After the programme was aired, Director-General Alastair Milne said that the documentary was 'very strongly founded', adding, later, that its research was 'rock solid'. The BBC chairman, Stuart Young, who happened to be Jewish, told his fellow governors: 'The Corporation has nothing to apologise for.' But Young was dying of cancer and strange things started to happen to *Panorama*'s witnesses.

One prospective Tory candidate declined to give a statement, after earlier telling the BBC's lawyers that he was a first-hand eyewitness to the alleged goose-stepping incident involving Hamilton in Berlin. Another Tory candidate provided the BBC's lawyers with a detailed account of what had happened in Berlin, only to recant in the last few days before the trial. The eyewitness was no more. Philip Pedley, the former YC chairman, wrote a courageous letter to party chairman Gummer to complain that witnesses to the Berlin goose-stepping were being leaned on to change their evidence. Gummer defended British democracy against the menace of the far Right as follows in a letter of 29 February 1984: 'My job is single-mindedly to protect the interests of the Party. I am not in the business of attacking those who present truthful reports. I am in the business of ensuring truth will out.'

The man politically responsible for the report was Pedley. He too was sued, but when the BBC caved in Pedley refused to withdraw. Hamilton and his friends backed off, and withdrew their case against the young Tory. The BBC had paid the plaintiffs' costs up to 21 October 1986, when the corporation had caved in. The judge ordered that the plaintiff pay Pedley's costs from that day on. But Pedley's political career has been blighted. He almost won selection for a safe Tory seat, until a whispering campaign killed his chances.

There is a disturbing coda to the *Maggie's Militant Tendency* saga, which only came out much later. It is the Strange Case of the Freelance Journalist Who Didn't Cash a Cheque.

The leader of the Young Conservatives' inquiry team which reported on the far-right infiltration into the Tory Party was Demitri Argyropulo. He was, then, a young and politically ambitious Tory, a county councillor in Surrey and chairman of the Conservatives' National Advisory Committee on Education.

If you are out to get someone in a serious way, you get hold of his credit card statements. This is not difficult if you know the right private eyes, often people with good contacts in the security business. A credit card statement pins people down to places they regularly visit – the local petrol station, your favourite restaurant, a book or record shop you like to frequent.

In Argyropulo's case there were two, a garage and the HMV record shop in London's Oxford Street. On Monday, 2 January 1984, a few days before the YC report on infiltration was published, he went to the HMV shop to exchange a faulty LP he had bought a few days before. It was raining.

Argyropulo went to an information desk inside the shop and reported the faulty record to a shop assistant later identified as Jonathan Walford. He told Argyropulo to go to the record bins and try to find a replacement copy. Argyropulo left his wet umbrella at the information desk.

Argyropulo failed to find a replacement copy of the faulty record, but did find five others that he wanted to buy. They were all in the sale, most priced at 50p. The total cost was £4.48. He returned to the information desk to find that his umbrella had been removed; Walford told him that it was in the front security office. Argyropulo left the records, which he had placed in an HMV bag, at the information desk and went to retrieve the umbrella. While he was doing so a member of the HMV staff took the records past the cash registers and placed them on the floor between the front security office and the door. (The distance between the security office and the exit was some three yards. The

distance from the records to the exit was some two yards.) After
signing for his umbrella, Argyropulo asked where his records
were. A member of the shop security staff pointed to where they
were, by the exit, and Argyropulo went out and picked them up.
He had not yet paid for them, and was immediately apprehended
by a store detective. The police were called, and Argyropulo was
taken to Marylebone Police Station and later charged with theft.

The committal hearing on the theft charge took place the
following day, 3 January 1984. The YC inquiry on infiltration
had been running since September 1982 and was almost ready.
Word of its potentially explosive content had leaked out. The
report was approved by the Young Conservatives' National
Advisory Committee with no votes against, and delivered to
the party chairman on 28 January. *Maggie's Militant Tendency* was
broadcast on 30 January. Argyropulo's local paper, the *Leatherhead
Advertiser*, carried a front-page story on the shoplifting allegation
on 2 February. It killed his political hopes. Copies of the article,
reproduced as leaflets, were discovered at Conservative Central
Office on 3 February. They were being distributed by right-wing
members of the Federation of Conservative Students and were
confiscated by Tim Cowell, a senior Central Office official.

The case came to court on 14 July 1984. The single most
important witness was Walford, who corroborated Argyropulo's
version of events and undermined that of the store detectives. The
jury returned a unanimous verdict of not guilty. Argyropulo was
awarded costs.

Some time after he had been arrested, a reporter on the
Leatherhead Advertiser, Rona Roach, told Argyropulo how the
paper had come to run the story. A freelance journalist had
telephoned the paper offering a story based on the shoplifting
charge, and then sent in a report. The cheque paid out to the
freelance was never cashed. When the paper checked the address
he had given them, they found that it was a derelict, uninhabited
building.

How come? Eh?

The broad attack of *Maggie's Militant Tendency* was well known. So was Hamilton's escape clause. He had sued and won. There had to be more and it had to be good. Back in Tatton, I started hunting.

Then one day the phone rang in my hotel.

'John Sweeney?'

'Uh-huh.'

'Of the *Observer*?'

'Yeah.'

'Call me Derek.'

'Derek?'

'Derek.'

Thus far, the phone conversation could have been scripted by Harold Pinter.

'How can I help you, Derek?'

'I'm the Tory Deep Throat. I can help you.'

Derek turned out to be a national figure in the Conservative Party, on first-name terms with half the Cabinet. He came up to Knutsford in person, bearing gifts: a bundle of documents, including a photocopy of Hamilton's MSI congress identity card which gave his surname in capitals, the date, 11–18 September 1972, and bore a hand holding a Fascist torch. Clearly, Derek Deep-Throat didn't like Hamilton that much.

There was more. 'You know Major and Brian Mawhinney wanted to kill Hamilton off.'

'What? Literally?'

He gave me a look of mild contempt.

'Politically. We heard that they were going to announce that it would be in the best interests of the party if Hamilton stood down. They were going to kill him off at a press conference, then go on to the attack and push Labour sleaze. There was a row going on at Doncaster council. They would use sleaze against Labour. We waited. And waited. And nothing happened.'

'What went wrong?'

'Someone tipped off the Tory Right. We heard that the big

hitters on the Tory Right told Major that if he killed off Hamilton they wouldn't like it.'

'Who, exactly?'

'We heard six names: Thatcher, Tebbit, and within the Cabinet Portillo, Lilley, Forsyth and Hague. The pressure on Major was too great to resist.'

'Why are this lot sticking up for Hamilton?'

'You've got to understand he's "one of us". Thatcher called him "our bonny fighter" just the other day.'

'Hey – a plot! Can I quote you on this?'

'Don't be stupid. But not a single Tory MP will come to Tatton and you won't get a Cabinet minister within miles of here. You watch.'

And Derek had more. Ten Tory MPs who had been on the 1983 trip to Berlin had signed a statement declaring that Hamilton had not given any Nazi salutes. Derek produced a photocopy. It must have been lying around at his club.

It read: 'We the undersigned, having attended the Berlin conference of the Konrad Adenauer Stiftung in August 1983, confirm that at no time did we see Neil Hamilton MP and/or Gerald Howarth MP goosestep, or give Nazi style salutes in front of the Sylter Hof Hotel or elsewhere in Berlin.'

It was signed by Ian Twinn, Simon Coombs, Michael Knowles, Michael Fallon, Martin Brandon-Bravo, Michael Clark, Alistair Burt, Geoff Lawler, John Watts and Edward Leigh.

Derek suggested I try some of the names on that list: 'There are some Tories who don't like Neil Hamilton. You'd be surprised.'

And then Derek left, as quietly as he had come.

Scene IV: The House of Commons, 12 December 1989

And so on 16 April 1997 I phoned Martin Brandon-Bravo. He was a Conservative MP, but one who had lost his Nottingham South seat in the 1992 election. He is also Jewish.

Within minutes he had faxed two pages of *Hansard*, the parliamentary record, to my hotel, the Cross Keys in Knutsford. They made interesting reading. The pages were an extract from a debate on the War Crimes Bill which took place on 12 December 1989. The argument that day was passionate and intense. Those in favour of the bill argued that it was Britain's moral duty to prosecute the perpetrators of the Holocaust who had found shelter in Britain after Hitler's war. Others, including a number of distinguished old-soldier politicians who had fought in that war, had argued that it was a violation of justice to bring forward after such a long time trials relating to crimes committed half a century ago in another country. The defendants and the witnesses would both be old and infirm, and the evidence likewise. Furthermore, the War Crimes Bill would require a change in the laws of admissibility of key evidence, such as video evidence. It was a debate which spoke to everything right and proper about the House of Commons.

I read the faxed pages closely. The first reported a speech by Conservative MP Ivor Stanbrook. He was one of many who expressed severe doubts about the bill, but in the context of his moral revulsion at the Holocaust. He prefaced his remarks by saying: 'Like everyone else, I am revolted by the knowledge of what the Nazis did to the Jewish and other communities during the war and I do not seek to condone, excuse or deny it . . . but emotions are a bad foundation for justice. . . . The motion asks us to set aside the most important feature of British justice – the right to a fair trial.'

The debate moved on and Labour MP Greville Janner, who is Jewish, then addressed the house:

After the war, I was a soldier with the British Army of the Rhine and served as a war crimes investigator. Our search section was looking for 10,000 people and we hoped to find them and the evidence to bring them to justice. There was evidence against those people of mass murder in concentration

camps, of the mass killing of civilians and of the shooting of
British prisoners of war who had escaped from Stalag Luft
Three. They were murderers. I am not surprised to see the
Hon. Member for Tatton [Hamilton] laughing. I can see
nothing laughable in this. It is one of the most serious and
important matters that has come before the house, and I see
nothing to laugh about in it.

The second page of the fax was more puzzling. Janner
continued: 'Half my family were rounded up by the sort of
people we have been speaking about today – local people. My
relatives were locked in a synagogue that was set on fire and they
died. I do not want revenge, only justice.'

Brandon-Bravo had marked in thick black pen the line in the
extract where Janner was saying: 'Half my family were rounded
up . . .'

'Why?' I asked him on the phone.

He explained that at the time he was Parliamentary Private
Secretary to the then Home Secretary, David Waddington. He
was on the government benches, his job to report back to his boss
the mood of the House on this critical and controversial
legislation. Brandon-Bravo said: 'At the point where Janner said
"half my family were rounded up . . ." he' – Hamilton – 'made
the remark: "the wrong half".'

But there was a problem with the evidence about the 'wrong
half'. Brandon-Bravo explained that Hamilton's remark had not
been recorded because *Hansard* reporters have a discretion not to
print what is said by seated MPs and those not formally addressing
the House.

No *Hansard*, no story. Unless . . . would Brandon-Bravo
confirm that Hamilton made the remark?'

'Yes . . . I have absolutely clear memory of that.'

He did more: 'In nine years in the House of Commons that was
the most offensive remark I heard from the floor of the house. I
felt ashamed that somebody on my side of the House should treat

this business as if it were funny. I am a very proud Conservative but I wish somehow there was a way of rooting out people like Neil Hamilton.'

I phoned Hamilton the next morning and told him I had a number of issues to put to him. I read out the extract from *Hansard* which covered Janner's work as a war crimes investigator: 'After the war, I was a soldier with the British Army of the Rhine and served as a war crimes investigator. Our search section was looking for 10,000 people. . . . There was evidence against those people of mass murder in concentration camps—'

Hamilton: 'Don't waste my time. I've got better things to do.'
And the line went dead.

Scene V: Inside Sweeney's head, Knutsford

I put the phone down and worried. You could say – and people did – that all this ancient stuff about Hamilton was academic, fruitcakey, not the point. In nineties' Britain the electors, the journalists, the movers and shakers are not interested in digging up these smelly bones.

Maybe. Gustave Flaubert once wrote: 'Our ignorance of history makes us slander our own times. Things have always been like this.' This is a consolation, but also a reminder that the battle for decency against the other side is a constant.

I love my job as a reporter and I believe in it too. During the Romanian Revolution I saw something amazing. On Christmas Day 1989 I was walking down the main drag, the Avenue Nicolae Balcescu, not far from the International Hotel, where the Securitate's hidden spools, in Saul Bellow's phrase, had 'turned behind heavy curtains'. Down the avenue came a flatbed lorry, on it a man throwing out newspapers. The Romanians, wrapped up in scarves and coats, ran clumsily after the lorry like the hungry after bread. They were desperate to read the first honest news for forty-five years.

In the days that followed the Revolution I sought out Romanian journalists. They were, by and large, a pretty disgusting bunch of creeps who had done nothing to challenge the status quo of the Genitals, sorry, Genius, of the Carpathians. But there was a measure of shame there, too, and frustration. When they had tried to get something out, to hint at Ceausescu's evil, no one had tuned in, no one in the West was listening. The Queen did knight him; he did come to Buckingham Palace, after all. No one had listened, even when they had dared to tell the truth.

It was the same back in the thirties, when Malcolm Muggeridge worked for the *Guardian* in Moscow and he stumbled across the horror story of the Ukraine famine in which maybe as many as 20 million people died. Arthur Koestler passed the winter of 1932–3 in Kharkov, then the capital of the Ukraine. 'Children looked like embryos out of alcohol bottles,' he later wrote.

At that time the dean of the Moscow press corps was Walter Duranty – a clever, subtle, cunning Englishman working for the *New York Times*. Duranty was the favourite of the Kremlin spin doctors. They came up with an ingenious ploy to suppress Western coverage of the Ukraine famine. The number one, hot, hot, hot story at the time was the Metro-Vickers trial, in which five British engineers had been charged with spying against the Soviet Union. But tickets to the trial were tightly controlled. In return for keeping mum about the famine, the Kremlin would allow selected reporters into the trial. Duranty bought the deal. The famine story, raised by Muggeridge and A.T. Cholerton of the *Daily Telegraph*, was brushed aside. No one was listening.

I imagine, too, the despair and the anguish of British reporters who covered Berlin in the thirties, the slow torture of the Jews, the repression of free journalism, the buckling of the rule of law under the relentless pressure of the Gestapo. And back home, no one was listening. Worse, the then proprietor of the *Daily Mail* was something of an enthusiast for Herr Hitler; the owner of the *Times*, likewise, and the then editor of my own paper, the *Observer*, asked his reporters to tone things down a bit.

I know what Muggeridge in Moscow and the others in Berlin went through, when no one was listening. It happened to me, as Yugoslavia smashed itself to pieces. I saw it coming and wrote and wrote and wrote about it, and no one seemed to be listening.

I wrote about the first death – though you could pick any number of first deaths – in the wars of Yugoslavia. He was a student, very tall, a basketball player, a Pogues fan. When the Belgrade students protested against the suppression of democracy in their city and the war policy of Slobodan Milosevic, the police were sent in to fire over the heads of the crowd. The Pogues fan was too tall and got it in the neck.

And then the war came. What is war like? Oh, Jesus, it's horrible. You don't see, you are not allowed to see, what incoming artillery can do to people. How it can blow off the side of a thirteen-year-old girl's head and put her father into coma and take a wodge like a slice of melon out of her mother's brain. How a shell pushes a wave of air in front of it, so powerful it can explode your eyeballs without touching you. In Osijek Hospital in 1991 I saw a man with bandages where he should have had eyes, otherwise completely untouched. You don't forget that sight.

In Dubrovnik, a few months later, I got the shakes and had to get out. I had been shot at and shelled on and off for months and my nerves had gone. Problem was, there was a siege. My first attempt was to jump on to an EC monitor's gin palace which was allowed free passage in and out of Dubrovnik. They threw me off. As the boat edged away from the harbour, I leapt on to it again: Sweeney's Leap. It was a good leap, but they stopped the boat, threw me off again and left me on the wrong side of the siege. Phil Davison of the *Independent* saw it happen, and poured some good whisky down my throat.

I was still shaking when I went to the hospital to check out the latest casualties. In the ward was a little lad with salt and pepper hair, the same age – five – as that of my own son, Sam, at that time. He had been injured with shrapnel very close to the groin.

As soon as I saw him I burst into tears. In the next bed was the Director of the Dubrovnik Music Festival, a friend of Yehudi Menuhin, who had also been injured. He gently remonstrated with me in perfect English: 'You should not do this job if you get so upset.'

I wanted to say that this – the boy – is nothing. That I had seen meat lorries full of dead Croat soldiers, people in Burundi with hacked heads, a man with no eyeballs in Osijek. I wanted to say that I could take it. Instead, I wept.

I escaped from Dubrovnik by hiding in the ladies' toilet on a ferry for women and children only, got my head screwed back on, went back, did Bosnia, Iraq, Rwanda, the rest.

It is, at times, a terrible job; at other times it is wonderful, funny, moving, worthwhile. But of all the terrible things in the world that I have seen and witnessed, the worst for me is those who know but don't care, who react to human misery with apathy and self-interest. Those who know but do nothing. And in my heart I knew that Neil Hamilton was such a man.

ACT THREE

. . . unsex me here,
And fill me from the crown to the toe top full
Of direst cruelty . . .

Scene I: The Longview Hotel, Knutsford

One lunchtime a white armoured car with 'UN' painted on the side in black turned up outside the Longview. From within, the armoured car's pith-helmeted commander saluted Bell and addressed him: 'We're with the United Nations sleaze-keeping force. But we shall be patrolling throughout the night to make sure that everything stays calm.'

But, as has often been the case with the real UN, the armoured car commander failed to deliver on his promise and buggered off after a few silly publicity snaps had been taken.

Inside the Longview, everything was far from calm. Hamilton had stolen the initiative and humiliated Bell in front of the nation. Tatton had blown everything else off the agenda: what Major, Blair and Ashdown got up to was much duller than the campaign in north-east Cheshire.

Somehow, Bell had to win back the initiative. Alastair Campbell pushed and pushed him. Why not have a second Battle of Knutsford Heath? Why not hit him hard and challenge Hamilton on the evidence? Bell thought about going into battle again, and demurred. He did, however, sign an 'attack dog' letter on Campbell's advice.

'Dear Mr Hamilton,' he wrote, using the letterhead of the Longview Hotel because the Bell campaign notepaper did not yet exist, 'it was nice to meet you. I am glad that the campaign is off to a friendly start.' (This is what is called, in England, irony. American readers should skip this bit.) 'Now that you have been confirmed as the Conservative candidate, I confirm that I will be challenging you on the issue of trust. I will stand as an independent, campaigning on an anti-corruption platform.'

Bell continued:

I am prepared to give you the benefit of the doubt on the unproven allegation which remains outstanding against you. This is that you received cash from Mohammed Al Fayed for asking questions and undertaking other activities in Parliament for him. Mr Al Fayed says he paid you, his employees report preparing envelopes of cash for you, and you dropped a libel action against the *Guardian* which continues to allege that you took cash. Nevertheless you vigorously deny that you accepted any money. The voters will have to decide who is telling the truth in advance of Sir Gordon Downey's report into the matter. I gave you an assurance, on one condition, that I will not be making the charge that you took cash from Mr Al Fayed during this campaign. The condition is this: you should give an undertaking to resign as an MP if you are elected but Sir Gordon finds you guilty of taking cash. I hope that you will give that pledge to the electors of Tatton.

This was a silly error. Godot would never find anyone guilty of anything. Only juries in British courts can do that. Whatever form of words Godot would come up with on Hamilton's conduct – and they would not be flattering – they would not include the word 'guilty'. The 'g'-word played into Hamilton's hands, reducing the scandal about his conduct to a binary call of guilty or not. Nor did the threat implicit in Bell's condition cut any ice with Hamilton. The Godot Report would not flop next to anyone's bowl of Ready Brek until after the election was lost and won.

Bell went on: 'My campaign will concentrate on your admitted wrongdoings which, even if you are innocent of the charge which you dispute, make you unfit to hold the office of Member of Parliament for Tatton. Let me list your wrongdoings so that the issues of the campaign are crystal clear.'

He brought up eight issues in all. 'You accepted gifts, hospitality and payments in kind from Mr Al Fayed whilst acting on his behalf in Parliament and in your dealings with ministers, thus breaking the rule that MPs should not be for sale.'

Bell then brought up the free holiday in the Ritz Hotel in Paris in 1987, though he did not go into details. This was a pity, as the six-day orgy of gateaux, champagne and 'Fillet-of-Challans-duck-cooked-pink-and-served-in-a-salamis-sauce-garnished-with-soufflé-potatoes' were pretty mouth-watering details in what was a dullish paper war. Bell also caned Hamilton for accepting 'free hampers from Mr Al Fayed', which was not exactly a knockout punch.

His next paragraph was harder for Hamilton to laugh off: '. . . further you failed to declare these payments in the Register of Members' Interests, thus breaking the rules of Parliament'.

Bell continued:

You accepted £10,000 from Ian Greer as a commission for your work in Parliament and in lobbying ministers on behalf of various companies. You failed to register this or tell ministers about it. You took £6000 from US Tobacco, via Ian Greer. You failed to register this payment and failed to tell ministers about it when you lobbied them. You told Sir Gordon Downey that this 'was wrong and I make no bones about it'.

In the final paragraphs of his letter he accused Hamilton outright: '. . . you lied to Michael Heseltine. You told him that you had no "financial relationship" with Mr Greer. That was a lie.'

Bell finished off with a bang: 'I do not give you the benefit of the doubt on these charges. They are the basis of my campaign. You have failed to provide convincing answers to any of them and indeed admit the most damaging facts.'

Oh, no, he didn't. After the letter was published in the press the first in a Niagara of solicitors' letters thundered down on Bell. Hamilton threatened all manner of retribution if Bell repeated his charges. In public Hamilton gave a doomsday warning: 'If you continue along the lines of your open letter, it promises to become the dirtiest campaign in modern times. Your emblem will not be a whited suit but a whited sepulchre.'

Some of the hacks weren't exactly sure what a sepulchre was. Hamilton explained: 'It's in St Matthew's gospel, as I'm sure you'll realise, because you're all God-fearing types. A "whited sepulchre" is an expression which means hypocrisy because it's white on the outside but unclean on the inside.'

The immediate difficulty for the Bell campaign was to come up with a fitting reply to the 'whited sepulchre' crack. Bell ordered his team: 'Find something from the Bible and tell me what to say.'

A Bell supporter wrote in with a suitable verse from the Bible, Exodus 28:3. 'What's that, then?' said one of the team.

Bell explained: 'It's about not taking bribes.' The verse ran: 'And thou shalt take no gift: for the gift blindeth the wise, and perverteth the words of the righteous.'

The next batch of legal letters from Hamilton's lawyers, Crocker's, were less heaven-sent. Bell was confronted with a series of grisly dilemmas. First of all, he did not want to get into yet another slanging match with the Hamiltons; he did not want a replay of Knutsford Heath with m'learned friends involved too. It was not his style to go round abusing people. If people wanted to vote for Hamilton, then fine, they should go ahead.

He told Ed Vulliamy of the *Guardian* (another old Bosnia hand), who passed through Knutsford one day: 'I have to be fair to Mr Hamilton. I am not a political attack dog. If Hamilton wins, I shall shake him by the hand and wish him well. I wonder if he would be a good loser – I'm not so sure.'

But, equally, it was not in Bell's character to back down under pressure, least of all to the Hamiltons. A third problem was that much of the specific evidence against Hamilton was not completely out in the open. The withdrawal of Hamilton's action against the *Guardian* was conditional on the documents, disclosed during the run-up to the case, being returned to the originating parties. Although those bundles contained all the deadly stuff against Hamilton, they were not public documents. Another problem was that Downey had not yet reported and the evidence to that inquiry, too, was not properly in the public domain.

Bell had plunged in, entering thick fog without proper bearings. Of course he had had little choice, but within the murk Hamilton was on home ground. It was his life and times that were at issue, not Bell's.

He had made a strategic mistake in writing the attack dog letter – something he regretted. 'If I had my time over again,' he said later, 'I would have ripped it up.' He did not speak to Campbell again, and from now on every attempt to push Bell into potentially risky territory was viewed with deep unease.

The effect on the Bell campaign was damaging. It became more than a little paranoid as the anaconda of Hamilton's lawyers tightened its grip. This all took place behind the scenes, in whispered conversations, but it bore down mightily on the man in the not so white suit. Still, not everything was going dreadfully.

Enter the Clean Machine.

The Clean Machine was neither clean, nor a machine. But it was to become Bell's own, a crazy, roaring, threshing, bumbling, chaotic – oh God! how chaotic – Heath Robinson contraption, loyal, for the most part, to him. At the very beginning there had only been the candidate and his daughter. Now, help was coming

through by the bucketful.   So many people volunteered
for the Bell campaign   that intense rivalries and
frustrations developed   within the engine room
of the Clean Machine.

   Screeching into   Knutsford came an
army of helpers,   quite a few of
whom knew   nothing about
the practice of   politics in Britain, sleaze, or   Tatton. They
did know a   lot about Bosnia,
though.

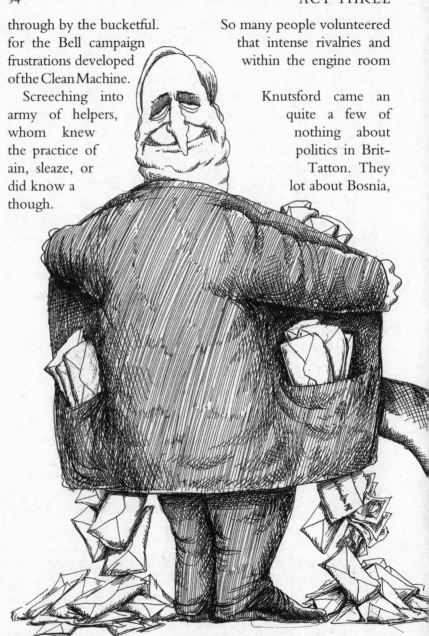

The largest was a slab of quartz called Nigel Bateson, who had been Bell's cameraman in the Gulf War and throughout the miserable break-up of former Yugoslavia. Red-bearded Bateson is a South African the size of Table Mountain, suited to the high veldt but looking pretty much out of place in a small dorp called Knutsford where no one had ever heard of biltong, still less knew much about spit-roasting aardvarks or, for that matter, pomping. Bell described him, with reason, as 'the best battle cameraman in the world'.

Every now and then Bateson exploded at some new atrocity from the Hamilton camp, discharging a series of expletives in Afrikaans which no one understood. Mindful of the aphorism of Marcus Aurelius, 'The art of living is more like wrestling than dancing',

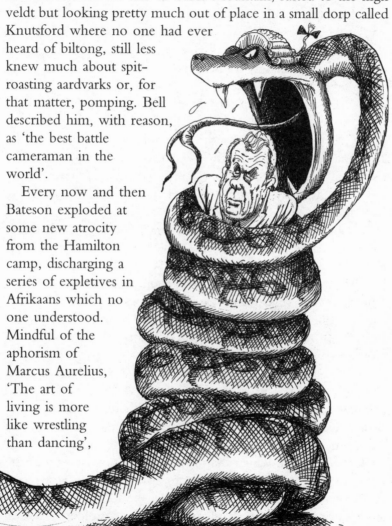

it became a private fantasy amongst some of the press corps to see
Bateson mud-wrestle Christine. Sadly, that never came to pass.
Who would have won?

Bateson immediately became Bell's driver and minder, hardly
ever leaving his side. He fixed things (and people) that didn't
work. And if they didn't work, he gave them a look that implied
their imminent annihilation. I have never seen him hurt a fly. But
no one doubted that he could hurt a fly, or an armoured division,
were he asked to do so. His first job was to check out a proper
office for the Bell campaign. There was one possibility, an old
showroom for Manweb, the local electricity company, in Princess
Street in the centre of Knutsford. When he went to have a look I
accompanied him for laughs. The showroom was bleak and
empty. There was a trapdoor. He lifted it: 'That's where we
put you, Sweeney, if you don't behave yourself.' He laughed,
chillingly.

Bateson slept every night in the former showroom. It had four
rooms – a large open room where the low-level and non-secret
campaign workers plotted in public, a small side room where the
low-levels plotted in secret, a back room – The Back Room –
where the high-level, secret campaign workers plotted in secret,
and a kitchen, where everybody swapped plots and secrets and
made tea. Out the back there was a courtyard, where the best
plotting of all went on.

Another old Bosnia hand, at one remove, was Bell's election
agent, Kate Jones. Her qualifications for this job were that she had
been the editor of his book, *In Harm's Way*, which is chiefly about
Bosnia. Kate One or K1 (because another Kate came along later)
was immediately pitched into the legal battle, fought from the
Back Room, from which she surfaced every now and then. She
wore the same slightly wild-eyed expression that Bob Hope, clad
in a brass-headed diving suit, did when he resurfaced intermit-
tently during his running battle with the Giant Squid in *The Road
to Bali*. To help her with the legal kalamari was a local barrister,
Anthony Crean, who looked irritatingly like Tom Cruise.

And then there were Bell's Belles. Shockingly, none of these three young women had ever been to Sarajevo, been shot at or shelled. They wore black, setting the chic for all of us sympathetic to the Man in the White Suit.

Like Melissa Bell, none of the three was hideously deformed. The tallest was Sophie Solomon, eighteen, who was reading Russian at Oxford in between stints as a DJ at the club Alien. Then there were the two Harrison sisters, dark-haired Antonia, twenty-one, who was about to launch into a career in advertising, and her blonde sister Sophie, twenty-four, a Granada TV researcher and 'wannabe presenter'.

The press became besotted with Melissa and Bell's Belles – to the exclusion of sleaze, Hamilton's involvement with the Italian Neo-Fascist movement (did no one care about he and Giorgio Almirante?) and even the battle over Manchester Airport's second runway. The newspapers set Melissa against Christine, starting with a headline in the London *Evening Standard*, which proclaimed: 'The Butterfly v. The Battleaxe'. No prizes were awarded for guessing who the battleaxe was, but just in case the *Standard*'s readers were supremely thick they got another clue in a subheading: 'Watch out Mrs H, there's a new blonde in Tatton.'

In a tightly packed field, Simon Sebag 'Teabag' Montefiore of the *Sunday Times* took the all-comers' prize for drooling and slobber. Of Melissa, he quivered: 'She speaks slowly and softly in a delicious but cold French accent, like Catherine Deneuve in *Belle de Jour* . . . the most elegant monster that has ever been made . . . looking tanned, thin and collected . . . the Evita of Knutsford.'

Of Bell's Belles, Teabag simpered: '. . . three intelligent, diffident, fearless Bellites, who also happen to be strikingly beautiful young women. . . . Her three graces, all of whom boast long legs and university degrees, are actually ruthless political cadres reminiscent of the Women's Battalion of Death that shamed the men of Russia in the first world war. . . .' Despite the excellence of Teabag's analogy, historians of World War I are silent on the extent to which the Women's Battalion of Death put on mascara before going into battle.

Nor did Teabag get a shag.

One of Bell's volunteers who was female but not twenty-four, a former journalist called Julie Tempest, tried to correct this media obsession: 'As a thirty-seven-year-old, I did try to start an alternative – Bell's Bags – which some of the more mature ladies subscribed to. Sadly we got no media attention.'

Tempest was working on the *Wilmslow Express Advertiser* when Hamilton was first selected back in 1983. 'At the time everyone was quite excited at this "bright young thing" coming to the new constituency and there was a general feeling that he was set for high office, possibly even Prime Minister. People found it romantic that he and Christine had taken time out of the campaign to get married.

'Ten years or more on, my mood was quite different. I hadn't followed the *Observer/Guardian* story closely but when Hamilton tried to ban the Sleaze book, I was incensed. I was in the local bookshop, Jardine's in Knutsford, and overheard a conversation with the sales assistant. It sounded interesting. What was being sold under the counter? It transpired it was the Sleaze book about which Hamilton's solicitors had sent out a threatening letter. I immediately bought the book and was sworn to secrecy about where I had purchased it. As the row over the Sleaze book grew – the local newspaper soon got on to the story – I felt that it would be a real travesty of democracy to allow Hamilton to stand and even win the seat in the general election.' She used her local contacts for the new phones to be installed quickly in the old electricity showroom. There was one hitch, though. Someone walked off with the telephone engineers' keys, leaving them locked out of their van.

Laura Gillan was a seventy-year-old Bell's Belle, whose admiration for the man caused her to travel eighty miles up the M6 to go canvassing: 'I would have supported him if he had stood for the Monster Raving Loony Party. Sometimes he possibly thought he had.' She recalls a particularly deflating experience while canvassing in Wilmslow. The door of a grand house was opened by, probably, the home help. She was followed by an extremely elderly lady who, seeing Laura's greying hair, asked: 'Did you vote for Lloyd George in the election of 1920?'

Noticing the slightly bemused look on Laura's face, she hastily amended this to: 'But, of course, you would only have been a child at the time.' Laura had not even been born, but it was nice to know that Bell had the Lloyd George supporters' vote sewn up.

Running policy for the Bell campaign was a younger, bonsai-banzai Martin Bell called Oliver Kamm, the candidate's nephew and lookalike. An investment analyst who did something clever with numbers in the City, Kamm was the campaign brain. If you walked by him quietly you could hear the hum of deep thought, like the buzzing you hear under an electricity pylon. Kamm said even less than his uncle, but what he did say was precise and worth listening to.

Keeping under control the hacks who popped up from all corners of the globe, and then some, was Bell's press officer, Kate Edgley, known as Kate Two (K2). A freelance journalist, she had a habit of signalling her cool contempt of the oafishness of the press by raising an eyebrow. Sometimes, she raised two. Had she been hideously deformed, she would have raised three.

Bell's Boys, like Bell's Bags, was an idea that never quite caught on. First in was Mark Whittle, a politics student at Leeds University and a mean piano player. His father, Brian, ran a news agency in the constituency. Then came a man with the name of a villain in a Victorian melodrama: 'It is you, Sebastian Doggart, who has ruined me so. . . .'

Doggart had been a freelance journalist working in Nicaragua – at least it made a change from Bosnia – turned theatre director. His campaign diary records the chaos and the chic of the Bell campaign headquarters when he arrived on Thursday, 17 April: 'The showroom looks somewhere between a Montessori class-room and Vogue House. There are wish lists on boards, coffee

cups everywhere, UN-style Bell posters on the walls and perfectly
manicured girls strutting around.'

The Clean Machine's volunteers competed amongst themselves to dislike the Hamiltons the more, proving the truth of
Nietzsche's crack in *Nachgelassene Fragmente*: 'There is a jealousy
in hating too: we want to have our enemy to ourselves.' There
was a constant sense of menace – real or imagined – from the
Hamilton camp. Occasionally, this tipped over the edge into
farcical paranoia. Doggart was hit by it at full blast.

He had been invited up by Crean, the lawyer, who was not
there when he arrived. He records his reception:

> Mark Whittle takes me aside and tells me that the office is
> divided into the front part, which is public, and the back part,
> which is private. I may not go beyond a certain point in the
> office until I am officially cleared.
>
> 'We have to do this,' he says, 'for fear of Hamilton spies.
> Two such moles have already been identified and expelled.'

'I tell him I fully understand,' noted Doggart, before adding, 'I
don't.'

There had, indeed, been two chaps who said they were from
Sandhurst and had volunteered their help to the Bell campaign.
But their behaviour was odd, their demeanour somehow not
quite right. They asked too many questions – who was who, what
was going on. Nor had they been to Bosnia. Bateson asked them
to leave. As Kissinger once said, 'Just because you're paranoid
doesn't mean there aren't people out there who want to get you.'

Doggart, who was encountering the paranoia in his first few
minutes in the Bell campaign office, knew none of this. His diary
details what happens next:

> Fear about my identity grows. A grey-bearded man called
> David who is in charge of Bell's schedule takes me through to
> the courtyard at the back of the office.

'Who exactly asked you up here?' he enquires.

'Anthony Crean invited me.'

'Well, I've never heard of such a man. It wasn't Geen, was it? Because my name's Geen.'

'No, it was definitely Crean.'

'Never heard of Crean. You'd better go inside until this is cleared up.'

'I feel lost somewhere between a cold war thriller and a farce,' wrote Doggart.

I return to putting stickers on posters. An hour later a good-looking man around 35 walks in and introduces himself as Anthony Crean. He tells me to wait a moment and he will sort me out. David takes me aside and again quizzes me about my roots. I explain to him that I have met the mysterious Anthony.

'Where?'

'He was here a moment ago.'

'I didn't see anyone. Show me.' Anthony is nowhere to be seen.

'He went out the back there.'

'That's only for authorised personnel, and there is no authorised Anthony.'

'No, really. I saw him go back there.' He leads me to the back where there is a bank of named pigeonholes.

'Can you identify the name of the man who invited you here?' he quizzes. There is no Anthony.

'No, but I saw him a . . .'

'This is getting too difficult. I think you'd better go out into the streets and talk to the people till this is sorted out.'

At that moment Anthony emerges from the back room. I hastily introduce David to him. It is clear he has met him before. They send me out and go into a huddle, which ends with David shrugging and saying: 'Well, he's your resource. You do what you like with him. But it's on your head.'

Anthony then takes me out for a little walk. He explains
there is paranoia in the office and says all he has to go on is my
word and my CV. I suggest he check up on me by calling some
friends which Martin and I have in common. He agrees and
then looks me straight in the eye.

'Do you swear that you have never had any formal links to
the Conservative campaign, or to Neil Hamilton?'

'I do.'

Doggart was passed. When he first told me what had happened
to him on his arrival at the Bell campaign, I told him that I had
mistaken Geen for a deaf barman and had asked him for a gin and
tonic, and then repeated my order more loudly. For some reason,
this story pleased Doggart.

And then Bell got help from the Liberal and Labour machines.
There were, to begin with, two of them. They were secret, high-
level campaign workers and you didn't know they existed, still
less talked about them. They were Back Room. The first to arrive
was Bill Le Breton, a clever, subtle man with a glint in his eye. He
had a wit as dry as the Gobi Desert and the deadpan delivery of
Les Dawson. Le Breton was President of the Association of
Liberal Democrat Councillors. Soon afterwards Alan Olive
arrived – an elections officer with the Labour Party, astute but
less dry than Le Breton, more jolly, more Roy Huddesque.

The agony for Bell and his agent, K1, was that everyone shoved
his oar in all at once. They had to face an expectation from the
Labour side that Bell should go on the attack, rubbishing
Hamilton mercilessly and placing him and sleaze at the centre
of the pantomime stage. In fact, the Hamiltons had brought the
spotlight on to themselves by staging the Battle of Knutsford
Heath. Others argued for caution, saying that Bell should play it
gently, allowing the electors to make their own judgement. There
was a national political dimension to this cleavage, as well. The
Labour Party high command, in particular Campbell, had wanted
Bell to come out and condemn Hamilton as aggressively as

possible. In a Conservative constituency, this always carried the risk that voters would be put off by such ungentlemanly behaviour. The Liberals whispered that Labour was happy to offer Bell up as a sacrificial lamb, for the good of their campaign nationally. They, led by Bell's old friend Paddy Ashdown, wanted Bell to win. At least, that's what they whispered when in plotting mode.

And then there were the hacks.

Very early on, David Leigh of the *Observer* and Ed Vulliamy of the *Guardian* were spotted by hacks from rival papers entering the Longview. The top-secret, hush-hush arrival at the Longview was even filmed by Peter Sharratt, making a fly-on-the-wall documentary for BBC2 which was shown after the election. Vulliamy, of course, was an old mate of Bell's from Bosnia. Leigh was not. What the two hacks had in common was that they were the joint authors of *Sleaze: The Corruption of Parliament*, a slim volume which was not entirely a celebration of Hamilton's parliamentary career. It did go on, rather a lot, about Al Fayed, the feasting at the Ritz and that sort of thing.

Hamilton, later, waxed indignant: 'We know that he was assisted by *Guardian* and *Observer* journalists throughout his campaign. So not only was his candidature procured ultimately by the Labour Party, but it was also very much controlled by the *Guardian* newspaper, which has been responsible for conducting the vendetta against me. So the idea that Martin Bell was in any way an independent candidate is an obvious nonsense.'

This might be fair, were it true. It was the Bosnia connection, not the Labour Party, that got Bell up to Tatton. Once the Hamiltons had zapped him on Knutsford Heath, Bell seriously wanted to win. And Bell is not a moron. He got a first-class honours degree from King's College, Cambridge, a town where the sheep crop grass untroubled. He is a man governed by his own mind; no one else's. He very quickly realised that he had been mistaken to rehearse the specific charges against Hamilton. It was not his style, nor would it woo the voters. He wanted to get to

Westminster, he wanted to beat Hamilton fair and square. And the best way to do that, he reasoned, was to ignore those in the Labour Party and in the newspapers who wanted him to excoriate Hamilton twenty-four hours a day. He reflected in his diary:

> Those who first invited me [people like Alastair Campbell] wish me to be more combative. This is not my nature and will lead to the kind of slanging match I wish to avoid: I see no purpose being served by the daily exchange of insults. I wish to run a 'high road' campaign, emphasising themes of trust and integrity. Also the 'H' word – honour – seldom heard in politics. As for the negatives, they are sufficiently implicit in the positives. And the battle Hamilton has to fight is not so much against me as against his own record. . . .

This was a strategic judgement, but it took Bell a week to figure it out. In the meantime it looked as though the Bell campaign had been paralysed by fear of Hamilton's lawyers and want of will to attack. Bell listened to Leigh and Vulliamy, the Professors Emeritus of Sleaze, partly because if Hamilton ambushed again he wanted, at least, to be aware of the principal charges against him. But as the campaign wore on, he said less and less about sleaze and let his positives imply his opponent's negatives.

Bell even listened to me go on about Hamilton's career-long flirtation with comic-book Fascism, to put it charitably, but he didn't act on it. The *Observer*, too, wasn't interested in the fine detail of Hamilton's connections with the MSI and what Brandon-Bravo had overheard. 'Too much Hamilton, Sweeney,' said one apparatchik of the hated boss class at the *Observer*. 'You're getting boring. Why don't you go to Wales to cover the election in Newport South?' I ignored him.

It seemed to me that what was happening in Tatton wasn't just, as some people were saying, a by-election in the course of a general election. It was more important than that – the cockpit of the entire election. The fight between Hamilton and Bell spoke to the very idea of democracy, that those who hold power must never be allowed to presume that they own it as of right.

Hamilton's playing with Neo-Fascist fire was a dark aspect of this presumption of power. Others got the point: a taxi driver and former England cricketer, Geoff Pullar, a gang of students in the Lord Eldon, and the landlord and regulars of the Freemasons' Arms in Knutsford. I remember banging on at the Freemasons', one day, about Giorgio Almirante, Neil Hamilton and the seven sons of Alcide Cervi, reducing the pub to an unaccustomed silence.

There was something nebulous and difficult, or so they thought in the Freemasons', about the sleaze allegations: 'Everybody's on the fiddle, aren't they?' I told them about the Hitler salute in the Reichstag. 'Hey, everyone's done an Adolf impersonation in their time, haven't they?' But taking a freebie off Almirante? Giggling during discussion of the War Crimes Bill? Laughing at a man who lost half his family in the Holocaust? 'The wrong half . . .'? There was a strain of behaviour in what Hamilton had done down the years which disturbed the drinkers. And I had the evidence to back up what I was banging on about: 'Tory trio meets fascists' (*Sunday Telegraph*, 8 October 1972), 'Our racism must be that of meat and muscles . . .' They shook their heads and ordered another round. Perhaps they thought I was just a fruitcake.

But what about the vast bulk of the voters? The ones I hadn't bought pints for? The ones not touched by Melissa's delicious but cold French accent? Or the Women's Battalion of Death strutting their stuff in black? Or Bell's Bags? Or the Lloyd George supporters for Bell? The electors of Tatton sat behind their net curtains, impassive as Easter Island gods, giving nothing away.

Scene II: On the Major battlebus

In the middle of the election campaign, the *Observer* ordered me to leave Knutsford and follow a boring grey man in spectacles round the country. There were three problems with this assignment: first of all, I had been completely hooked by the battle for Tatton and did not want to leave it for a moment; secondly, I quite like John Major and find it hard work writing rude things about him; thirdly, there was the little matter of what had happened to the *Observer* writer who had covered the Prime Minister's campaign the week before. He had ended up on the front page of the *Sun*: 'DRUG SCANDAL ON PM'S JET – WRITER IS FIRED FOR HEROIN IN LOO.'

The tabloid screamed on:

A journalist has been sacked for taking heroin as he flew with the Prime Minister on his election plane. Tory Party chairman Brian Mawhinney tipped off police after 'reformed' junkie Will Self took the drug in a toilet. Last night 35-year-old Self was fired by the *Observer* for failing to deny that he had taken drugs. He was accompanying John Major and wife Norma to the East Midlands with other journalists when passengers saw him go to the loo. He was said to look nervous but came out minutes later relaxed and calm. *Observer* bosses issued a statement last night which read: 'Serious allegations have been made against Self which he has failed to deny. As a result his contract with the *Observer* has been terminated.'

Hours after the front page had hit the presses, I caught up with Major wandering around a shopping centre somewhere in Cheshire. He's good on the stump, unusually gentle and easy-going. What makes him enigmatic is that he is so seemingly insignificant, dull and boring. Major has the body language of a Ford Sierra dashboard and the facial mobility of a traffic cone. He has the conversational style of a traffic cone talking to a Ford Sierra dashboard about sports studies. Despite all this, there is a personal courtesy and a charm mixed in with the stiff insignificance which is very disabling.

Once I was sent by the *Observer* to Huntingdon to annoy him over some forgotten outrage. I had a go, but after a while it seemed slightly unsporting to give someone a hard time as he went round chatting about strawberry jam at a constituency fete. I gave up and started nattering to another hack about this and that. There was a slight tap on my shoulder. I turned round: it was the Prime Minister.

'Excuse me, could I pass by. . . .' Had it been Mrs Thatcher and I had been in the way, you knew you would have been coshed by a handbag and knocked to the floor.

Every now and then the wires inside his head get slightly mixed up so that he doesn't get it quite right. The first day I went to monster Major during the election campaign I was wearing a silly straw hat and he clocked it and came over and said: 'That's a very colonial hat.' Tropical, yes; colonial, no. He pressed on and chatted to an Asian family and their kids, all of them clearly terrified by the pock-pock of the Nikons and the dead coypus gobbling up the sound: 'You may not have made Chester Zoo, but . . .' he tilted his entire body to the meejah'. . . what about these?'

I had never seen him so relaxed. He was almost demob-happy, aware perhaps that he was soon to go on a long holiday. But this very relaxed air makes you like him more. He's a nice man, et cetera, et cetera.

I had brought with me some 'Martin Bell For You' stickers. But who to give them to? I checked out the hacks who could be trusted. In the spring of 1990 I had gone on an archaeological tour of Albania, the first tourist trip into the country since the Romanian Revolution. On the coach there were four Muslims from Bradford, protesting against the officially enforced atheism in that country. There were three people we called with our easy contempt 'the legits'. And there were seventeen journalists, pretending to be interested in Albanian archaeology. What the rest of us were really interested in was to collect the full set of Balkan revolutions. On the trip was an oaf who dropped a hunk of cheese in the teacup of the beautiful translator. The other translator, my friend Agim, looked left and right, surreptitiously, as if checking whether the Segurini were listening. Then he said: 'In Albania, we have a saying: "No forest without pigs." '

One of the hacks who, like me, loved that story was Peter Popham of the *Independent*, now chained to the Major bus. I handed over a sticker, which he wore on the inside of his jacket. A pal from a well-known broadcasting organisation, who would not thank me if I named him, took one too. Our 'Martin Bell For You' stickers cleverly hidden, we followed Major round the shopping centre, flashing at each other. You've got to keep yourself amused when you are reporting the Prime Minister.

Back on the Major battlebus the man from the *Sun* crept towards me: 'You're from the *Observer*, aren't you? Any comment on the sacking of Will Self? Eh?'

The other hacks twitched. Story. I was aware of a dozen heads turning towards me.

I kept my counsel.

'Silence?' said the man from the *Sun*.

Ann Leslie of the *Daily Mail* – a pal, even though I loathe her politics – cracked: 'Uncharacteristically silent for Sweeney.'

And then I recovered my powers of speech. 'As to what is being said of my friend Will Self, I can only say this . . .' the hacks had clicked on their tape recorders, waiting for the line, '. . . a man is innocent until proven guilty.'

Thank you, Neil Hamilton.

I had never actually spoken to Self before and, although he is a writer I admire, he wasn't a friend in any true sense of the word. But I didn't want the *Sun* to know that.

The hacks on the bus were fascinated by what was going on in Tatton. To them, it was much more interesting than traipsing around the countryside following a boring grey man in spectacles. This is partly because the hacks were cocooned from the prime ministerial presence. He was in his own battlebus, complete with Norma, fixers, staff, creeps and Conservative Central Office gargoyles. Next came the snappers' battlebus, where the conversation, at best, went like this:

'Light's crap.'

'*I am* at f15.'

'The desk didn't like the shopping arcade. They didn't make.'

'Light was crap.'

'The desk doesn't understand.'

'The light was crap.'

'The desk.'

'Fuck the desk.'

'Light's crap.'

On the third bus were the scribblers, herded around like pampered cattle in pens, who mooed soundbite questions at the boring grey man in spectacles. Every now and then, he mooed back. In Tatton I was in the middle of a battle, with the heavy artillery of legal threats whizzing over my head, Fascists marching inside my brain, Adolf Hitler saluting Lord Eldon, a man I respect greatly in deep trouble. With Major, it felt like being in a boring shopping arcade – which was, in fact, where we were.

The consensus on the scribblers' bus was that Hamilton was winning and had beaten Bell hollow at the Battle of Knutsford Heath.

'Thing is,' I said, 'Bell isn't that kind of bloke. He is courteous. He doesn't like offending women like Christine. . . .'

'I know what happened,' said Ann Leslie, with a hint of smug knowingness in her voice.

'What?'

'Martin approached the Hamiltons as he would approach a Serb road block. The idea in his head was to placate them, calm them down, then get ten miles further along the road and be very rude about them.'

'Right.'

When I got back to Tatton, I relayed this metaphor to Bell. He immediately saw the power of it, and used it again and again. Thank you, *Daily Mail*.

The Major battlebus convoy stopped at some ghastly venue while Major wowed his troops in private and the hacks ate awful pies. I hit the phone, working away at Giorgio Almirante. In a break between phone calls a dead coypuist from ITN or Sky came over.

'You're from the *Observer*, eh?'

He ran his sleeve against his nose, as if snorting heroin.

Big joke.

I have witnessed a woman, eight months pregnant, shoot up with heroin because her craving for the drug was greater than the love for her unborn child. This happened in Dublin, where I was writing a   story about Veronica Guerin, the brilliant

Irish journalist
assassinated
for going
against the

drug barons. You can, if you know where to look and pay the junkies a little money, watch people shoot up heroin in any city or town in the British Isles. I believe heroin to be an abomination. But there was something about the soundman, something nerveless and stupid, that made me hold my tongue. I was getting just a little of what I had been handing out to the Hamiltons, and I didn't like it one little bit.

Late that afternoon, a surreal scene.

In the middle of the battle for who rules the United Kingdom, flat calm. A runway somewhere near Chester; a scattering of big sheds; a backdrop of trees, fields; in the foreground to the left a blue British Midland jet, to the right a control tower, topped by a frenzy of radars. The landscape void of humanity.

Flat calm.

Then a man in a black suit walked from right to left, surrounded by other men in black; behind them a funeral procession of black limousines crept along. But something was missing. The media had all been pre-packed away in the plane, so only Dave, the scribblers' battlebus driver, and I were there to watch the Prime Minister enjoy a simple human pleasure. He was going for a walk.

Dave – maroon jacket, thinning curly hair, nice man, steady driver – drank in the scene, then decided his vote: 'You know, I was going to vote Labour because of all this sleaze business, but I do like John Major. I've worked with him before, last time.' He recalled: 'I was at Edgbaston a few days back and he came up to me and he hadn't seen me for five years and he said: "Hello, Dave." '

And with that simple but magnificent feat of memory, the most unfathomable man in British politics had won back yet another voter of Middle England to his cause. The polls were saying Major would lose. Maybe.

Then the plane grunted down the runway and took off. The motorbike escort riders, perhaps for the hell of it, perhaps for the practice, gave Dave and me a treat as the coach slogged back towards Manchester. They played tag, blocking off the traffic at roundabouts, then zooming past, block, zoom, block, zoom – a sweet taste of power.

But it was all an illusion. The block, zoom was for the prime ministerial limo and the Special Branch Land Rovers behind us; once they had overtaken the coach, the outriders and the Branch disappeared into the distance, as one day, soon, they would disappear for Major. Maybe.

That night he went on *Question Time* and someone asked him about Neil Hamilton and Skoal Bandits. Hamilton took money, via Ian Greer, from US Tobacco. The company was punting chewing tobacco to British consumers. Chewing tobacco causes cancer of the mouth. While the Department of Health was thinking about banning it, Hamilton started lobbying hard for the company's freedom to market Skoal Bandits. He also took a free first-class flight to America, courtesy of US Tobacco. He also gave the stub to his accountant, so that he could claim tax relief on a first-class ticket he hadn't paid for.

What did Major make of Hamilton's advocacy of Skoal Bandits? This is what he said: 'I don't know if [Hamilton's behaviour] was wickedness or foolishness, maybe deserving of censure, but not of such censure that a whole career is thrown away.' Not much of an endorsement for Hamilton; not much decency either. Derek Deep Throat had said that Major had wanted to give Hamilton the bullet. The Prime Minister certainly did not show any great enthusiasm for Hamilton. Major's answer was a glimpse of the powerlessness of power, the lack of room for manoeuvre that restricts any Prime Minister. And it was also an indication that, when it came to the test, Major was not – could not be – a nice man. No man of power can be.

The next day Major skirted the IRA's alarums and arrived in Bolton to see a metal phallus crane-lifted on to a set of concrete bollocks at the new Wanderers' ground. He put on a white Wanderers sweat-shirt with number ten printed on it. The hacks were penned behind a cow fence, mooing quietly.

'It's only ten miles to Tatton,' I said, cheerily.

Everyone scowled at me.

A little later I managed to get close enough to Major to ask him a question he couldn't just ignore.

'Going to Tatton to support Mr Hamilton?' I asked, cheerily.

'As you know, where I go is something I can't discuss for obvious reasons—'

'I know,' I said, on the defensive.

'So don't ask me!' he snapped back. Smart and not in the least bit nice. Then one of Major's Crouch Kamikaze stopped me dead. These strange creatures, clad in sky-blue, crawled around at knee height so they wouldn't be spotted by the cameras, throwing themselves between Major and the hacks the moment things got potentially embarrassing.

That night Major wowed the faithful in Manchester. You could hear the dentures clack-clack their obeisance even before he opened his mouth. The joke of the night? 'Tony Blair in Amsterdam will be like a fly at a spiders' convention.' Bad joke, bad entomology; spiders are solitary creatures. But good, nasty politics – the idea that Tony Blair would be Chancellor Kohl's puppet was leaked into the public mind. And the poison of that

was a million miles from the Nice Man with the Air of Flat Calm.
To pull off that trick is not nice, but it was clever.

I returned to Tatton knowing that many Tories would –
choke, spit – vote for Major to remain Prime Minister. And
that meant burying Bell and re-electing Hamilton.

Scene III: The Brick Red Lubyanka

Meanwhile, the campaign was going smoothly within the walls of
the Brick Red Lubyanka that is the Tatton Conservative Constituency Association. ITN's camera team was allowed a rare peep
and caught Hamilton and Christine in confident mood.

Hamilton: 'We've had an excellent reception.'

Christine: 'We really have.'

Hamilton: 'Absolutely first-class.'

Christine: 'It's been really humbling. It's been really great.'

A floppy-fringed schoolboy emerged from a back room and
introduced himself to Hamilton.

Hamilton went into the back room. The boy followed.

Hamilton: 'Hi, how are you?' They shook hands. 'I've just
written to you today. We put it in the post this morning.'

Christine (from the next room): 'Have we put it in the post or
could we have saved ourselves a stamp?' She looked towards the
back room and then walked away.

Hamilton stood square-on to the boy, in a gauche, sinking-
into-his-neck posture, with arms folded. Both the boy, who was
slightly taller than Hamilton, and the candidate avoided eye
contact. Hamilton shifted from foot to foot. The boy, in T-
shirt and Barbour-type jacket, fiddled awkwardly with a note-
book.

Hamilton: 'So, um' – suddenly, his tone was more hushed.
There followed a long pause, then Hamilton looked away from
the boy and down at the ground – 'um, plenty of things to be
done. Are you in the sixth form?'

Boy: 'Yeah, I'm in the sixth form.'

Where better to learn about the reality of the modern Conservative Party than from Neil Hamilton?

The Hamiltons were on home territory. They didn't have to campaign. They knew everybody who mattered in the constituency: the landowners who allowed their estates to be planted with Hamilton posters, the farmers who put up Hamilton placards in their fields, the businessmen who knew that the Conservatives were the natural defenders of their profits.

They didn't have far to go to find profitable enterprises. Just across the road from the Brick Red Lubyanka was Knutsford's Rolls Royce, Bentley and BMW showroom. One day they paid a majestic visit.

Christine: 'It's wonderful news. Business is booming in Knutsford.'

Salesman: 'More cars than they've done in America, so . . .'

Christine: 'All in this little showroom in Knutsford . . .'

Salesman: '. . . all in Knutsford.'

Hamilton: 'Isn't that fantastic? I'm delighted to hear . . .'

Salesman: 'All to local people.'

Hamilton: 'Really? All to local people?'

Christine: 'I only wish we were in the market to buy one.'

Hamilton: 'If only MPs were paid more, I could buy one.'

Salesman: 'This is true. This is very true.'

Hamilton had the Rolls Royce owners' vote sewn up.

The great mystery for everyone studying Tatton was 'What's going on in the minds of Tory voters?'

The boundary changes meant that Tatton was now the fifth safest Tory seat in the country. According to the *Times Guide to the House of Commons*, if electors voted along the same lines as they did in 1992, then Hamilton would scoop up a national vote of 32,235. This would be a 62.2 per cent share of the vote: about as near as you could get in Britain to the vote share enjoyed by a Ceausescu or a Honecker. The boundary changes meant that

Hamilton's notional majority went up from roughly 15,000 in 1992 to 22,365 in 1997.

Labour's notional vote in the revised constituency, if everyone voted as they had done in 1992, would be 9870; the Liberals would get 9387 votes. The two anti-Tory votes added together come 11,000 short of Hamilton's monster 32,000 votes. Hamilton, by the luck of the boundary draw, looked impregnable.

He could lose thousands of votes and still coast into Westminster. And Bell's projected total presumed that all Labour and Liberal supporters would vote for him, discounting the evident displeasure of many in Tatton that the 'media candidate' had been parachuted into the constituency from nowhere, or, to be precise, from Sarajevo.

For Bell to come anywhere near hurting Hamilton, there had to be an unprecedented collapse in the Tory vote. But precious few Tories had come out against Hamilton: Squirrel Nutsford was dithering, while Cussons and Martin had been given the black spot.

On the contrary, Christine, in a cardigan of blazing Tory blue, told of one victory to two ladies also in blue: 'We had a wonderful telephone call in the office the other day, I don't know if you know, but from somebody living in Great Budworth and she said: "I've never voted Conservative in my life and I never will again, but I'm so angry and incensed by what the media have done, and in particular by what Martin Bell has done, I'm voting for Neil on the first of May." '

Meanwhile a new and horrible migraine gripped the Bell campaign. The attack dog hacks were starting to hoover up the dirt on Mr Clean, just as Matthew Parris had predicted in the *Times*.

By this time Bell had moved out of the Longview and had based himself in a quiet flat, his den. Every now and then I was allowed in for a natter over a bottle of wine and takeaway pizza. It would be nice to describe my role as 'intelligence officer' for the Bell campaign, all-licensed spy, charged with telling Bell, Melissa and Bateson what exactly the other camp was up to. The reality was somewhat different. I was Bell's fool. I had some freedom to tell him things which others might not care to. I had been blunt about his failure at Knutsford Heath. But most of the time it was on with the jester's cap, as I waved my fool's stick around Tatton.

I remember Bell, Melissa, Kamm and Bateson worrying about the next hurdle, the horrors of the nomination process. The big South African ended up with a small consolation: 'At least, with a name like Bell, he will head the list.'

'Hah!' said the fool. 'You know he changed it by deed poll so that he could top the form. His real name is Martin Zzyxwyzzy.'

Bell's face degrumped, for a moment.

But when they went for the people he loved, there was very little any of us could do. Somebody had gone through the rubbish in the Bell home in Hampstead Garden Suburb. Bell's other daughter, Catherine, studying at a college in America, had to be rescued by security men when hacks monstered her. The sleazeballs were camping outside his friend's home. His friend was a private person. Why did she have to be persecuted?

I remember being in the den when he took a call from his friend. When it was over he looked up with that slightly dazed expression he has when faced with life's cruelties. 'Now I am beginning to realise what the Hamiltons have been going through,' he said and shook his head.

I looked away and examined my soul and found it wanting.

Bell sensed that his two failed marriages were about to be exhumed. The mother of Bell's two daughters, Hélène, his first wife, is French and works for the French Treasury in Polynesia. They met in Spain, married in London and raised the children in Washington, where Bell was then the BBC's correspondent. While in Washington he had an affair, and left Hélène for the woman who became his second wife. Polynesia is a long way from Knutsford. Bell hoped that the hacks would leave her alone.

Although the affair which led to the break-up of his first

marriage had taken place seventeen years earlier, Bell knew that
he had to act. On Friday, 11 April he went on the offensive,
swallowed a bitter pill and in the Back Room of the old electricity
showroom gave a pre-emptive interview to John Hellings of
Rupert Murdoch's *News of the World*. He didn't enjoy the
experience.

Hellings: 'Why should it be such a secret?' Bell tries to interrupt
but Hellings goes on: 'No one from the *News of the World* is
suggesting that you shouldn't have one or that there's something
wrong in having one.'

Bell: 'Can I just, can I just, can, can. . . . If you give me a
shorter speech, I'll give you a quicker answer.'

Hellings: 'Good.'

Bell: 'There were reporters combing the countryside. Please
come and talk to me.'

Hellings: 'Well, that's what I'm doing. And you said beat up on
me. Well, I don't want to beat up on you.'

Bell: 'Beat up on me on the financial issues. . . .'

But the hack was having none of it. He wanted to know about
Martin's private life. Under pressure Martin conceded a little
about his second marriage.

'The relationship was disastrous, and this is also on the record.
There was a fundamental disagreement between us about the
amount of time I spent with my children.'

Interview over, the candidate hit the phone, telling a friend the
latest sin he had been accused of:

'. . . I paid a bribe to somebody in Bosnia not to kill me.
Well, actually I might have done, you know, but if so I'd have
had to come up with a receipt. This is the kind of crap I'm
dealing with. Absolute crap. . . . Yeah. . . . OK. I've no idea, all
I know is that there are unknown people scouring the country, I
mean it may be they think they can save the election by
discrediting me. I'm just running my campaign here. There's
a major smear campaign going on. Major smear campaign,
which I shall learn to live with and I'm going to stay the

course and I'm not going to be intimidated by it. OK. Thanks. Bless you. . . .' He put the phone down. 'Unbelievable. I'm now supposed to have paid children in Northern Ireland to throw stones at the military. And I was then withdrawn by the BBC. This is the biggest smear campaign.'

He went to the little office in the campaign HQ and sat down at his typewriter. He doesn't use computers.

'I am very pissed off. I'm going to get these bastards. This is going to be the sleaze issue that plays against them.'

Later he held a press conference, his anger just reined in: 'These people, whoever they are, have not gone for my politics, which are truly independent and non-party. They have not gone for my honesty, because they will find no wrongdoing in my financial records and they know that. Instead they have gone for my private life. I urge these cowards and sleaze merchants to desist, and I believe that we shall draw strength from the shady manoeuvrings of shady people.'

Whoever they were, it wasn't the sitting member and his wife. Hamilton said later: 'Well, it was absolutely nothing to do with us—'

Christine (interrupting): 'He's had twenty-four hours of bad press coverage. Well, we've had two and a half years of it. I mean poor Martin Bell. . . .'

Hamilton: 'Yup. I never at any stage mentioned his personal life and that wouldn't have been my style. I wanted to fight this campaign on the issues. It was Bell who personalised the campaign against me. We never responded in kind, although we could have done.'

That Sunday, 13 April, the tabloids flopped through the letterbox of the Longview Hotel. They were all pretty dreadful reflections on the obsessions of British popular journalism. 'MARTIN BELL CHEATED ON HIS WIFE – ANTI-SLEAZE CANDIDATE CONFESSES TO THE NEWS OF THE WORLD'. Under the headline 'WHEN THE MAN IN THE WHITE SUIT BROUGHT ME TEA IN THE MORNING' the *Mail on Sunday* tracked down Bell's second wife, the American TV reporter Rebecca Sobel, from whom he was also divorced long ago, to her home in Los Angeles. Bell hadn't spoken to her in years, but she told the hacks: 'He's funny and has a lovely dry wit. He's thoughtful, not cold or cruel.'

She added that Bell would make 'a superb, honest' MP and praised his courage in standing for election. As 'dirt' goes, this wasn't ever so dirty. The *Mail on Sunday* even threw in a halo on top of Bell's head, making him look like the Saint. A film of the same name had just been released.

That Sunday, Bell read the papers and reflected on the events of the past few days:

It's been an extraordinary week. I really did think when I started I was in for a 48-hour career in politics. I couldn't believe that Neil Hamilton would not stand down. I know the Conservatives, and I'm not pro or anti Conservative, but they are good at holding on to what they've got. And why should they give away one of their safest seats? Well, it looks as if they're going to and now I'm stuck with it and I'm going to go through with it and sometimes, increasingly, I'm enjoying it. And now, this Sunday morning, I discover that I have the endorsement, not only of two parties, but of both my ex-wives. I am absolutely delighted.

On Monday, 14 April, Bell got the endorsement of the local Liberals after their candidate, Roger Barlow, agreed to stand down. Bell said: 'Now both opposition parties have endorsed me, and by a larger majority than the local Conservative Party endorsed Hamilton, I can pursue my fight against corruption in the House of Commons.'

That was the party line stuff. Until this point, Bell had been able to hide behind the fact that, until formally endorsed by Labour and the Liberals, he could not be expected to identify his policies or put out campaign literature. Now, that defence was gone. He was out on his own. Little did he know that he was soon to be ambushed again, not by Hamilton or Christine, but by a seven-foot-tall creature of indeterminate sexuality.

In the Brick Red Lubyanka, everything was running smoothly to plan. ITN filmed five middle-aged envelope stuffers stuffing envelopes. In his election literature Hamilton was subtly patronising, describing Bell in one election leaflet as 'a decent man' – albeit one 'duped into standing as a Labour stooge'.

Tory Blue Jumper (as she stuffs): 'What alternative is there? There's no alternative. I've always been a Conservative. And I'm staunchly Conservative this time. Nothing that's happened in the last few weeks has made me waver one iota. Because I think the intervention of Mr Bell is quite astonishing and appalling.'

Her fellow stuffer, a woman with grey bun, wispy bits, glasses down her nose, held on with chain, snapped: 'Fantasy.'

A third stuffer, spectacles and a agreed: 'We've patronised awfully big way.'

a man with moustache, been in an

Grey Bun: 'Yes.'

Specs and 'tache: 'By the media, largely. And by a singular failure by the local social democrats and Labour, who have orchestrated this campaign, the bottom line of which is "Let's get Hamilton out, at any cost." '

Stuffers (chorus): 'At any cost.'

Specs and 'tache: 'The voters of the constituency have not been considered in any way. Plus the fact, we're now, I think, as a constituency, we're a laughing stock. We've got so many strange candidates, some of which want, you know, you really do, kinkyboots and goodness knows what else.'

Not everything said at the Brick Red Lubyanka was untrue.

Thus far, the campaign in Tatton had only been moderately surreal. That changed dramatically on Tuesday, 15 April, on the steps of Macclesfield town hall, where the candidates travelled to file their nomination papers.

The road to Macclesfield was touched on in Bell's diary that day: 'Bosnia was surely easier than this. Driving down the hill into Macclesfield with Nigel Bateson, my cameraman there and in the Gulf and now on unpaid leave of absence to help me, we conclude it is much like driving down the Mount Igman road into Sarajevo under fire. Much the same gradient but different dangers.'

Scene IV: Macclesfield town hall car park

Enter Bell.

Enter Miss Moneypenny.

Miss Moneypenny, of Miss Moneypenny Glamorous One XS Party, was dressed to kill for the second ambush of the campaign. She was a hymn to cross-dressing in green and black hooped leggings, six-inch-high clogs with black espadrille-type ties around her ankles, purple regal fur jacket with Dracula-type neck and black and white spotted lining and matching crown. A garland of £5 notes hung around her neck. Her face was caked in yellow foundation, red overdrawn lips, red-lined cheekbones, black eyes hidden behind two millipedes of false eyelashes. On top of her head was an understated birdcage. Not many people wear birdcages on their head, even in Tatton. She looked like Tweetie Pie, had you taken bad acid.

Miss Moneypenny was not any ordinary transvestite. She was one who was interested in politics, in particular having her picture taken next to Bell and Hamilton. Her presence was part of a cunning wheeze by the owners of a Birmingham nightclub, called Miss Moneypenny's, to cash in on the massive media presence in what the *Guardian* was calling Planet Tatton. For whatever reason, there was something about Miss Moneypenny which scared the pants off Bell, whose moral and physical courage had never been confronted by such a curious threat before. Artillery: yes; stalking transvestites: no.

Miss Moneypenny, dripping £5 notes, chased after Bell as he limped across the car park: 'Hi, honey. You wouldn't take any of this, would you? No, we know you wouldn't take any of that. You're good on the battlefield, I hear, as well. We're going to put up a good fight, honey. We're going to see what war's really like, honey. . . .'

Bell did something no one had ever seen him do before when faced with danger. He legged it.

Earlier Miss Moneypenny had chased Hamilton to the entrance of the town hall, squawking her manifesto: 'I want to put the tat back into Tatton. We want to know what you are doing for today's youth.' Then, as Hamilton had disappeared into the town hall, she posed for the cameras, draping herself over the railing and pouting. Then more shrieking, like that from an extruded bird of paradise: 'Miss Moneypenny's transformer. Putting the tat back into Tatton. Miss Moneypenny's transformer. Putting the tat back into Tatton. Thank you.'

Inside the town hall, Hamilton was keeping up the pressure. Bell had intended to file his candidature under the title 'Independent, anti-corruption'. This represented a success for the hard-line, Labour-ish tendency in the Bell camp. The idea was to put sleaze right up at the top of the polling card. But inside the town hall he was warned by the acting returning officer, Brian Longden, that the description 'anti-corruption' could leave him open to a legal challenge. Bell spent about forty-five minutes with Longden, whose long face suggests Mildred's put-upon husband in the TV sitcom *George and Mildred*. It was clear that the legal challenge wouldn't be coming from Miss Moneypenny. Bell could have Tippexed out the 'anti-corruption' title but the campaign team knew that Hamilton would make much of that retreat, giving him the opportunity to say that Bell was backing down. So they withdrew the papers and determined to get a fresh lot of nominations, using the description 'Independent'. They had another twenty-four hours to get it done properly. Bell, Melissa and Bateson returned to the Bell HQ, father and daughter looking depressed, the South African muttering strange incantations in Afrikaans. The Bell campaign announced that they would be holding a press conference at 4p.m., where they would explain to the puzzled hacks why the nomination was being postponed for a day.

Hamilton had been the first to leave Macclesfield town hall. He emerged at the door, only to be monstered by Miss Moneypenny. He and Christine retreated for a few minutes, then came out. He made a brief statement to the hacks milling round: 'Martin Bell has invited me to stand down. I have submitted my papers. It is not too late for him to stand down and he is clearly desperate to do so' – Miss Moneypenny lurched in the background, like a sexually confused giraffe – 'and return to Hampstead, where he lives. He has come to Tatton as a Labour stunt and the Liberal Democrats and Labour have denied their own supporters a vote.'

The Hamiltons made off. Not long after, the hacks started to get calls on their mobiles. Hamilton would say more at a press conference to be held at a poignant venue, Knutsford Heath, at

3.45p.m., a quarter of an hour before the Bell presser. It was a smart move.

While Bell was spending more and more time in the Back Room, Hamilton was asserting his freehold rights to the Heath and the constituency it embodied.

The day became more, not less, surreal. The sun had got his hat on and come out to play for Hamilton's open air press conference.

Scene V: Knutsford Heath

Enter Hamilton, Christine, Blonde Groupie, Grey Bun and General Wojciech Jaruszelski.

Hamilton looks natty in dark suit and flowery tie; Christine dignified in blue and white pin-striped jacket, blue rosette, obligatory string of pearls, and with white schoolgirl slides holding her hair off her face.

Enter hacks, dead coypus, attendants.

Enter Man in Leotard.

He is tubby, clad in a clingfilmesque red and blue leotard with white stars on it, matching tights – one red leg, one blue – red, white and blue striped swimming hat, and trainers. The leotard is cut beneath his hairy chest, held up by thin straps over his beefy shoulders. He sports round black spectacles with lenses the thickness of milk bottle bottoms.

Enter Two Dancing Girls. They sport combat camouflage trousers, matching tank tops and long brown hair.

Man in Leotard and Two Dancing Girls lumber towards the Hamiltons.

Hamilton: 'Um, who's this coming?'

Christine: 'Oh, God.'

She stares at Man in Leotard and Dancing Girls.

Hamilton: 'We'll try and keep them at arm's length.'

General Jaruszelski: 'Before we do anything we'll just remind them about the RPA [the Representation of the People Act].

We're bound by the RPA until the nominations are closed. Neil can talk to print journalists but obviously can't talk to broadcasters. If broadcasters talk to print journalists we can't stop them.'

Hamilton and General Jaruszelski go into the throng of hacks, while Christine, Blonde Groupie and Grey Bun hang back in a separate group.

Hamilton, addressing the hacks: 'We know that Mr Bell doesn't have any policies, but now he doesn't have a party either as I understand it. And the candidate who wants to make government more open is not terribly open' – Man in Leotard hovers on the edge of the press conference – 'even about his party label.

'Now I gather from what you would call impeccable sources that he has attempted to call himself an anti-corruption' – Two Dancing Girls a-jigger and a-jive – 'candidate. Can I just remind Mr Bell of what he said on this precise spot just a week ago when I said to him he was welcome as an independent candidate but not welcome as an anti-corruption' – Man in Leotard sashays towards the Dancing Girls – 'candidate because I have denied all allegations of corruption made against me. Mr Bell said this of the anti-corruption label: "I have not chosen this title, I am going to stand as an independent."

'He said that he may talk about trust in this campaign. Mr Bell has obviously betrayed that trust and forfeited' – Dancing Girls wiggle their hips, erotically – 'any right to be a candidate in this election. Just to mirror what he said to me yesterday, it is still not too late for him to stand down and scuttle back to Hampstead where he belongs.

'So, if Mr Bell is attempting to turn this campaign' – Dancing Girls approach Man in Leotard suggestively, stroking his plump thighs – 'simply into an extension of the *Guardian*'s character assassination campaign against me, then what he is doing is prostituting' – Man in Leotard shudders in simulacrum of carnal ecstasy – 'himself, and he is wrecking the election for the electors of Knutsford and Wilmslow and Alderley and all the other places

in the Tatton constituency who have been denied the opportunity to vote for mainstream parties, particularly the Labour Party
and the Liberal' – Man in Leotard gives a *moue* of suppressed
passion – 'Democrats.

'This is part of a cynical electoral ploy, which was admitted by
John Prescott when he came here last week, to order the local
Labour candidate out. This is part of the Labour Party's national
campaign strategy, of which Mr Bell is wittingly' – one of the
Dancing Girls gyrates, sensuously – 'or unwittingly an essential
part to keep the non-issue of sleaze in the headlines. So if Mr Bell
is serious about anti-corruption I ask him to follow the lead which
he obliquely set on the smears' – Man in Leotard and Dancing
Girls huddle together – 'which have been directed against him.
Because where are these smears coming from? Because they're
not coming from the politicians. They're coming from the more
responsible sections of the media.

'He spoke at the weekend of an unprecedented campaign of
innuendo' – the more plump of the Dancing Girls stops gyrating –
'and slander against him, a smear campaign. What Mr Bell is
engaging in in this constituency is a smear campaign' – Man in
Leotard stops gyrating – 'against me. He has betrayed the trust of
the electors of the Tatton constituency even before he has been
able to nominate himself as a candidate, so' – the less plump of the
Dancing Girls stops gyrating – 'I call upon him now to withdraw
and for mainstream candidates to contest this constituency in this
election.'

The first hack off the mark was Jim Hancock – no dancing girl,
he – of BBC regional TV: 'If he files nomination papers as an anti-
corruption candidate what action will you take?'

Hamilton: 'Well, that remains to be seen.'

Hancock: 'Would you go to law?'

Hamilton: 'Well, the system is that you have to, as I understand
it, that you have to take an objection before the close of
nominations, but any action which is taken is decided on
subsequently. So one can't stop a candidate from putting up

under a particular label, but if he subsequently were to be elected then he places himself in danger of an election court unseating him.

'But this campaign is, I agree with Mr Bell, about trust, and I would like Mr Bell to hold to his word to me last week and to stand in this election on a clean and decent campaign on the issues in front of the people of this country. This is not a corruption campaign, because last week he said that he gave me the benefit of the doubt on the allegations of corruption which have been made against me.

'So, if we take that out of his campaign, what is left? Nothing. My advice is for him to go home.'

Hack: 'Have you objected to the returning officer about his candidature, sir?'

Hamilton: 'I can't object because I don't know what he's calling himself.'

Another hack: 'Have you indicated that you might object?'

Hamilton: 'I can't disclose to you the contents of any discussion I might have had privately with the returning officer this morning, but Mr Bell gave me an absolute assurance last week that he was not going to stand in this constituency on an anti-corruption label.' Hamilton's voice rises, an edge of menace in it. 'An absolute assurance. If he has gone in to the returning officer this morning with nomination papers bearing that description, then he has either told me a deliberate lie last week, knowing that that was his intention, or he has made a U-turn without telling me, in betrayal of the trust which he asked the people of this constituency to place in him.'

Hancock: 'If he decides to stand as an anti-corruption candidate, the returning officer cannot stop that happening. He has very limited powers.'

Hamilton: 'Well, the returning officer does have certain discretions, but if the returning officer were to allow him to stand under a particular label, obviously that application could be subject to a judicial review and, subsequently, the possibility of an election petition, and that would have to be decided by an election court. But these are all hypothetical questions because we don't know what Mr Bell has decided to call himself. We tried to get it out of him this afternoon – I can't understand why he's so coy. This is an election, and in an election you are supposed to lay out your stall, not close it up.'

Hancock: 'Are you asking the returning officer to disallow a description "anti-corruption"?'

Hamilton: 'I can't comment on any particular nomination paper until it has been submitted. But I am quite happy to make a comment when we know what Mr Bell wants to call himself.'

He was getting away with murder. Or so it seemed to me. Throughout the election in Tatton I worried about the extent to which it was fair to challenge Hamilton on what he said, and on what he didn't say. I settled on being like the Dinsdale Brothers in the *Monty Python's Flying Circus* sketch. Once, they nailed an associate's head to the floor. Oh, yes, they did that, said the victim, adding:

'They were cruel, but fair.'

Sweeney: 'How absolute was that assurance, sir?'

Typesetters do not have the capability, but if it were possible the 'sir?' would be printed here in a font known as Ironics.

General Jaruzelski, muttering to Hamilton: '*Guardian* journalist' – not true. I work for the world's oldest Sunday newspaper, established in 1791, not some provincial johnny-come-lately like the *Manchester Guardian*.

Sweeney: 'Was it as absolute as your suggestion to the Deputy Prime Minister that you had no financial arrangement with Ian Greer? Was it as absolute as your suggestion to the then Conservative—'

Hamilton: 'We don't talk to Guardian Group newspapers.'

Sweeney: '. . . Party Chairman, Mr Gummer, that you did not—'

Hamilton: 'Any other questions?'

Sweeney: '. . . give a Nazi salute in the Reichstag in 1983?'

Hamilton looks at me, cobra-eyed, as if to say, 'Don't mention the war!' Or, to be more precise: 'Don't mention the Reichstag!'

Someone – could it be Christine – cackles: 'Oh, come on!'

Blonde Groupie (ridicule in her voice): 'Come on, now.'

Sweeney: 'Hold on a second. Could you please answer the question. How absolute was Mr Bell's assurance? Was it as absolute as your assurance to the Deputy Prime Minister?'

Hamilton: 'What Mr Bell said to me last week was, "I have not chosen this title of anti-corruption. I am going to stand as an independent." So I put it to Mr Bell, I put it to Mr Bell that he has one choice. Either he's going to maintain his promise given to me one week ago or he's going to break that promise. Either he's going to stand as an anti-corruption candidate, and told me a deliberate lie last week. Or he is now trying to break his word, given to me last week. Either way, he forfeits all right to call himself a candidate of trust in this election.'

Point made, Hamilton drawls to a close. While he poses for the snappers, Christine approaches Julia Hartley-Brewer of the *Evening Standard*, whose nickname on her first local paper was, unfairly, Julia Heartless-Bastard. She is sitting on the grass, about to make a call on her mobile. Other journalists are milling around as the press conference breaks up.

Christine: 'Julia. Who . . .' – she gestures towards Man in Leotard – '. . . is that?'

Heartless-Bastard: 'Tommy Sex.' (For it is he.)

Christine: 'Tommy Sex! He is a candidate?'

Heartless-Bastard: 'I think so,' (machine-gun laughter) 'yes.'

Christine (to herself): 'Fine rippling muscles.' (Walking back to her two friends, Blonde Groupie and Grey Bun): 'He is, he's a candidate called Tommy Sex.'

Blonde Groupie (in Mrs Fawlty-on-the-phone tones): 'Oh!' Then, as the realisation of the naughtiness of it sinks in, she shrieks: 'Ooooh!' and does a Les Dawson-style smack on Christine's arm. They both gaze at Tommy Sex. The cut of his leotard leaves practically nothing to the imagination. They face each other, their bodies and faces convulsing with giggles.

Christine: 'Hea-ther!' (said in mock indignation to Grey Bun). 'Shuh. . . .' Blonde Groupie is by this time almost jigging on the spot in her excitement. Realising that she is being filmed, she brings her hand up to her mouth to silence herself.

Grey Bun (who doesn't seem to have got the joke): 'Standing here?'

Christine nods.

Grey Bun: 'Tommy did say that there were a number of err . . .'

Christine: 'Shhuh . . .' (turning her back to the camera) '. . . look out . . .' (she puts her hand up as a warning sign to her friends) '. . . they're all. . . .' (Christine turns back to face the camera, her face recomposed. She and Blonde Groupie, who has also stuck her straight face back on, walk away.)

Tommy Sex: 'Mrs Hamilton, we'd certainly like to sing a song for you. It's a top tune.'

For Grey Bun, the penny has just dropped. She is now gawping at Tommy Sex, snorting with laughter, displaying her teeth.

Tommy Sex: 'She can join us if she wants. Come on, Mrs H. Give us a song here, come on.'

Exeunt omnes, leaving Tommy Sex and the Dancing Girls to their gyrations on the heath.

A short while afterwards, Bell held a quickie press conference at the old electricity showroom. Clearly irritated by the mind-games from the enemy, he snapped: 'Can this be Mr Neil Hamilton, the most discredited member in the Mother of Parliaments? Mr Hamilton has typically thrown his lawyers at me. We have the people, he has the lawyers. Judge that for yourselves. We want to fight this in the towns and villages of Tatton. He wants to fight it in the courts.'

Later, the Bell campaign got a visit from Edward Bear, dressed in a bear suit and offering a pot of honey to Bell.

Behind the scenes, the agonies continued. The hard-liners

thought that Bell should call Hamilton's bluff and persist with 'anti-corruption'. The moderates thought he should stick with 'independent'. As the battle raged within the Back Room, precious time and energy were lost. While the Hamilton leaflets were ready to be printed and posted, not a single Bell leaflet had yet been agreed and approved by the lawyers, let alone printed. If Hamilton's intention had been to constrict the Bell campaign with the lawyers, he was succeeding.

In the old electricity showroom, everything was running into the muck. Nothing went right, not even the drawing up of the nomination papers. After Bell had been kiboshed at Macclesfield by the threat of Hamilton's challenge, new nomination papers were drawn up. Only at 10p.m. was it realised that a mistake had been made on the nomination paper. Sue Addison, a Knutsford Bellite, spent until midnight ringing and visiting her friends to get new seconders. She got people out of bed – they opened their front doors in dressing gowns. She couldn't use her husband's friends because they'd all been in the pub before and had been used on Miss Moneypenny's nomination paper. As it turned out, this new 'stand-by' nomination paper was not used.

Getting nominated had not been easy for a fourth candidate in the battle for Tatton, Lord Byro, also known as David Bishop, a poet and painter and decorator from Nottingham. His Tatton Diaries record the struggle:

April 14: Knutsford. Having collected ten signatures from the local pubs, went to Knutsford library to check the electoral roll. Three of the people who signed weren't on it so had to go to Macclesfield Town Hall for a new proposal sheet. On the way back, bus overheated and has to stop outside the Dixon Arms [Hamilton stronghold, where the selection meeting had been held]. Lo and behold, whom do I espy sitting in the lounge but Hamilton and his wife. I say to the bus driver:

'Do you mind if I nip in for a minute?'

'O.K. by me,' he replies. Burst in on the Hamiltons.

'I'm Lord Byro.'

'Oh, so you're Lord Byro,' says Christine.

'Yes, and your husband's a scallywag and so are you. Staying in the Ritz for nothing. You've both had your snouts in the trough for years.'

'You be careful what you say,' says Christine.

'I'll just say what I like. Anyway I must go. My bus is waiting.'

Exit me leaving the Hamiltons and their entourage looking rather bemused.

Lord Byro took up residence in the Freemasons' Arms. He could always be relied on for a haiku of anti-Hamilton doggerel over four pints, if you were in the need. I often was.

The next day, Wednesday, 17 April, Bell filed his nomination papers under the title 'independent'. Caution and the moderates had won. He was one of a preposterous ten candidates standing in Tatton, more than any other seat in the country. In alphabetical order, Bell headed the list.

His proposer was Laurence Hobday, a former Tory councillor who was engaging if, er, somewhat vertically challenged. Hobday looked like Ronnie Corbett but his monologues were funnier. He had quit the party in dismay at Hamilton's antics and was a key card for Bell whenever he was criticised for being a Labour or Liberal stooge.

Hobday appeared for a photocall to sign the nomination form. The following day, driving past a newsagent, he spotted a billboard saying 'TOP TORY BACKS MARTIN BELL'. He recalled: 'Wondering to myself which cabinet minister had come out in favour of Martin, I went in to buy a copy of the *Knutsford Guardian*. The "top Tory" turned out to be me.' Hobday's eminence was partly due to the embarrassing fact, for the Bell camp, that there were very few Tories who were prepared to say in the open that they would not support Hamilton. The old mafia code of *omertà* – silence, or be killed – certainly seemed to be active in the minds of the Tatton Conservative Constituency Association.

Next on the candidates' list was Lord Byro. His nomination was accepted under the title: 'Lord Byro Versus The Scallywag Tories Party'.

Hamilton came next, proposed by Panda Bear – constituency chairman Alan Barnes.

Top gun for the Natural Law Party was Michael Kennedy, the author of a worldwide best-selling book, according to the *Knutsford Guardian*, on the Special Air Service, entitled *Soldier I, SAS*. (I am always sceptical about what is written about Britain's elite regiment, having played chess with a few of them while they were protecting the British ambassador in Albania in a hotel in the middle of a shoot-out between the Shik and the rebels. Clear-headed killers the SAS may be, but they're crap at coping with the King's Indian.) Kennedy told the local paper he had an honours degree in French with Latin, which would come in handy if any of his electors wanted to levitate while listening to a reading of Caesar's Gallic campaign.

A second independent was Sam Hill; a third independent was Simon Kinsey, a naval officer, unimpressed by Hamilton; and speaking up for the Albion Party, was John Muir, an eerily normal businessman. He told the *Knutsford Guardian*: 'Tatton has been turned into a media circus.' He could say that again. 'Tatton has been turned into a media circus.' He could say that . . .

A fourth independent was Ralph Nicholas. Unusually, he was not fighting on the sleaze issue. He had criticised Bell for turning Tatton Liberal Democrats and Labour supporters into non-voters.

Next came Burnel Penhaul, commonly known as Miss Moneypenny the Transformer. She described the platform of Miss Moneypenny's Glamorous One XS Party: 'My party is the excess party standing for glamour, flamboyance, non-conformity, sex, life, escapism, equality, comfort and style.' She made no mention of boosting the name of a nightclub in Brum.

Last and not necessarily least curious was Julian Price of the

Juice Party, which stood for 'personal integrity, wisdom and innovation', as if Tatton's electors did not have enough of that from the others.

Sadly, for those of us who believe that infinite variety is one of the joys of our great democracy, Tommy Sex did not stand. His dreams of election glory, or, to be more accurate, certain failure, were doomed after his shadow Chancellor, Frank Pontoon, blew all the campaign funds on the 2.15 at Newmarket.

Even though the nominations were done and dusted, Hamilton had one last trick up his sleeve. He lodged a formal objection to the returning officer, Longden, over Bell's use of the word 'independent'. Hamilton said: 'Bell is a stooge of the Labour Party with Liberal Democrat support. He is making a mockery of the election in the Tatton constituency.'

Hamilton's objection was rejected.

The Bell campaign's notepaper, which had finally arrived, depicted an oak leaf and acorn on the top left. It looked like a drawing from a primary school nature table, but was no less charming for that. That Wednesday Bell set out his stall in his leaflet in traditional staccato style:

> I was until recently a war reporter on television. I do not have any personal political ambitions. I belong to no political party. I have been asked to stand as an independent candidate in Tatton by people both inside and outside the constituency. . . . My aim is to offer an electable alternative and to unseat Mr Hamilton.
>
> I shall not campaign on charges of corruption which are still disputed. On this he is entitled to the benefit of the doubt. But he is not entitled to the benefit of the doubt on instances of admitted wrongdoing. These include misleading the Deputy Prime Minister and taking money from a lobbyist without declaring it.

The charges against Hamilton were vastly scaled down from the attack dog letter, in what could well have been seen as a

victory for Hamilton's lawyers. But the tone of the 16 April letter
was less hysterical, more authoritative. The rest of the letter
bashed away at the policy angles, a teeny-weeny bit Eurosceptic
– 'we are an island people' – thoughtful, nicely balanced between
tradition and innovation. 'I shall be a champion of the Armed
Forces, and especially of the families of those concerned. I owe
that to my friends in the Cheshire Regiment.'

The letter finished in the famous clipped style of the man who
once said: '. . . grimmer than before, but no less determined'. He
wrote:

> If and when elected, I shall serve the people of Tatton to the
> best of my ability; I shall receive no undeclared income; I shall
> accept no directorships; I shall take no free holidays; I shall tell
> no lies. I shall do all I can to remove the stain of corruption
> from public life. The rest of the country is looking to Tatton for
> a better kind of example. Together, I believe that you and I can
> provide it.

It was impressive stuff, powerful in what it implied rather than
in what it uttered. Hamilton's lawyers, Crocker's, did not like it.
They wrote back the next day, Thursday, 17 April, in a two-page
letter which turned on the heat: 'The remark that you will "do all
you can to remove the stain of corruption from public life" . . . is
a clear accusation that Mr Hamilton is corrupt, an accusation the
gravity of which is redoubled in the context of an election
campaign.'

The letter ended with a pretty formulaic legal threat: '. . . our
client reserves his right to commence proceedings against you
claiming damages for libel following the publication of the report
by Sir Gordon Downey. If, as is confidently expected, the report
clears our client of the charges of corruption, the damages he will
be seeking will be very substantial indeed.'

You get this stuff in newspaper offices all the time – well, I get
it all the time – but for quite a few of the Bell team it was

unpleasant and scary. 'They're trying to demoralise us,' said one of the team in the *Independent* the next day. 'It's all done as a distraction because they know that our campaign has been set up from scratch. We've had to respond to everything.'

The pressure on Bell's time was immense, made worse by the fascination of the world's media by the Battle of Knutsford Heath. Press officer K2 recalls: 'I was fielding zillions of press enquiries from all corners of the earth. There were a few feeble attempts at dirt-digging but all most journalists wanted was to interview the man in the white suit. "I'm a friend of Martin's, we were together in Bosnia . . .," went the patter. "I'm afraid he's far too busy for interviews but you are welcome to follow him on the campaign trail," went my reply.

'On the other side of the office was a call from Japan Broadcasting. There were three phones, all on the same line, but no transfer facility. Sometimes somebody would hold the phone at full stretch while I took the call on the opposite desk. Sometimes I would clamber across the room, stepping over the knee-high wires from my own computer I had brought from home, to reach the phone. I felt like a stock exchange dealer, putting one phone after another to my ears, as New Zealand, Canada, Italy, the Netherlands, Belgium, all wanted the latest on Tatton. They'd phone up, and a few hours later they'd appear. Kunihiko Kishimoto from the Jiji Press, Japan, Christophe Lamfalussy from *La Libre Belgique*, Mark Sainsbury from TVNZ, Anjali Mody from the *Indian Express*, François Sergent from *Libération*, Werry Crone from *Trouw*, wherever that is. . . .

'The intensity of the media interest, with the constant intrusion of camera crews, irritated rather than encouraged the troops. Greeting Thomas Abraham from *The Hindu* – India's national newspaper – after his long journey from another continent, I hoped he hadn't heard the mutters of "There are no votes in Bangalore." Of course, Martin built his career doing precisely what the world's press were now on his doorstep to do, so he wasn't about to turn them away. But in an operation which rarely had a working photocopier, where filing meant separate piles of paper on the floor, where strategy was planned little more than a day in advance, the idea of an operation capable of manipulating the situation was laughable.'

If they couldn't catch Bell, they wanted to interview Melissa and film Bell's Belles strutting their stuff. Melissa and Bell's Belles obliged, beginning to get some idea of what Princess Diana goes through. But, politically, this media interest – they often didn't bother with the Hamiltons – paid little dividends. It did mean that much of Bell's precious time was wasted. At lunchtime that Thursday he spent twenty valuable minutes walking up and down and being interviewed by old friends from the Canadian Broadcasting Corporation. For Bell, professional and personal courtesy required that he should give his old colleagues time. But Hamilton's dig at Bell – 'the media candidate' – obscured the reality. Every time he talked to foreign TV cameras, he wasn't talking to his electorate. Worse, ordinary people, particularly pensioners, were frightened by the gnashing piranhas of the press who accompanied Bell everywhere he went.

And still he hadn't got any leaflets out.

On Thursday evening the Bell team went for a drink in the Lord Eldon. Often, the Bell campaign seemed more like a pub crawl than an orchestrated attempt to gain office. The mood was difficult, tense. The spell of Hamilton's lawyers was working all too well. With only two weeks to go, Bell's lawyers had not agreed the terms of his election literature. Nothing had been sent out through the post. The Bell campaign was stalled. Jonathan Freedland of the *Guardian* was in town. A clever, sharp chap, he had covered Clinton's re-election in the States. He was appalled at the lack of technique within the Clean Machine, so much so that he went up to Bell when he was supping his pint. Hamilton had his soundbites – 'innocent until proven guilty' – but where were Bell's? I, too, had a go, urging Bell to get out on to the streets, to forget the lawyers, to leave the Back Room to get on with the legal battle.

'Walk across the constituency, Martin,' I suggested.

'Can't walk. Got a bad leg,' he said, grumpily.

'What's your soundbite?' persisted Freedland. He had spent too long on Fifth Avenue. What was right for the Big Apple was wrong for Knutsford – in particular, wrong for a fifty-eight-year-old man who hates soundbite culture. Wrong for a man who loves the English language and has a first-class Cambridge degree to prove it. Wrong for a man who had worked on eighty assignments including eleven wars and one of whose mates is Kofi Annan, the new Secretary General of the United Nations. Desperate to take the heat out of the scene, I started to babble . . .

'If you can't walk, get a horse. A white horse. It would be brilliant. You could ride across the constituency from one end to the other—'

'Sweeney,' Bell fixed me with a stare, as if I was quite mad, 'you have some wonderful ideas from time to time, but I must say that your strike rate is getting pretty low.' He stared into his beer.

'You've got to—' started Freedland, but Bell thumped his fist down on the table, making it bang.

'I know what I've got to do. I've got to get those leaflets out. Once they're out, then we'll be fine.' He looked up and fixed the two of us with a mighty scowl. You don't argue with Martin Bell when he is angry. Freedland and I had overdone it, he by being too Clintonised, me by being a fruitcake. Bell looked up, sensed our dismay, sipped his beer and said: 'Every campaign has its low point, and you've just seen ours.'

But there was no mistaking it. We were witnessing Bell's Wobbly Thursday.

On Friday the atmosphere at the Bell team morning briefing remained hawser-tense. Doggart's diary records the scene:

Bell's agent Kate Jones gives a morning briefing to the ten members of the permanent team, of which I am now formally a part. A hardened campaigner in his fifties interrupts her to say that he has spent the last few days collecting signatures, only to find that the wording has been changed without consulting him.

'We had to take out the word corruption,' she replies.

'Why?'

'I don't see why I should have to explain that.'

'Because not doing so shows a lack of respect and trust.'

'Look,' she says wearily, 'if you don't want to work on this campaign, you're totally free to leave.'

'I don't have to be spoken to in this way. I've been involved with many electoral campaigns, and I've never seen one so badly organised.'

'Fine. Well, if you don't like it, you'd better leave. Take an hour to think about it and let me know.'

'I don't need an hour.' With that he gets up and storms out, clutching the pile of petitions he has collected.

Millbank-man Alan [Olive, the Labour Back Room man] runs after him fearlessly and grabs the petitions. A scuffle breaks out in full view of some bewildered constituents in the front office, and the volunteer is eventually thrown out.

That Friday, Hamilton and Christine were sighted walking towards the old electricity showroom. There was a panic attack at the Bell campaign HQ. Doggart's diary again records the scene:

Alan Olive tells me to stop him coming in and staging a Battle of Bell Headquarters. This is my first sight of the enemy, garnished with a big blue rosette and chequered blazer, topaz-eyed and droopy chin. He is accompanied by Christine and two other die-hard blue rinses, as well as a media melee. Their progress is delayed by hostile passers-by. One shakes Neil's hand and then holds up his palm on which is a 'Martin Bell For You' sticker. A van driver shouts 'money, money'. Eventually, he reaches the door of the campaign headquarters and hands over a letter. Cameras whirr, and the Hamiltons disappear.

Bell retaliated in a packed press conference
shortly afterwards. He came out of the
Back Room, anger and frustration
at the legal mullarkey
evident in the firm
timbre of his voice.
This time he did not
look down at the floor:
'I have met some

heavy-duty, world-class thugs in my time, and Mr Hamilton is certainly not in that category. I can only repeat what he said about me a few days earlier: he's a perfectly nice man but totally unsuited to politics.'

One step forward, two steps back. The next drama took place shortly after the press conference ended. It became obvious that one of Bell's Bags had got through the best part of a bottle of Glenfiddich and was speaking too loudly and stridently. An argument followed, in which she denied being drunk. She was sent home, fuming.

On Saturday morning, the *Guardian* ran Freedland's piece. Under the headline 'An innocent overawed', he savaged the Bell campaign:

There's something odd about a man in a white suit. He looks like a photo negative, the reverse of the norm. He is all light where there is usually shade. It's right that Martin Bell, the would-be independent member for Tatton, should look that way. For he is the reverse candidate. In an era when politicians are condemned for being all style and no substance, Mr Bell is the very opposite. It may cost him dear. That he is a man of integrity and honour no one doubts. He approaches voters in Handforth or Wilmslow, his suit and slight limp instantly reminding them where he's been and what he's seen.

Principle is not in short supply in Mr Bell's mission to clean up politics. What is missing is technique. Mr Bell's campaign is a negative of the one fought nationally by New Labour; strong on principle, but almost painfully unprofessional. Everyone in the office is charming and self-evidently decent. But the atmosphere is closer to that of a *Blue Peter* appeal than a guerrilla campaign to oust a stubborn man from the fifth safest Tory seat in the country. Members of the public are greeted by a sweet lady in a dog-collar. The phones go unanswered. No one can find a copy of a policy statement. There is not a single battle-hardened election veteran in sight.

[They were hidden away in the Back Room, arguing with each other.] Instead the campaign manager is Mr Bell's 24-year-old daughter, Melissa, whose good looks have garnered a raft of front-page photographs. She is bright and committed, but has barely seen a British election, let alone fought one. Mr Bell's agent, Kate Jones, who is in publishing, admits: 'I don't know the first thing about electoral law.' There is no morning pep talk to the team, no speech from the candidate to fire up the troops. There is no consistently-used slogan. Little discipline is exercised over the candidate's time.

Freedland's piece cast everyone into gloom. It made for grisly reading. What was worse was that a lot of it was true. It prompted a spate of letters in the *Guardian*. Melissa stuck up for her dad:

We noted Freedland's critique of the Bell campaign and his easy disdain for our idealism. But that is exactly what the people of Tatton are telling us is wrong with the General Election. That it is about parties rather than people. I am proud of my father's idealism and prouder still of his stand. Was Mr Hamilton prepared to let Mr Freedland spend a day with his campaign? The people of Tatton deserve to know.

The 'sweet lady in a dog-collar' was the Rev. Pauline Pullan. She too had a go at Freedland, but conceded some of the truth in his attack: 'Only shortage of time has prevented us from becoming the smooth-running, well-organised unit we would wish to be.'

But time was short.

The most damaging letter, and the one picked up by the other papers, came from Sander Meredeen, the volunteer who had been ejected on Friday morning. His contribution to the letters page of the *Guardian* was devastating:

Martin Bell's campaign was in tatters, much worse than as described in Jonathan Freedland's otherwise excellent report. I've just quit the volunteer team after three days spent largely sitting around doing very little because there is no professional management, no clear lines of communication, no inspirational leadership. . . . I found a fumbling, stumbling, unco-ordinated team of volunteers, expected to work without clear leadership under a campaign manager [Melissa] who, for all her charm, lacks the necessary skills to manage a successful campaign. . . . Campaigns are not won by volunteers sitting on their bottoms in offices; by a candidate who stands around, looking lugubrious, like a little boy lost. Martin Bell should get out there, start smiling and start telling electors what he believes in and what he's going to do about local buses, local schools and local health services. Above all, he should sort out that management team. Or he'll lose.

Peter Sharratt, the cameraman for the BBC fly-on-the-wall documentary which was going to be shown after the election, had been banned from the Back Room. He wanted a view of what was going on behind the scenes. Knowing that no one would see the footage until after the election was over, I spoke the truth: 'Things are going very badly for Martin. Hamilton is hitting him with his lawyers, so all the energy of the campaign is being taken up by spending hours and hours and hours in the back room of the new campaign headquarters worrying about the lawyers, worrying about threats of legal action from Hamilton. And he's winning the mind game. Hamilton is winning. Martin, and the rest of them, are demoralised. It's absolutely terrible. Martin is my champion, Martin stands for everything I believe in in life, decency, fair play, integrity, and he's losing, at the moment. If things don't change, then Martin Bell will lose and Neil Hamilton will win.'

I meant every word of it.

ACT FOUR

... This avarice
Sticks deeper, grows with more pernicious root
Than summer-seeming lust ...

Scene I: Knutsford Civic Centre

In my time as a reporter I have seen some things you could not
believe, had you not seen them with your own eyes. On
Christmas Eve 1989 I remember a shipyard worker on the
Danube, somewhere between Timisoara and Bucharest. He
was suspended in a rickety bucket from a crane, wiping out
the giant letters 'Nicolae Ceausescu' from the roof of a shipyard
building – air-brushing on an industrial scale. In November 1991
I remember feasting at a Serb banquet, thrown by the Yugoslav
People's Army, on beef stew and slivovitz off white linen in the
gutted ruins of the Hotel Dunav as the unburied dead of Vukovar
lay yards away. I remember a ballet dancer, a Muslim man, who
had been tortured in a truly terrible Serb detention centre,
describe his life before the war. 'I had a Maserati, a beautiful
house with a garden. And a pink swan,' he said. A pink swan? 'A
pink swan,' and he opened his arms, and a pink swan unfolded its
wings.

And, hand on heart, I can say that the Charter 88 Democracy
Day candidates' debate in the Tatton election is up there with
some of the most bizarre political events I have witnessed in my
life.

It took place on the evening of Tuesday, 22 April. They
trooped on stage: Bell, independent, on the left; then, to the right
of him, Ralph Nicholas, independent; Michael Kennedy, of the
Natural Law Party; David Bishop, poet, of the Lord Byro Versus
the Scallywag Tories Party, sporting a top hat with a sleaze special
offer, 'Poet for Sale, 10/6', tucked in the rim; Miss Moneypenny,
sporting yellow bridal dress and birdcage; and, on the right, John
Muir of the Albion Party. Muir was the only one who looked
remotely like a career politician, and appeared all the more odd
for that. He sat, looking as butch as is possible when sitting next to
a transvestite, leaning forward, forearms on the table.

For the audience, the below-the-belt view beneath the table
provided an interesting contrast. Miss Moneypenny's black and
yellow hooped knees were clamped together, her feet apart;
Muir's knees were spread as far apart as his trousers would allow,
his tie dangling at fig-leaf length. It looked like a badly cut film
strip of a knee dance. The debate, such as it was, was chaired by a
man of the cloth who was a dead ringer for the vicar in *Dad's
Army*.

Hamilton wasn't there. Shortly before the meeting, General
Jaruszelski had issued a press release:

Neil Hamilton will not be taking part in the Charter 88/
Democracy Day meeting at Knutsford Civic Centre this
evening. Neil Hamilton is holding his own public meetings.
Neil was invited last week to take part in the Charter 88 debate
as a 'one to one' with Martin Bell. This arrangement was not
permissible under election law, because it excluded other
candidates, and because it involves expenditure 'other than
by the election agent'. We understand that Charter 88 have
now invited some or all of the other candidates to tonight's
meeting, and some of them may be attending. This does not
change the status of the Charter 88 meeting in regard to
electoral law.

This was an odd communication. There is nothing in British electoral law that forbids two, three or x to the power of 10 candidates from debating together. But the Representation of the People Act does set out, in its provisions on broadcasting, that candidates should be treated fairly. That means the BBC and ITV could not broadcast the event if Hamilton was not present; that would have been unfair on Hamilton in the eyes of the law. No Hamilton, no broadcast. But to say that the Democracy Day debate was 'not permissible under election law' was an assertion worthy of the real General Jaruszelski, not his lookalike.

Minus Hamilton, the debate went ahead.

Bell's press officer, K2, had been worrying about the candidate's grumpy face for some time. 'The nearest I got to some kind of image manipulation was yelling "Smile!" to Martin just before the shutter snapped those deep-set eyes and his overly serious, sometimes pained expression. Just before he went on stage for the candidates' debate, I even attempted "Make love to your audience". He smirked at me. When he got on stage, he looked as grumpy as usual.'

I sat at the back with Richard Cussons, the Tory Party member who had spoken out against Hamilton at the selection meeting to little avail. True blue though Cussons was, he was developing a nice line in subversion. A stationer and newsagent, he had put a new special offer in his shop window, offering brown envelopes at knock-down prices. Also there, dumped untidily at the bottom of the window, was an old copy of *Private Eye* featuring Hamilton and Christine. 'How much would it take for you to resign?' asked one bubble. 'About £10,000 in a brown envelope,' replied a second bubble. As the debate took place Cussons and I tried not to giggle too much, but it proved impossible.

Bell spoke first, clearly, his voice powerful, articulate, impassioned. He was, indeed, getting better. It is easy to keep a straight face through Bell.

Next came Ralph Nicholas, an insignificant, podgy-looking man with a mop of dark, greasy hair, the kind of person who is

murdered in the first five minutes of a detective movie. Nicholas
had launched his campaign at the Swan pub in Mere a few days
earlier to seven journalists, including a TV crew from BBC
Northwest. On that occasion, he was strikingly rude about
Bell, claiming: 'The only reason that Bell has got so much
publicity is because his daughter works for Reuters.' There
had always been an anxiety in the Bell camp that theirs was
the media candidate. This was the first time that they had to cope
with the charge that he was the media candidate's father. At the
candidates' debate, Nicholas got off to a sour start by rubbishing
Bell once more.

'People don't want a media candidate. People don't want to
know about sleaze. I don't stand on an anti-sleaze candidate, the
man on my right's doing that,' said Nicholas. 'I don't stand on an
anti-corruption candidate.' To be fair to Bell, he was not standing
on anyone at the time. Nicholas had been a councillor for the
Manchester district of Trafford from 1990 to 1992 before he quit
mid-term. He had taken retirement 'due to stress', begging the
question why on earth he wanted to become Tatton's MP. 'What
the people of Trafford want . . .' The rest was lost in giggles as
people in the audience – Cussons, me – called out, 'You're in
Tatton, not Trafford.' He went on to dig a deeper hole for himself
– 'We must reform the poll tax' – forgetting that it had been
abolished by John Major when he first took over from Lady
Thatcher. Nicholas was giving a pretty good impression of one of
those people who have been abducted by aliens and suffer 'time
lapse syndrome'.

The man from the Natural Law Party, which believes in yogic
flying, had not been abducted by aliens. He was an alien. Or, at
least, he had the same delicate features – too big a head
surmounted by thin, spindly limbs – and jerky body language
as the aliens whose flying saucer crash-landed and who were
dissected by US government scientists in the 1947 Roswell
incident. The Alien's command of the earth language known
as English was adequate, though incredibly boring. Even more

boringly, he did not yogically fly. His manifesto was recklessly self-anhilating, headed: 'What me? Vote for the Natural Law Party? You must be joking!'

By the standards of the candidates' debate, Lord Byro of the Lord Byro Versus the Scallywag Tories was a serious politician with much to offer the electorate. His manifesto advocated the setting up of a

> Parliamentary Anti-Sleaze Squad (PASS) to be headed by Neil Hamilton, ex-Tory MP. With his knowledge of the House of Commons' tearoom and gossip and the ways of the scoundrel Mohammed Al Fayed, Mr Hamilton would make an excellent poacher turned gamekeeper. Christine Hamilton to be his secretary so she can keep an eye on him. I have calculated that the money confiscated by Neil will be enough to cut the Public Sector Borrowing Deficit at a stroke and would enable my party to renationalise water, gas, electric, British Rail and British Telecom. (Bob Hoskins to be sacked.) 20% VAT increase on Harrods brown envelopes. This should be enough to keep the Post Office in public ownership.

Lord Byro's other vibrant measures included forcing

> 'Dishonest' John, Heseltine, Lilley, Portillo, Clarke to serve six months in a high-rise flat on Manchester's Moss Side on bread and jam and then given Restart interviews on the National Lottery Show, the Spice Girls to serve 14 days penance in Holloway, Large Breweries to be charged with vandalism against old pubs, old-fashioned Sundays to be restored and Manchester airport extension to be stopped.

This strong set of policies was reduced in the *Knutsford Guardian* to just two: 'Opposes the extension of Manchester airport and will campaign for the renationalisation of major British industries.'

He made a speech about the single currency and how the
Tories got rid of the imperial system years ago: 'Sixpences,
threepenny bits, inches, tons, acres: just to appease European
businessmen.'

He then read out a poem, 'Asylum in the Sea'. His poetry isn't
quite Keats, mind:

> Land of PurgaTory,
> home of BSE,
> scoff your Sunday dinner
> laced with CJD.
> Served with Yorkshire Water,
> what a dainty dish.
> And it's no use
> going fishing
> cos there ain't no ruddy fish.
> Sun goes into orbit,
> Hogg's head on the block. .
> Farmers in the Tower,
> Beefeaters run amok.
> Land of PurgaTory,
> going round the bend.
> John Bull and Blue Moollenium
> Apocowlyptic
> end.

The speech of John Muir of the Albion Party left the audience
baffled. His opening remarks concentrated on a fire in his house in
London. While sympathising with his trouble, it was hard to see
why a house fire in London constituted reason enough for him to
become the member for Tatton. He had three policies: to
introduce a Bill of Rights; to do something about Europe –
no one was quite sure what; and he took a firm line on house fires.
The trouble was that he answered every single question by
introducing variations on these three themes. He looked oddly

normal, besuited, a businessman at a sales conference. The problem was that in the company of the Alien Abductee, the Alien, Lord Byro and Miss Moneypenny, his normality struck one as all the more eerie. He was Mr Eerily Normal.

Miss Moneypenny's make-up – perhaps in deference to the alien element – had entered a fifth dimension. The black lines had multiplied, streaking across her face like tongues of fire; diamond studs marched across her eyebrows; her lips glistened with Christmas card glitter. Her speech, however, was something of a disappointment. She may have been wearing an empty birdcage on top of her head, but from the content of what she had to say it seemed possible that she had an empty birdcage inside her head too. That impression changed, however, when she uttered the immortal words: 'I've got a first-class honours degree in chemical engineering.' The audience gasped. She was not just a pretty birdcage.

Questions were invited from the floor. An elderly gent with a fine head of silver hair and a neatly groomed moustache got to his feet. He spoke with deliberation: 'First of all I'd better admit that like the last speaker' – surely not? – 'I'm also a graduate chemical engineer, but I'm sorry, I didn't bring my bridal dress too. What I would like to know from all the other candidates, apart from Martin Bell, is why are they standing, because they will be taking votes against Mr Bell. Could Miss Moneypenny answer the question first?'

Her voice crackled a little, then out came a mannish simper: 'I have as much right as any of these people here to stand.'

The hall sat in silence, and then we all burst into applause. It was an affirmation of the democratic principle; what elections are all about. That it came from a man/woman with a birdcage on its head, there to publicise a Brummie nightclub, made it no less moving.

Lord Byro was asked what he could do for the people of Tatton. 'I don't think I could live up here, because the houses are too expensive for a start,' he replied.

Cussons put up his hand and asked Lord Byro why he was wearing a blue rosette. The poet quoth: 'It's an Elvis Presley rosette. I won a first prize at Gracelands.'

Mr Eerily Normal was asked by a clerical gentleman where he stood on the proposed by-pass for Alderley Edge. 'I would say that the first measure that I would like to see introduced would be a new Bill of Rights. It's as simple as that.'

'Your position on the Alderley Edge by-pass?' reminded the vicar.

The sense of farce was intensified by the constant shuffling of too few microphones to go round. The debate was punctuated with painful pauses as the candidates, trying one moment to look and sound like political rottweilers, politely passed the microphone up and down the line like cucumber sandwiches at a vicarage tea party. Every now and then, the microphone yogically flew across the table. If you looked closely, it was possible to see a disembodied hand – like Thing in the Addams family – emerge on to the table and move the microphone. Looking closer still, one could observe a figure – the kind traditionally called Igor in the horror movies – connected to the hand that made the microphone yogically fly. Perhaps Igor was obeying the Natural Law.

Someone addressed a question about sleaze to the Alien from the Natural Law Party. He replied: 'The corruption is not at Westminster, it's in the collective consciousness of the nation. And that is where the Natural Law Party can make a significant difference.'

While the rest of us tried to locate our collective consciousness, the Bell camp's hitherto restrained and quiet Professor Brainstawm, Oliver Kamm, exploded logically. 'You described your party's programme as being founded on principles that are scientific and irrefutable. The greatest philosopher of science of this century, Sir Karl Popper, maintained that the criterion of a scientific proposition was that it be falsifiable – a contingent explanation capable in principle of being refuted by empirical

evidence. I respectfully suggest that, in describing your programme as scientific and irrefutable, you were literally talking
nonsense. . . .'

We watched, open-mouthed, as a slavering, wild-eyed
Kamm continued to rip chunks of the Alien's brain out with
his teeth. ·

'You further claimed that your party's principles have been
validated by scientific journals. Would you please provide a full
list of refereed scientific journals that are entirely independent of
the Natural Law Party and of the Transcendental Meditation
movement and are of the status of, say, *Nature*, that have
confirmed the claim that it is possible to float in the air without
physical support?'

Bell told Kamm that his late father (also Kamm's grandfather),
the novelist Adrian Bell, would have been proud. Kamm said
later: 'The candidates' debate was a waste of time, given that
Hamilton didn't turn up. I was annoyed at this, so I took it out on
the Natural Law Party candidate.'

The council was phoned so that someone could come round
and sweep up the remains.

Scene II: The Brick Red Lubyanka, St George's Day

Meanwhile, Hamilton was indeed playing hard to get. It seemed,
from the perspective of the Bell camp, that he was deliberately
using the RPA to suppress media coverage. The more people saw
of Bell versus Hamilton, the worse it was for the sitting member:
that was the line from the old electricity showroom. So the
Hamiltons had changed tack. They were now trying to keep their
heads down, run a low-key campaign and presume that the silent
32,000 would do the rest.

Hamilton had agreed to go on *Newsnight* for a live head-to-
head debate with Bell, chaired by Jeremy Paxman. The BBC
producers spent three days agreeing the format of the debate.

Incidentally, Hamilton insisted there should be no mention of Godot's inquiry into cash for questions, but then he finally agreed that a small percentage of the debate could cover standards in public life. The *Newsnight* team then had to track down the other eight candidates and persuade them to waive their right to appear on the programme. Miss Moneypenny refused to waive her/his/its right to take part in the debate and was going to be allowed to have her (etc.) one minute of fame. On Saturday morning *Newsnight* producer Charles Colville went up to see Hamilton. He said: 'I was told I had wasted my journey because he doesn't want to take part. . . .'

But Hamilton did take part in a stunt by the bookies Ladbroke's. They offered both Hamilton and Bell £500 each to back themselves, with

the proceeds going to charities of their choice. Bell had been willing to go ahead at first, but urgent consultations in the Back Room argued against it. The worry was that the £500 might be regarded as part of the Bell campaign's election expenses. So only Hamilton turned up, scooping up the £1000 bet and all the publicity. General Jaruszelski was quick to pounce in the pages of the *Wilmslow Express*: 'We think Bell is worried about meeting Mr Hamilton because each time he turns up he comes off worse.'

That was true of the 'Most Seen Politician' in the appearances league table, calculated by the *Guardian* and Loughborough University. The league table registered 'the number of appearances as one of the main players in a story, all media'. By 21 April, Blair was leading with 531, Major next with 517, Ashdown 167 and Hamilton fourth with 140. For a backbench MP to get more media hits than the Chancellor of the Exchequer, Ken Clarke (81), the Deputy Prime Minister, Michael Heseltine (78), the Deputy Leader of the Labour Party, John Prescott (56), and Lady Thatcher (51) was a stunning achievement. Bell wasn't doing too badly, though. He was sixth overall, with 84 hits. As far as the media was concerned, Tatton was tops.

Inside the Dixon Arms in Chelford, five blokes, three in cloth caps, were caught chatting about the Tatton election by a Channel 5 camera crew.

First Bloke with No Cap: 'Well, I wouldn't mind screwing his wife. How's that for a start?' (He points and winks – with an 'eye' – at camera.) 'Get that on.' (To general guffaws.) 'Don't forget. Get it on.'

First Cloth Cap (sinking into his grey anorak): 'I'd think you've lowered your standards. I think you've lowered your standards.'

First Bloke: 'No, I want to get into money.'

Second Bloke with No Cap: 'Well, he's not guilty until he's been proved guilty, is he?'

First Cloth Cap: 'My personal opinion is that I think he is. Sticking my neck out.'

Second Bloke: 'What's your opinion, Peter? You know the guy better than anybody.'

First Cloth Cap: 'Peter's not standing.'

First Bloke: 'No, his days are over. He's been caster-ated.'

First Cloth Cap: 'I mean they're all guilty.'

First Bloke: 'Yeah. They're all guilty. They're all in the job to earn money. I've never seen Miss Moneypenny. I'd like to meet her.'

First Bloke's wish was about to come true. Miss Money-penny minced into the Dixon Arms in Chelford wearing a red tutu, black and white top with wing shoulders and red and yellow hooped sleeves, black gloves, green head-dress with silver ball atop, spider's legs' eyelashes over a yellow foundation make-up, white bobbles on wire protruding from her chest, green and black hooped tights and twelve-inch-high black spotted white platform heels – as you do when you nip in for a quiet pint.

Miss Moneypenny's manifesto launch was somewhat uncon-ventional. It took place in the hall at the back of the Dixon Arms, where Hamilton had been reselected by the Tatton Conservative Association. She was accompanied by two wiggling dancers in black and white waitress outfits, sporting micro-skirts, showing suspenders and strumming imaginary guitars. Miss Moneypenny sang while strutting up and down the stage, protruding bobbles on her chest bouncing, her left hand holding a microphone, her right arm by her side, her black-gloved hand flexed outwards and moving from side to side.

Her voice was so-so: 'Does anyone know the way? Can you hear someone say? We just don't know what to do. Does anyone know the way? There's got' – knee lift – 'to be a way to' – she crashes down a few octaves – 'blockbusterrrrrrrrrr.'

The sweet siren sounds as the camera cuts to an audience of three cameramen and a dozen punters in a room full of empty tables with white cloths on. The music thuds away. Close-up on the punters: two middle-aged blokes in glasses, one with a beard, the other showing a few greasy strands of hair sticking out beneath his cloth cap, dragging their cigars in boredom. An elderly red-faced gent, white light reflecting in his glasses, heaves himself forward in his chair, puts his head down, creating several chins, and mutters to himself. Two elderly chaps, heavy jowls, puffy eyes, look on, open-mouthed. It wasn't like that in my day, you can almost hear them think.

What was going on inside the Brick Red Lubyanka? It was the most fascinating place in all of Tatton, but I was not flavour of the geological epoch. One day, while sitting in the White Bear, on the other side of the roundabout from the Tory HQ, I saw my fellow hack Stummer from the *Independent on Sunday* knock on the door. He recalls what happened:

My visit to the constituency party headquarters started well. I managed to talk my way past the intercom, security camera, through the heavy doors and up to the reception desk.

'I wondered if I might be able to talk to Christine for a few minutes?' I asked a party worker. Then Christine appeared and said:

'Well, as long as you're not that man from the *Observer*, I suppose I—' At that moment the doors behind burst open.

'Mrs Hamilton, Mrs Hamilton!' boomed a man in a black suit and Clint Eastwood black hat. 'I just want to ask you—'

Christine's response was swift, shrill and merciless:

'Get OUT! Get OUT! Both of you get OUT! I thought you weren't with that madman Sweeney!'

Seconds later we were both outside in the rain.

'Sorry about that,' said Clint.

Hamilton's leaflets were now out. Slick, beautifully printed and in glorious technicolour, they depicted Hamilton on his own; with Christine in the sunshine; with Christine in the rain, 'Opening a much-needed pelican crossing'; and with an old codger, 'Neil delivering meals on wheels during National Volunteers Week'. The old chap looks anxious, presumably because he has never tasted 'breast of Bresse chicken larded with foie gras cooked in vin jaune served with a quenelle of polenta with San Daniele ham' before. Or, maybe, this particular consignment of meals on wheels had not come from the kitchens of the Paris Ritz.

Hamilton's leaflet attacked Bell as a supine stooge: 'Labour stunt is a denial of democracy,' it read.

> In Tatton the General Election was turned into farce when Labour and the Liberals withdrew their candidates. Martin Bell was parachuted in from London as a Labour Party election stunt. What an insult to you the voter! . . .
> Decent people are revolted by muck-raking and trial by media. I hope you will register a protest by voting for me.

Of muck-raking and trial by media, there was an infinite variety for decent people to be revolted by. The *Mail on Sunday* was still needling Bell. Nigel Dempster makes his living dribbling acetic anhydride on the rich, the famous and anyone who flickers across his bluebottle's compound eye. His column on 20 April was headlined: 'Could this true Tory's girl be Martin's Belle?' The story named Bell's friend and reminded readers of his two divorces.

The *Daily Mail* joined in the fun. On 23 April there was a subtle little demolition job by Lynda Lee-Potter, Christine's favourite journalist:

> Our latest political star continues to look tortured and as though he's expecting a bullet in his back. This may be the effect a lifetime spent in the war zones of the world has on your facial muscles. It may simply be that he's terrified, justifiably, of Christine Hamilton. However, we should not be fooled. Foreign correspondents, in my experience, are resourceful, selfish and survivors. They can somehow rustle up a chilled Martini in the desert and arrive on time at destinations to which there appears to be no known route, carrying everything they

need in a small rucksack. They have even been known to track down a half-decent bottle of wine in Bucharest. They are totally self-sufficient but convey an alluring helplessness and attract the kind of leggy young beauties who are currently rallying around Mr Bell. The one thing Melissa need never do is worry about her father being lonely.

War reporters, if they can be bothered, can also write bitchily to order. The photograph of Lee-Potter heading her column reminded me, eerily, of someone. Then I remembered. Lee-Potter is the spitting image of Andrei Chikatilo, the Russian serial killer executed for fifty-two killings in Rostov. I wonder if they are, by any chance, related?

On St George's Day, a Wednesday, Hamilton launched his campaign proper with a brief press conference on the steps of the Brick Red Lubyanka.

Enter stage right Hamilton, Christine, Panda Bear and General Jaruszelski.

Enter stage left dead coypus, Simon Hoggart of the *Guardian*, Steve Bell, the paper's cartoonist, and assorted hacks.

Hamilton was wearing a St George's Day red rose above his blue rosette. With his check jacket and floral tie, he looked like the test card on the first day of colour transmission on Albanian TV. (The *Telegraph*'s David Rennie was an admirer of Hamilton's *tendresse* for check. He wrote: 'His enemies have painted an image of him in which he is regularly to be seen sidling into a Mayfair office block to collect envelopes of cash from an Egyptian tycoon. What does he wear? Trust-me bank manager stripes? Humble-but-decent tweeds and flannels? No, he opts for Terry-Thomas-style "bounder's check". Hamilton could hardly have made a more defiant choice.')

Hamilton begins with his usual line about introducing a novel element into the campaign: politics. His face quivers as he speaks. He looks nervous. His hands shake as he clutches one of his leaflets.

He opens: 'As a minister in the last Parliament, I initiated the government's attack upon red tape and regulation. We've not made enough progress in that respect and too often we've been driven as a government – and this is not a unique failing of this government, of course, it's a failing of all governments – too often we've been driven by hysterical headlines in tabloid newspapers, which have caused us to raise business costs. . . .'

Enter Lord Byro.

He is sporting a ludicrously tall black top hat which looks as if it was made in a primary school arts and craft class, with a red St George's Day cross on a white background, cut out of that day's *Sun* newspaper, Sellotaped on to it. He has stoked up on patriotic fervour with a couple of drinks in the White Bear so that he is now able to confront, as his diary puts it, 'Liealot and the Dragon'. His voice cuts in over the top of Hamilton.

Lord Byro: 'Vote for somebody else! Liar, cheat, scallywag. What about the *Guardian* allegations?'

Christine: 'They're the liars.'

Hamilton ignores him, intoning: 'I only want to answer questions on the issues.'

Lord Byro: 'Liar.'

Christine: 'You're the one who is lying!'

Hamilton's hand cuts a swathe in the air: 'Let me handle it, it's my press conference. My campaign is about real politics—' – car hoots loudly – 'real politics is put forward only by me as the Conservative Party candidate in this constituency.'

Lord Byro: '. . . somebody from Al Fayed, Mr Hamilton.'

Enter Sweeney.

Sweeney: 'Mr Hamilton. Mr Hamilton.'

Lord Byro: '. . . stay at the Ritz.'

Sweeney: 'Mr Hamilton, I want—'

Lord Byro: '. . . you denied it last week.'

Hamilton: 'This is, er—'

Lord Byro: 'I asked in the Dixon Arms last week, did you stay at the Ritz, and you said you didn't. And you did stay at the Ritz. Sorry, it's in the *Guardian*.'

Christine: 'You're the one who's lying.'

Lord Byro: 'The *Guardian* said you stayed in the Ritz.'

Hamilton (having to shout over the top of Lord Byro, Sweeney and others): 'If somebody want to ask me a sensible question, I'll be happy to try to answer them.'

Sweeney (Foghorn booming above the lot of them. To Lord Byro): 'Excuse me a minute, sir – could you please be quiet?' (To Hamilton): 'I wish to put a question to you, Mr Hamilton. It is this. A good number of Conservatives do not support you. Among those are local Conservatives in the constituency and a former Conservative MP whose name is Martin Brandon-Bravo. He says that you made, in his hearing, the most offensive remark he heard in his nine years in the House of Commons—'

Hamilton: 'If you have any questions on the issues—'

Sweeney: 'On 12 December 1989—'

Hamilton: '. . . I'll be quite happy to try and answer them.'

Enter Mr Eerily Normal of the Albion Party.

Mr Eerily Normal: 'I have a question on an issue. On the issue of sovereignty, Mr Hamilton. You say that sovereignty rests with Parliament and that the United Kingdom, as the party that you represent, delivered its, er, retention as, er, empty of sovereign importance.'

(Everyone, at last, has been silenced by the enigma of a question that nobody understands.)

Mr Eerily Normal (continuing): 'Sovereignty in my opinion rests with the people of this country. It is on loan to Parliament. And only on loan to the people to decide exactly how they wish to disember . . ., to di . . ., to dissent . . ., to extend sovereignty throughout the country. So, it is an election, it is an election that that issue is raised. It's on loan by the people to Parliament.'

(A lorry is heard accelerating away, perhaps with the cognitive remnants of Mr Eeerily Normal's brain.)

Hamilton: 'I'm not sure I understand the question, but we have general elections every five years—'

Lord Byro: 'You took money from Mr Al Fayed, Mr Hamilton—'

Hamilton: '. . . to decide the future course of the country. . . . I am quite prepared to state my position on this and other issues now.'

Sweeney: 'Mr Hamilton, could you characterise your conversation with the Deputy Prime Minister on 20 October 1994?'

Hamilton: 'Any further questions on issues?'

Mark Whittle (Bell spy): 'You said you wanted to talk about issues—'

Lord Byro: 'But sleaze is an issue, Mr Hamilton—'

Whittle: 'How come—'

Lord Byro: 'Sleaze is the big issue.'

Whittle: 'For what reason were you not at the Charter 88 meeting last night?'

Hamilton: 'Because I wrote several weeks before the meeting to say that I had already got my own public meetings. I'm the only candidate in this election out of ten to have regular public meetings—'

Sweeney: 'Give us the details of one public meeting that you've held thus far, Mr Hamilton.'

Hamilton:'First of all, have you got any questions on the issues?'

Lord Byro (over the top of Sweeney): 'The issue is that you're a crook, Mr Hamilton. And your wife's aiding and abetting you in these lies that you're peddling.'

Hamilton: 'The *Observer* is perfectly entitled to come to my meetings if it wants to.'

Lord Byro: 'You have not answered my question, Mr Hamilton.'

Hamilton: 'Anybody got any questions on the issues?'

Lord Byro: 'Yes, you're a crook. That's an issue.'

Guardian cartoonist Steve Bell (no relation): 'Will you be having a debate with Mr Bell?'

Hamilton: 'Well, Mr Bell seems remarkably elusive. I've four times asked him even to have a private meeting with me—'

Lord Byro: 'You were invited to the debate last night, Mr Hamilton, but you didn't turn up—'

Hamilton: '. . . and he's refused or ignored my invitations. He could have seen me here yesterday—'

Lord Byro: 'You were invited to the debate last night, Mr Hamilton, but you didn't turn up—'

Hamilton: 'He could have seen me here yesterday when we tried to raise some money for charity which Ladbroke's was putting up, but he didn't turn up. And it's anyone's guess why he didn't turn up. I don't know why he's running scared of meeting me. Possibly, as my agent said yesterday, it's because he knows that every time he meets me he comes off worse.'

Lord Byro: 'Why didn't you turn up last night, Mr Hamilton?'

Sweeney: 'Mr Bell takes the view that you shouldn't take money from big business.'

Hamilton: 'Well, we seem to have exhausted the issues.'

Exeunt Hamilton, Christine, General Jaruszelski and Panda Bear to the Brick Red Lubyanka.

Lord Byro recalls in his diary: 'Hamilton is shaking like a leaf. I'm starting to feel sorry for him so I clear off back to the pub.'

Hamilton may not have enjoyed his press conference and he suffered some of our anger at the aggression of his lawyers and his failure to show up at the candidates' debate. But he didn't have to campaign. All he had to do was to keep his head and wait for his 32,000 voters to deliver his seat. Except at the beginning there was no sign that he was panicking, despite our absurd attempts to put pressure on him. Once he got into his stride he was always fluent, smart, quick with a riposte. I felt a deep sense of failure. He seemed impervious to any attack. Only a stake through the heart would do it.

Later, I went for a beer with Doggart. He records the following in his diary:

I go for a drink with Sweeney who is sceptical about Martin's chances and desperate for a break against Hamilton. Sweeney eats, drinks and dreams Hamilton. 'Don't you think you're victimising him? When has any individual in public life been subjected to such a sustained and vicious assault on his reputation? Why didn't you do this to Maxwell?'

'I tried,' Sweeney said, 'but I was forbidden by the editor.'

Gloomily, Hamilton posters hung from the trees all over the constituency and, in particular, Knutsford Heath, which was private land and owned by Conservatives loyal to the sitting member.

Later, Bell told the *Guardian's* Simon Hoggart: 'You'll notice that all his posters are on trees and hedges, never in people's houses. Unless I'm mistaken, trees and hedges do not have a vote.'

Cartoonist Steve Bell, a Rasputin look-alike, took in the blue blossoms hanging from the limes and coined a fine Hamilton aphorism: 'Trees for sleaze.' I went round repeating it all day, so much so that people thought it was my joke.

Hoggart went into a pub with the candidate, Melissa, Bateson and the Belles.

Two blokes looked up from their pints. 'We couldn't vote for a man who drinks,' said one. (Northern humour does verge on the predictable.)

'This is medicinal,' said the other.

'Then you must be very ill,' the candidate snapped, but amiably.

'I expect you'd sooner be dodging bullets, wouldn't you?' said the first chap.

'I would, I would,' he replied.

Scene III: The Old Electricity Showroom

Ten days before polling day Bell's formal election literature, cleared by the lawyers, finally began to arrive from the printers.

Enter Bell.

The three Bell's Belles stand to attention on one side of a table in the old electricity showroom.

Sophie Solomon (calling out): 'Maaartin.'

Antonia Harris (handling papers): 'Do you mean these?'

Bell (hobbling towards the other side of the table towards the Belles): 'Yes.'

Bell's Belles (simultaneously): 'Ahhhhhhhhhhhh.'

Sophie: 'Who's a clever girl?' (Girls smile and giggle.)

Bell (toothy smile): 'What would I do without my girls? (More 'ahhhhing' from the Belles.) We're going to need some more as well.'

All the Belles: 'Are we allowed to, are we allowed to, are we allowed to put them out?'

Bell: 'Oh yes, we've been putting them out all afternoon.'

Chiming Belles: 'Ohhhh, Ohhhh, Ohhhh.'

Sophie: 'So they've been cleared?'

Bell: 'They've been cleared.'

Sophie: 'Oh great, we can run some more off, then.'

Bell (grinning):'It was saying some really dangerous things. And I would wish to take out a taint of corruption from public life.'

Sophie (exaggeratedly): 'Oh, my God.'

All Belles: 'Oooh. Ahhh.'

Sometimes, I wondered whether I was on the wrong side.

The content was the labour of many hands but the policy had been figured out by Bell's Professor Brainstawm, the celebrated Popperian Kamm. He had done his homework, tinkering with the original statement and playing around with the campaign policy to make it as boring and Tory attack-proof as possible. He outlined his thinking after it was all over:

The Tory leadership's line on Hamilton was that Tatton voters should support him on grounds of his policy platform, while Hamilton's line of attack was going to be that Martin's candidature had robbed the voters of the chance to make a judgement on the respective party programmes. Plainly the point of our campaign was to focus the election on the issue of the egregious unsuitability of the Conservative candidate to hold public office of any kind, while avoiding the implication that Martin was a purely single-issue candidate.

Martin is a genuinely non-party animal, and I have been talking politics with him for twenty years. I know broadly what his views are likely to be even if he hasn't arrived at them yet. I used to think of myself as standing on the extreme Right of the Left, while Martin was on the extreme Left of the Right. But he seems to have moved towards my position. He is a sort of Jackson liberal, Henry not Jesse; strong on both defence and welfare. In writing his manifesto, I wanted to make the issue of trust central and to make him immune from attack on grounds of his having no purpose other than the (entirely noble) one of unseating Hamilton.

The Bell policy manifesto – 'A fresh start for Tatton' – thus started with the question of standards in public life, and stated that while most MPs were honourable public servants, the rule was unfortunately not universal (thinking of no one in particular). It gave credit to the government for its economic management since 17 September 1992 – Black Wednesday, when the pound crashed out of the ERM; struck a stance of moderate Euro-scepticism; criticised the internal market in the health service; and supported active membership of NATO and the UN as the military and diplomatic arms of Britain's security. It was conservative stuff, though only with a small 'c' and theoretically bomb-proof.

Kamm was amazed when Hamilton attacked Bell on defence. 'He quoted out of context a call for greater coordination of European countries' foreign and defence policies. Given that

Martin is hardly a nuclear unilateralist, and that Hamilton has neither served in uniform nor seen a shot fired in anger, it would be difficult to think of an issue more likely to cast Martin in a favourable light.' The Euro-scepticism went down well with one newspaper, as Kamm recalls: 'On the strength of this, and also an aversion to the character and ethics of Hamilton, we won the endorsement of the *Times* in its guide to Euro-sceptic candidates to vote for – much to my surprise and slightly alloyed pleasure.'

One political rival was not very impressed with Kamm's homework. Lord Byro recorded in his diary: 'Go into Bell's office and grab his manifesto. "Get the jobless back to work" states one line. Where have I heard that before? If I'm elected I propose to legalise prostitution, pay them a state wage and call it "The Knobseekers' Allowance".'

The Bell campaign team now had the job of sorting, stamping and stuffing into envelopes sixty thousand campaign letters. On the day the first leaflets arrived work started at 9a.m. and did not finish until 11p.m. The old electricity showroom felt like an engine room fuelled by – this being England – cups of tea. Laura Gillan was one of the envelope stuffers: 'Big Nigel [Bateson] used to appear regularly at the envelope-filling table bearing cups of tea and coffee which, because we were sitting down and he is around seven feet tall and chunky, he had to serve to us kneeling.' The ladies, generally of a certain age, got a certain *frisson* from seeing the man mountain on bended knee before them.

Once Paul Cousans, a photographer for the *Times*, came into the Bell campaign HQ. The office was abuzz with at least a dozen volunteers stuffing envelopes. 'Yes, feel free to photograph them,' said K2. He looked slightly embarrassed before asking if there wasn't anybody younger to photograph. K2 looked around. The envelope-stuffing volunteers were all around fifty. She produced a couple of Belles. He was delighted and took his snap, with Bell's Belles in the foreground and Bell's Bags tucked away, smudges in the background.

I was hanging around when a call came through. It was from

Paramount movies, or somebody pretending to be from them. They were interested in making a film about Tatton. We wondered who would play whom. Bernard Hepton could play Neil Hamilton. Hepton had been good as the Commandant of Colditz in the old BBC story. As for Bell: Colin Firth, Ralph Fiennes, anyone in a white suit. Doggart thought Christopher Walken as Hamilton, Anthony Hopkins as Bell, Emmanuelle Béart as Melissa and Glenn Close in rabbit-killing mode as Christine. Or, maybe, Juliet Stevenson.

And, as ever in the old electricity showroom, fantasies of power and control over the candidate competed with the more mundane job of getting Bell elected. David Geen was always good for surreal copy – as if we were not getting enough.

Geen: 'I don't want too many more street walkabouts. He seems to be meeting the same shoppers on successive days and they're getting a trifle bored with him.'

And Geen again: 'We're the Jehovah's Witnesses. We're converting. Very few parties find themselves on doorsteps trying to do that. They are usually working to find out where their vote is to ensure that it turns out on the night. We're converting and we've only got one weapon and that's Martin. And we're putting him on as many doorsteps as possible to see as many people as possible. And he leaves behind a trail of touched souls. . . .'

The Rev. Pauline Pullen recalls a visit to the Bell HQ by one such touched soul: 'About two weeks before the election an elderly lady came in, saying she wanted to vote for Martin. She was adamant that this was where she had to vote. I gently explained to her that she would have a card at home explaining where she needed to go. She went off, then somebody else came in, convinced that if Martin was elected he would form the next government. David Geen said: "I've always fancied being Home Secretary." '

A fresh nightmare arose for the Bell campaign. By some appalling series of accidents they had somehow managed to offend Swampy and his friends, who were currently building treehouses and digging tunnels respectively above and below the planned site of Manchester Airport's second runway.

The second runway was Tatton's hottest local issue. When built, it would mean greater noise pollution and distress for people living in the constituency closest to the airport. For that reason Hamilton had been a vociferous opponent of the scheme, something to which he had alluded in his own campaign literature.

Long before the election had been called all the legal remedies had been used up. The runway was going ahead, the builders were ready to start work, but everything was on hold because a group of idealistic 'greens' had started to burrow beneath the proposed site. Down these holes, some of the star tunnellers had blockaded themselves in. Their protest was illegal, but also enjoyed widespread public sympathy. No one in Tatton wanted more aircraft noise or yet more of our precious countryside dug up; though, equally, no one wanted to hang around Manchester Airport on August Bank Holiday watching 'delayed, delayed, delayed' on the flight departure screens.

To make sure that Bell was seen to be on top of the issue, David Geen had arranged for him to go to the site and meet some of the protesters. Everything had been organised through a slightly deranged protester nicknamed Rod the Ranter.

As soon as they got to hear of the plan, K1, Melissa and Bill Le Breton decided that it was a bad idea. Bell should go to the airport, but he should go and look for himself, not be a captive pawn of either side of the argument. In particular he should not be seen anywhere near any dirty hippies, lest the combination offend Tory voters. Geen was instructed to change the diary, but not to let the protesters know about it in case they hijacked Bell's appearance. Fear of hijacks still ruled the Back Room. K2 was instructed to find a friendly photographer who would snap Bell at the site, but would be sworn to secrecy. Laurence Hobday, the ex-Tory who was the Back Room's political equivalent of WD-40 – 'Just spray on Hobday and everything will come unstuck' –

was instructed to go with Bell and inform him all about local concerns.

Like a scene from a John Le Carré novel, a convoy of three cars moved off from the old electricity showroom in secret. The hush-Vote-hush-Bell convoy drove to Wilmslow, where they had a secret rendezvous with Cavendish Press photographer Jennie Robertson. She left her car and got a lift from one of the vehicles in the convoy. It crept along a dual carriageway and surreptitiously skidded on to the kerb. Everyone got out, dived through a hole in the fence and emerged in a field adjacent to the site, a wasteland dotted with trees. In the far distance, if you squinted hard enough, you could make out a treehouse.

Robertson snapped a man in an off-white suit with a grumpy face talking to a man who looked like Ronnie Corbett. In the background you could make out wasteland and trees. Then, some sixty seconds later, everyone scampered through the hole in the fence again and hurried back to the cars.

Robertson recalls: 'It was like being part of the FBI, or the Secret Service. I had to leave my car in Wilmslow. It was very bizarre. There could have been a great picture at the runway site but it wasn't good enough. All you could see was the fencing around the site and red tarpaulin in the trees. I couldn't get anything. Martin wasn't relaxed, and all I got was him having a quick chat in an empty field and that was it. This sort of thing has to be set up properly. It was frustrating because I was doing it exclusively, but I wasn't able to come back with the goods. It's hard to come up with something different, and this could have been a great picture because the second runway was so newsy at the time.'

As a photograph showing Bell's concern about the second runway, it scored, like Norway's entries in the Eurovision Song Contest, 'Nul points'. Later, Robertson's boss, Brian Whittle of Cavendish Press, recalls: 'Jennie rang me up and said, "This is absolute crap. I can't do anything with it." '

A few shots had been wired off to all the national newspapers.

None of them wanted them. Whittle phoned K2 to protest: 'This has been an absolute disaster. We've got a picture in which we can't see anything, no protesters, no runway, only a field with Martin in it. I am not a happy bunny.'

But the secret airport visit did have one result. Rod the Ranter arrived at the old electricity showroom, enraged that he and fellow greens had waited three hours for the non-arrival of Bell and his team. Geen tried to placate Rod the Ranter, which only caused him to rant with yet more fury. The passionate troglodyte threatened to chain himself to the railings outside the office. From this moment onwards the Bell campaign had a new terror: that they would be targeted by Green Rage.

By a strange coincidence Lord Byro had taken time off the stump to visit the second runway site that day. His diary records his outing:

> Went to see Swampy and Co. at their protest camp. He wasn't there. Probably on the *Richard and Judy* show. Handed out a few leaflets then walked three miles back to Wilmslow. Bell and his media entourage turned up after me but didn't enter the camp – perhaps he didn't want to get mud on his White Suit! In the Freemasons' Arms in Knutsford that night some of the locals slag off Swampy. 'Dole-scrounger – I'd like to fill his hole with concrete,' shouts one. I have a surrealistic vision of Swampy's bowels bursting and covering Manchester Airport with crap.

Scene IV: Mere Bowling Green hall

That Thursday evening the Hamiltons staged their first event for the public in the Tatton campaign. It was at the Mere Bowling Green club, a slice of our green and pleasant land. Robin Stummer of the *Independent on Sunday* and I were chatting in the car park about the latest gossip when a Rover surged in, 'Vote

Hamilton' stickers on its side, Christine at the wheel, Neil riding shotgun. She made as if to drive the car into me and looked a little mad. I jumped back and made my way to the hall, where I sat right at the back, quiet as a mouse.

Enter Hamilton, in check jacket, pullover, grey trousers, stonking rosette.

Enter General Jaruszelski.

Enter Christine Hamilton in tweed jacket, trousers of a homicidal purple and a face no less hostile. She sat one seat away from me at the back and stared with a ferocity which was almost erotic. 'Female murderers,' wrote Shaw, 'get sheaves of offers of marriage.'

The play began. Eighteen people dribbled into a hall which could seat eighty. Crueller: of those eighteen, I recognised that three were scribblers from Fleet Street, two were technicians from ITN, and one was a spy from the Bell campaign, Sebastian Doggart. Of the 32,000 who had voted for Hamilton in 1992, only twelve Tories – it seemed – had turned up for what was the very first meeting of his campaign.

Hamilton strutted and fretted his half hour upon the stage. But the absence of supporters clearly had him rattled. There was something about the stage, the village hall, the lack of bums on seats, that suggested bad amateur dramatics. What we were watching was not an election campaign, but a rewriting of *Macbeth* for the nineties: 'Is this a brown envelope I see before me?'

But once he got going, Hamilton's confidence grew. He is an articulate and skilled speaker with a pretty wit, rubbishing 'what Kelvin Mackenzie calls the unpopular press . . .'. There was a certain poetry about Hamilton citing Mackenzie as an authority. Mackenzie is the most brilliant moron in Britain. When he was the editor of the *Sun*, I doorstepped him for the *Tatler* magazine and asked him the John Mortimer question – 'Do you believe in God?' – at quarter to seven in the morning, through his letterbox, before the milk came. By way of reply, I got only a demonic chuckle.

Hamilton spoke admiringly of the journalist who once put a photograph of the victim of the West Ealing vicarage rape on his front page. And he denounced the journalist-turned-politician who had never done, never would do, such a thing.

Hamilton had set out his case against Bell. It was no soundbite, but a long argument. To savour the game he was playing, readers should stick with it: the extravagance of his final thought can only be appreciated if you wade through the whole thing.

The election has been hijacked and the electors don't really have a choice between the various political parties who are going to decide the future of this country. The way in which Martin Bell emerged perhaps casts some doubts about his credentials to use the term 'Independent'. He claimed that he was here because he had been invited by lots of local people. Yet you and I know that this spiffing wheeze of withdrawing the Labour candidate and inducing the Liberals to follow suit – then replacing them with Martin Bell – was a plot that had been forged at a London dinner table.

This followed a suggestion by the official photographer to Tony Blair in this campaign, the man who did all the photos for the Labour Party manifesto, who happens to be amongst his other commitments the long-term live-in lover of a Labour front-bench spokesman in the House of Commons. He made no reference to the fact that Tom Stoddart and Bell had both been injured in Sarajevo in the summer of 1992; or that Bell had written the preface to Stoddart's book.

It was, then, the Labour Party who fixed the Liberals, and Mr Bell's first press conference happened to be organised by the Labour Party and the bill was initially paid for by the Labour Party. I don't suggest that Bell is necessarily a sympathiser of the Labour Party, but what I do say is that this is a cynical election stunt in which he was induced to participate, the consequence of which has been that the electors of this constituency have been denied the choice available everywhere else in the country.

Christine, weirdly, had started to cup her hands to her ear, a gesture to get him to speak louder. It was entirely unnecessary because he could be clearly heard. It was almost as if she could not bear to watch her man suffer without doing something, without the therapy of action. He ignored her.

I think this was an anti-democratic turn of events, not least because since he's been here Mr Bell has shown himself conspicuously incapable of formulating any sensible policies to substitute the Liberal and Labour policies.

He's standing on an entirely bogus issue of sleaze or anti-corruption. As he purports to be the candidate of righteousness and truth and high standards in public life I find that somewhat surprising, because one of the things he said in the now famous Battle of Knutsford Heath was that he had not chosen the title of 'anti-corruption' for himself. That was a title he did not seek to use. Yet, lo and behold, what did we find at Macclesfield was that he was designated an 'Independent Anti-Corruption' candidate. So for a man who complains that politicians don't keep their word or tell the truth it wasn't a very auspicious beginning. And a rather insecure foundation upon which to build the house he seeks to inhabit for the next five years.

Mr Bell is wholly unfitted to form any opinions on the allegations which have been made against me. . . . Mr Bell has seen none of the material I have shown the inquiry, and has, in fact, rebuffed invitations from me to show him the relevant material so that he could form a view. Four times I have issued that invitation and four times I have been met by a wall of silence. So what he seeks to make the main issues in this election about me has no grounding. And what he is doing is to undermine one of the fundamental tenets that a man should be regarded as innocent until proven guilty. And we shall know in a very short time what the outcome of the Downey inquiry is because within a very few weeks of Parliament resuming because it is already complete and sitting in a safe – unfortunately for me. Because nobody would like more than me to have this report published. This election would have been much easier for me to fight if his conclusions had been made public before Parliament was prorogued. So I'm actually the principal victim in all this.

'. . . I'm actually the principal victim in all this . . .'. I sat there, open-mouthed. Was Hamilton a visionary in the Nietzschean sense? The philosopher once wrote: 'The visionary lies to himself, the liar only to others.'

He sat down to a polite death rattle of applause. Suspicion, doubt, disbelief hung in the air. The empty seats mocked him with their silence.

Hamilton invited questions. Of the twelve Tories there was a perfume of old ladies; a brace of Crusty Majors; a posh couple; the Hamiltons' muscle, Mr Heavy the Bouncer; and, odd man out, a spiky-haired chap with a thick silver chain around his neck, dressed in jeans, black T-shirt and leather jacket. He had a barrow boy's swagger and would have looked more at home in *EastEnders* than Mere Bowling Green hall.

Two questions were from loyal Tories. The less boring of them came from a ruddy-faced Crusty Major who appeared to have been on the Planet Zog for the past month: 'Chairman, I'm having a little difficulty with this meeting. I thought I was just coming to an ordinary meeting at Mere. Now, we seem to have press here, video recorders and things, can you tell me what's going on?'

Hamilton smoothly batted the marshmallow of a question over the boundary: 'I don't think that the media interest in this meeting has anything to do with my views on political issues at all. It would certainly be out of character for anything as serious to occupy the minds of so many members of the fourth estate.

But, clearly, what's happening is they're hoping I'll say something
embarrassing that can become the focus of a story.'

True, something embarrassing would have been nice.

The posh couple turned out not to be loyal Hamiltonians at all.
The woman did the talking. She had long, thick, brassy blonde
hair, a slightly husky voice, scarlet lipstick, plaited hairband,
plucked eyebrows, and several Krugerrands of jangling jewellery
dangling from her neck.

'Mr Hamilton, I am a lifelong Conservative and I am coming
today, I'm afraid, to beat you with a very big stick, and I feel really
guilty about it actually now because I hate kicking dogs when
they are down, I really do. I hate to kick a dog when he's down,
but I'm afraid I'm going to hit you with a big stick. . . .'

Sticks and dogs? Was she an animal liberationist? The RSPCA?
Was Hamilton cruel to animals? I found myself waking up and
writing the headline: 'HAMILTON THE KITTEN KILLER: HE DINED
ON DEAD PUSS AT THE RITZ.'

'It is a vital issue,' she continued, 'and it affects the whole
democracy of our country. The whole democracy of our country
is at stake right now. And we are talking about truth and we are
talking about justice and we're talking about Mr Major's belief in
truth and justice and trust and your belief in the belief that an
Englishman is innocent until proved guilty. . . .'

Stummer and I were on the edge of our seats. This was going
to be the big one, this was going to blow Hamilton out of the
water, this—

'Well, we are about to be proved guilty before we have had a
chance to prove our innocence. I am a victim of Lloyd's. . . .'

Pah! Her accent may have been posh, but her text was a
Marxist rant at the iniquities of capitalism. Her specific beef with
Hamilton was that she and her husband had lost their money
when he was Trade Minister, and responsible for the insurance
market. The posh couple were Lloyd's Names, people who had
blown their fortunes by playing and losing at the insurance market
casino.

That meant there were only ten loyal Tories, standing on a wall. . . .

Mrs Not-So-Wealthy-Now went on and on, angst in her pants: 'This is contradictory to the concept of justice you both promote so earnestly and therefore a violation of our human rights by the mere fact that by actually paying up, before we have a chance to sue – and we will never get the chance to sue, because the price of justice and the access to justice is much too high in this country. . . .'

If poor people are stoical when they lose their money down the dogs, I wondered, why should rich people be different when they lose their money down a dodgy dogtrack called Lloyd's of London?

She looked as though she was winding up: 'This is a complete travesty of justice and represents a deliberate attempt by the Conservative government to conceal the truth that has damaged so many people's lives. Lloyd's are guilty of fraud and extortion and this government is colluding with them—'

Mercifully the chairwoman of the meeting, a rosy-cheeked headmistressy type in a yellow blouse, was getting bored too: 'Would you please come to your point?'

Mrs Not-So-Wealthy-Now: 'Yes, I'm coming to a point. Mr Heseltine, when confronted with the letter, refused to acknowledge its existence publicly. When I persisted after the meeting, he brushed me aside and fled the scene. Why, why, why, I would like to know? If you are a party of democracy, you must stop defending fraudsters and stand up for the truth if you are to win my vote or thousands of other victims of Lloyd's vote in the future. You must do something now. We are about to be bankrupted.' She reinforced the point with a swing of her gold-braceleted arm.

Hamilton expressed his enormous sympathy, said he would look into it and calmed her down. When he had finished, she said: 'Thank you very much.' No wonder she had got ripped off.

The most surreal question came from the spiky-haired chap. 'I'm not a Conservative Party supporter. . . .'

And then there were nine Tories standing on the wall . . .

'I know you know what we think about the candidature of Ian Bell, erm Martin Bell, ha ha ha, I'll get the name right. We find the whole episode entirely undemocratic, we've written a leaflet about that. You've seen it. I believe you not unsurprisingly agree or sympathise with parts of that. It seems entirely obnoxious to us in the political and democratic process. . . .'

Hamilton leant forward, looking earnest, his hands together as if in prayer, nodding, blinking agreement as Spiky went on.

'I've been up and down the country, and the overwhelming mood I find is that people are genuinely disenchanted and I would suggest that this event in Tatton has happened on the back of that general disenchantment. In actual fact, because of the paucity of political debate generally, because of the paucity of what is taken to be democratic argument in this country currently, it is possible for the *Guardian* and Martin Bell and others to do that sort of thing. . . .'

Spiky closed and waited for the response of the sitting member.

Hoisting his fly zip up, Hamilton got to his feet and did little to conceal his delight at the strange turn of events: 'Well, one of the most surprising developments in this campaign was the endorsement I received from *Living Marxism*.'

You could have knocked Her Majesty's Press down with a brown envelope. Spiky turned out to be Alex Turner from *Living Marxism* magazine. No Tory he. The audience in Mere Bowling Green hall had been treated to *Living Marxism*'s take on Tatton.

Hamilton continued his speech of thanks: 'I have to admit I'm not a subscriber to *Living Marxism*, but I did enjoy reading that article. . . . It is true that in this general election campaign, debate on meaningful issues has virtually disappeared, and in this constituency to the most extreme degree. And that is regrettable. So it looks as if we are going to form an unbreakable popular front between the Conservative Party in Tatton and *Living*

Marxism, but, at least in this limited respect, I think it's a
respectable view to hold. And so I welcome the serious contribution which *Living Marxism* has rather surprisingly made to the
campaign in this constituency.'

Any more questions?

Sweeney: 'Can I ask a question about—'

Rosy Cheeks:'Sorry, I'm sorry, but I did say "One last
question." '

Hamilton: 'If it is a serious question about an issue then I will
respond. But if it's the sort of question that you've been trying to
ask me all week, I won't.'

Sweeney: 'In 1972, you took a free trip off the Italian Fascist
Party' – groans and cries of 'Boring, boring' – 'and you gave a
salute—'

Hamilton: 'I thought it was too much. This gentleman is from
the *Observer* newspaper and he's been trying to disrupt my
meetings all week—'

Sweeney: 'You said this: "Europe is sick, where there is chaos
there must be order, and where there is—'

Hamilton: 'This is a man without a sense of humour.'

Sweeney: '. . . there must be strength.'

Rosy Cheeks: 'Thank you, sir. A few moments ago I did say
that we would take only one question and we have taken that
question.'

Sweeney: 'So the question is—'

Rosy Cheeks: 'Thank you.'

Sweeney: 'Why did you take a freebie off the Italian Neo-
Fascist movement in 1972?'

Rosy Cheeks: 'Thank you. Thank you.'

Sweeney: 'And the answer is what?'

Rosy Cheeks: 'Thank you very much.'

Sweeney: 'What is the answer to my question?'

That was about as far as I got. General Jaruszelski nodded to Mr
Heavy the Bouncer who came over and stood an inch from my
face.

Mr Heavy the Bouncer: 'I'm asking you to leave. Could you
leave, please?'

Christine stared at me, snarling: 'He's twisted.'

I walked out, ordered a gin and tonic at the bar and took in the
scene: bowling trophies gathering dust,
a Crusty Major guzzling
alcohol in the
corner, a
barman
wiping a
glass dry
with a tea
towel. As
I did so,
an image
swam
into my
mind's
eye.

Of a severed head.

Twisted, eh? Oh, I guess so.

After Bell had been injured in Sarajevo in late August 1992, my courage was seeping away. I couldn't face the Big City, so instead I went with photographer Jez Coulson to Banja Luka, the largest city under the control of the Bosnian Serbs. At that time, the Serbs were dragging Muslims off the streets. They did not reappear. At night, Banja Luka rang with gunfire. I met the Swiss head of the Red Cross. He was a brave man who was staying in the city for as long as he could take it. He shook with fear. 'They are killing Muslims at night, in the day, all the time.'

Later, the Serbs executed the local head of the Red Cross in Banja Luka. And they blew up two mosques that had adorned the city since the late Middle Ages.

But to stay in Banja Luka, then, to visit the camps, one   had to get on the right side of a Bosnian Serb propaganda major.

And he had a photograph to show me. It was a grisly image of a severed head – a Serb, so he said – executed by Muslim fundamentalists. The severed head rested on a wooden box while the bearded fundamentalists looked on, grinning.

The photograph may indeed have been that of a Serb, though it could have been of a Russian, the image taken in Afghanistan years before. But the larger truth it purported to represent was a lie. The Bosnian Serbs were murdering Muslims wholesale. One photograph, of uncertain provenance, did not alter the balance of evidence: the terror of the refugees, the tears of a Muslim woman whose son had last been seen disappearing into a police station, the tremor of the hands of the Red Cross man.

A little while later, I saw the same photograph of the severed head adorning the wall of the Bosnian Serb press office in Pale, the black joke 'capital' of the black joke state of the Srpski Republic. The office belonged to Sonja Karadzic, the daughter of the psychopathic psychiatrist, and pure poison. The severed head had been reproduced on the front page of a magazine called *Living*.

Odd.

Living is a perfectly harmless supermarket mag, full of riveting stuff about knitting patterns, hints for picnics and how to improve your sex life. Apart from the knitting, I'm a fan. It doesn't normally run severed heads on its cover.

I took a closer look. Underneath *Living* was a large rectangle of black. Aha. The anti-Communist propaganda of the Bosnian Serb joke-state made its acolytes unhappy with the word 'Marxism'. So 'Marxism' had been blacked out from the full title of the magazine: *Living Marxism*.

Living Marxism and the Bosnian Serbs and Neil Hamilton, eh? Why not? The Trots on *Living Marxism* were sympathetic to Hamilton because they, too, were being 'persecuted' by the Evil Empire of the Guardian Newspaper Group. The explanation was simple: Bosnia, again. *Living Marxism* had taken the side of the Bosnian Serbs from the beginning of the war. *Living Marxism* didn't like the Evil Empire, in particular, and had run a long piece saying that the Bosnian Serb concentration camps weren't so bad. ITN, which had broadcast the first TV footage of the worst camp, Omarska, sued for libel. ITN's chief witness is Ed Vulliamy, of the *Guardian*, who was with the ITN team at Omarska. Therefore, *Living Marxism* and Hamilton were like Noddy and Big Ears. The Trots didn't quite endorse Hamilton – that was his flick of gloss paint – but they were sympathetic to his cause. It was so cynical it was almost funny.

Then, again, I had met a survivor from Omarska. He had loaded the dead on to flatbed lorries. They were driven away and dumped down a mineshaft. One day he had loaded his brother on to the lorry. Not so funny.

I gulped the gin and tonic and replayed Hamilton's line in my mind: 'I'm actually the principal victim in all this. . . .'

Hanging on to the bar of the Mere Bowling Green Club for grim death was a Crusty Major. He fished out something from inside his jacket. It was a photocopy of a Matt cartoon in the *Daily Telegraph*, depicting a TV reporter intoning into his microphone. The caption read: 'This is Bosnian TV, reporting from strife-torn Tatton.'

The Crusty Major barked a laugh, sipped his pint and said: 'I'm a lifelong Tory, but I'm not going to vote' – he motioned to the door of the hall from which I had been ejected – 'for that bugger.'

Outside, it seemed, the wood began to move.

Later, I caught up with Bell, Melissa and Bateson on the stump. 'Hey, Martin,' I said, 'I think you might win.'

'Oh, shit,' he said and everyone else in the car laughed.

The following Sunday my piece in the *Observer* came out, complete with my description of Christine wearing 'trousers of homicidal purple and a face no less hostile'. The ITN crew teased her about the phrase.

Christine, sporting a red and black striped boating blazer, string of pearls, blue rosette and her purple homicides, roared with laughter. She reached down to her trousers. 'They're not worthy

of such attention. Ha, ha, ha! They're jeans. I wear red all the time
and I don't have a lot of blue. So I had to go out and buy some
bright blue   outfits, and the idiot journalist
from the *Observer* couldn't
even tell that they were blue
and he called them purple,
which is absolutely indicative
of the *Observer*'s
level of getting the

facts wrong.
I've got
two pairs.
But they're
wonderful,
they're bright
blue, they're
Thatcher blue.
Anyone but an
idiot knows that.'
   I wandered into
shot as she stormed
off: 'It was a trick of

the light. The colour of the trousers. Everything else in my piece was true.'

But the really weird thing about Christine's response didn't hit home until I was in the pub. She had objected to the colour 'purple'. She had made no objection to the adjective 'homicidal'. You could write a book about that.

Up and down, down and up, the Tatton election roller-coaster lurched. For the Hamiltons, the meeting at the Mere Bowling Green hall must have been the absolute low point of the campaign. For them, things started to get better.

That week the *Wilmslow Express Advertiser* splashed: 'REBEL PEACE DEAL BOOST FOR HAMILTON'. Reporter Lawrence Matheson knocked out the story in deathless, breathless prose: 'Beleaguered Neil Hamilton has struck a shock last-minute peace deal with Tory rebels. In a surprise U-turn, outspoken critics, including Tatton Tories Derek Squirrel and Frank Keegan, say they will now back Hamilton after he promised to resign should the Downey Report find against him and the party whip be withdrawn.'

This was bad news for Bell; it looked like the Tory grassroots was burying its doubts and coming back to vote for Hamilton.

Squirrel Nutsford, then the current deputy mayor of Knutsford, and mayor-elect, defended his switch back to Hamilton to ITN: 'What this letter does, it gives the Conservative voter the opportunity to vote feeling that if there is a problem, it will be dealt with by Parliament. And I think that's really all we sought to do. Because basically we are Conservatives, we want the Conservative Party to be elected and we want a Conservative member for this area. I would hate to think that we had an independent candidate for the area, because that again would be outside our control, and we certainly don't want a sitting member who actually becomes an independent because it is a very rock-solid Conservative area. So, I think we did the right thing and I think actually it helps Neil Hamilton and will play an important role in the amount of votes he gets at the general election.'

Squirrel Nutsford squirreled on: 'What this has done has helped people focus back on the Conservative Party because they can vote for the Conservative Party on the basis of this letter, I believe.'

Frank Keegan, the other former Hamilton sceptic and Kojak look-alike, thought the sitting member would thank Squirrel Nutsford and him for the letter: 'This has done him an enormous favour. Three people stopped me in the village yesterday morning, people I knew were Conservatives but I don't really know their name, stopped me in the village and said, "Well done, we needed something to allow us to go out and vote on May 1. And this helps.'

Squirrel Nutsford cut in with a stout defence of the sitting member: 'Whatever your view of Neil Hamilton is, you've got to admit he's a tough politician. He's a good politician, he speaks well, and he's conducted himself with vigour throughout this whole difficult process, for example. And I think for that reason he will get people's support. Martin Bell, who I've no doubt is a very nice man, is not a politician and I think Neil has that advantage over him. I think Neil will get in. . . . And I think that the letter we have written, or the letter we've had in reply, will help that issue enormously.'

The Squirrel development caused misery and turmoil in the Back Room. It meant that all the clever calculations were off again. The Back Room had a fair idea that the Labour and Liberal vote was firming up for Bell. But that buttered no bazookas with Hamilton's 32,000 votes. If enough Tories stayed loyal to Hamilton, thanks to this new formula that he would quit if Godot found against him, then the election was lost.

More bad news for Bell came. Someone was posting copies of *Sleaze* by Leigh and Vulliamy through letterboxes in Knutsford, with a chain-letter note asking recipients to read it and pass it on. At £9.99 a copy this was quite an investment. General Jaruszelski faxed K1: a constituent 'says that a copy of the book *Sleaze* was delivered to her home together with your "Martin Bell Reports"

leaflet on Sunday morning. Does this mean that you are using
Sleaze as election literature as part of Martin Bell's campaign?'

Hamilton didn't bother to wait for the reply. He immediately
accused the Bell team of 'dirty tricks'. K1 wrote an urgent letter to
Longden, the returning officer:

'I want to make it as plain as I can that no copies of this book
have been so delivered by the Martin Bell campaign (and nor will
they), I have authorised no such expense (and nor will I) and that
we dissociate ourselves entirely from such actions.'

And mavericks – presumably Bell supporters – had spray-
painted Hamilton posters with £ signs, most spectacularly on the
big blue sign on the front of the Brick Red Lubyanka which
declared it to be the Tatton Conservative Constituency Association. Hamilton waxed nasty, ranting about serious legal action
against the Bell campaign if he was exonerated by Godot, as he
confidently predicted.

Hoggart records the reaction back in the old electricity
showroom: '"This is no laughing matter," Kate Jones warns
us. "These irregularities are truly dangerous as Hamilton could
use them to annul the election result." She looks on the verge of
tears.'

K1 had to deal with the legal Giant Squid. The pressures must
have been hideous.

The Clean Machine continued to scale new heights of political
organisation. Michael Solomon, father of Sophie, one of Bell's
Belles, was given campaign letters, asking people to use their
postal vote, to deliver to old people's homes. In the flurry of
activity he misunderstood, and thought they were letters thanking
people for signing the Bell petition. So he went to an old people's
home and gave the residents a rousing speech thanking them for
having given their support to Bell and his campaign to clean up
British politics.

A frail old lady raised her hand.

'Yes?' asked Solomon.

'You're very tall. Can I have a glass of water?'

Scene V: The streets of Tatton

Blonde bob: 'I mean he isn't a criminal. He's suggesting that he's a criminal.'

Studenty type: 'And not declaring it for income tax. He's admitted that.'

Blonde bob: 'If he hadn't declared it for income tax, the tax authorities would have been down on him.'

Studenty type: 'But he's protected as a Member of Parliament. He's abused the law, he's bent the law.'

Robust woman approaches the scene: 'If he was a policeman he would have had to resign. If he was a teacher he would have had to resign. The man's crooked, and anyone who votes for him must be crooked.'

A different part of the constituency.

Enter Hamilton in a cowdung-green V-neck.

Punter: 'You know I was in government myself, so I know. Yes. A trained service officer. I know there's quite a lot of, er . . .' – he sniffs, exaggeratedly – '. . . queer things go on in government. Which I could, er, but I, I—'

Christine: 'You could write a book about it.'

Punter: 'Exactly. I think we all could. We won't do. But yes, I hope that everything goes OK for you.'

Hamilton: 'Well, thank you. We know that I'm innocent.'

Punter: 'Well, you know yourself, don't you?'

Hamilton: 'And I wouldn't be putting myself through this trauma if it were otherwise. So, er, we have to fight for what we believe to be the just outcome.'

Chekhov once wrote: 'The most intolerable people are provincial celebrities.'

Hamilton had *Coronation Street*'s Ken Barlow.

Bell, to begin with, had no endorsements. Then they started to flow in. Early on, I had asked him who his favourite writers were: Shakespeare, G.K. Chesterton, his father, the East Anglian novelist Adrian Bell, and John Le Carré. Bizarrely, I know Le Carré a little and had got drunk with him in Hampstead only a few weeks before.

I sent a fax off to Cornwall and a hand-written one whizzed back the same day: 'Whether as an Englishman or as a journalist, Martin Bell stands for many of the qualities I most admire. I regard him as a perfect champion in the fight against Parliamentary rot and the corporate abuse of democracy' – signed John Le Carré.

Sir Alec Guinness sat down at the Connaught Hotel on 22 April and started to write a letter:

Dear Mr Bell
   Just a line to wish you good fortune on 1st May. . . .'

The phone rang. It was Doggart, trawling for celebrities. The man who played Le Carré's Smiley in *Tinker, Tailor, Soldier, Spy* and Obi Wan Kenobi in *Star Wars* returned to his letter:

I had just written the above sentence when the telephone rang with Mr Doggart's invitation to come to Knutsford. An extraordinary coincidence. Alas, I cannot come; I have to be in London for the next three days and then again next week until polling day. In any case I would be of no use to you, much as I would like to be. You have huge moral support from everyone I know. Would it be 'sleazy' of you to accept the enclosed small cheque? I only proffer it as your campaign expenses must be formidable. It will at least help out with a morning coffee or two. If you can't accept it give it to your favourite charity.
        Every good wish,
        sincerely,
        Alec Guinness

   P.S.   You are much too busy to acknowledge this so please don't bother.

The Force was with Bell.

Next came a badly typed letter from the man who, among other great things, wrote the screenplay of *Tinker, Tailor, Soldier, Spy*, Alan Bennett.

> Dear Mr Bell
>   I gather you are accessible to messages of support and encouragement and I am happy to send mine which is, I may say, wholly unsolicited. I fervently hope that you and the electors of Tatton will see off Mr Hamilton, who is not, as his wife insists, innocent until proved guilty but guilty out of his own mouth. Good luck and I'm sure you have the support of decent people everywhere, whatever their party.

Smiley's People were rooting for Bell. Slightly more untidy than Bennett's typing was a letter from an eight-year-old boy called Chris and his six-year-old sister, Rebecca. She wrote: 'I have a song for you. Bell Bell the wonderful Bell. Bell Bell kindest Bell.' She included a sequence of drawings featuring a non-grumpy, smiling Bell saying, uncharacteristically: 'I am glad I have won' and 'The Bad Man' in a prison, tears running down his face and a bubble from his mouth saying: 'I hate Bell.' She and her brother Chris enclosed a cheque for £1. Doggart records: 'Martin's eyes fill with tears and he insists on writing a letter to them straightaway.'

Then came the coppers. John Stalker, the former Deputy Chief Constable of Greater Manchester, whose inquiry into skulduggery amongst the security forces in Northern Ireland was stopped and who was forced to withdraw from duty in strange and sinister circumstances, turned up. Stalker had never met Bell before, but he dived in: 'Hello, I'm John Stalker and I'm supporting Martin Bell.' Posters went up on the wall in the old electricity showroom: 'The more I saw of Martin Bell, the more I realised he was an honest guy who will represent the people of Tatton well – John Stalker.'

What's more, he had good contacts.

One day Stalker organised for Bell, Melissa and Bell's Belles to go to Manchester United's ground. The 'girls' were late and Bell and Bateson went off without them. Melissa and the Belles raced up to Manchester, desperate to catch up. Antonia Harrison faxed me with her reminiscence. 'We girls,' she wrote, 'spent the journey applying make-up in the hope of meeting the first team, e.g. Giggs, Beckham and Cantona. No such luck. Only the second team!! We were greeted by Alex Ferguson saying: "Martin, I thought you'd brought the Spice Girls, what a bevy of beauties!" He told the second team to hold themselves back!!!' (I've kept her deployment of exclamation marks.)

Then came another cop, albeit one from another plane of reality. They were filmed together, working the streets of Tatton:

Stalker: 'Nice to see you.'

David Soul (for it is the star of *Starsky and Hutch* and the number one pop star of the seventies, swirling his hand around his face, speaking in an LA drawl): 'Yeah, nice to see you too.'

Stalker: 'I'm the real cop, I suppose. Or was until the last few years.'

Soul: 'Yeah, well I'm a real actor actually.'

Stalker: 'Yes, I know.' (Laughter.) 'It's a sort of juxtaposition of a lovely Cheshire town and—'

Soul: '. . . and a couple of has-been cops.'

Where had Bell got these people from? the Hamiltons must have wondered. In fact it was Bosnia all over again. Soul had watched Bell argue on television that, confronted with mass murder, it was not enough to report neutrally. By coincidence, Soul had been working on a plot line for a new TV series in which an American reporter had come to exactly Bell's position. The two men met, and became friends. Although a hugely well-known face, Soul is something of an old-fashioned American radical. He was there at the Battle of Wounded Knee, when the US government moved in against Native Americans protesting about their lack of rights. For Soul, the Battle of

Knutsford Heath had echoes of that engagement. For us hacks he was a godsend, great copy and, for an American, not too bad at coping with irony. Every time he appeared we used to hum the theme tune of *Hawaii Five-O* – the rival TV cop show to *Starsky and Hutch* – then say: 'Book him, Chang, murder one.' He took this in good part.

Soul was an immediate and amazing success on the campaign trail, particularly attracting women of a certain age – from the late twenties onwards. Bell, however, had a definite *cachet* with an older age group. One toothless grannie came up to him once and confided: 'You're the best thing since *Picture Post.*'

On the stump with Soul, Bell's patter had improved virtually beyond all recognition.

Bell: 'Hello, I'm Martin Bell and this is my friend David Soul. You may remember him: he was Hutch. . . .'

Soul (smiling at Tatton housewife who had just been getting the spuds on): 'Hi! I hope you'll be supporting my friend. . . .'

While I was travelling in a car with Jojo Moyes of the *Independent*, she foolishly confided in me that at the age of seven she had had her first crush – on David Soul. Jojo's favourite hit had been 'Don't Give Up on Us, Baby'.

As soon as entered the Bell, Soul and the gang Knutsford Drop-In Centre, a smallish,

crowded set of rooms on a council estate, I happened to mention Jojo's secret to Soul at the top of my voice.

'Hey, that's kind of cute,' said the ageing rock star with a heart of gold.

'Fuck off, Sweeney,' said Jojo.

That morning at the centre it was karaoke time for a group of mentally impaired teenagers and their carers. The latter were youngish or middle-aged ladies, looking after a group of people society does not smile at. Soul took up the microphone and serenaded Jojo and the carers. It seemed as if it was the first time a Hollywood star had serenaded anyone in the Knutsford Drop-In Centre. By the time he had finished, the joy-struck faces made it seem as if we were all in the Hollywood Bowl.

Later, in another council house area, Soul and I walked into a sweetshop. 'Hi,' I said, 'this is Hutch and I'm Starsky.'

'Give over,' said the lady behind the counter.

'Could I have a packet of Marlboro, please?' asked the honeyed tones.

'Oooooooh, he doesn't half talk like 'im.'

'It is him,' I said.

'Give over.'

'Show her your credit card, David.' He opened his wallet.

'Ooooooooooooooooh,' she said, orgasmic.

In the Lord Eldon that lunchtime, the door opens to whistles, cheers and camera flashes. In walks Christine in Purple Homicide suit with matching umbrella. Hamilton follows in bounder check, with hang-dog posture, arms dangling awkwardly by his sides. Christine chats to people about canvassing in the rain, the secret of long life and a millennium tapestry being made in Knutsford. Hamilton's conversation only flows when he has the opportunity to trot out a party political line.

Hamilton: 'Well, are we all having a nice long lunch?' He laughs, threading his fingers together for want of knowing what to do with his arms. 'It's a good job beer's a food, isn't it? And at 99p a pint, you can't afford not to.'

Christine: 'Who's going to join us in not having lunch? Or are you all not having lunch? All not having lunch. Right. Jolly good.'

Hamilton, approaching somebody at the bar, abruptly lifting his right arm from the elbow in soldier-like motion to shake his hand: 'Now, how are you? Lovely to see you.'

Christine, accosting Old Boy in shirt, tie and jacket: 'Sorry about this. It's the second time—'

Old Boy: 'There's no need to be sorry about it.'

Christine: 'It's the second time you've had your lunch invaded.'

Old Boy: 'I'm not worried about that. I'm worried about all these people who think they're going to set the world on fire.'

Christine: 'What, you mean the media?'

Old Boy: 'Oooh, yes.'

Christine: 'Well, as long as they're buying drinks and giving good business to the pub, that's what we need.'

Old Boy: 'No one's bought me a drink.'

Christine (winking): 'No one's bought you a drink. What would you like?' (Winking again.) 'You're on the Tetley's – on the cheap Tetley's – aren't you? No, no. What are you drinking?'

Old Boy: 'Don't worry about me.'

Christine (a third wink, as she walks to Hamilton's side at the bar): 'Don't worry.'

Old Boy (to himself since Christine has walked away): 'All I'm worried about. . . .'

Christine (turning to the rat pack): 'I'm certainly not going to say, "Would anyone like a drink?" with all you lot around.' (They laugh, miserably.)

Hamilton (waving them away): 'They're all on expenses anyway.'

Old Boy: 'It's like a bloody circus around here.'

Hamilton (standing): 'Yeah, it is.' (He turns to face a man standing by his side and raises his pint.) 'Hello, Basil.'

Old Boy (to the backs of the two men standing by his chair):

'By the way, Martin who?' (Hamilton gives a clearing-his-throat chuckle.)

Basil: 'I don't know.'

Hamilton: 'Doctor who.'

The sitting member turns back to face Basil. The two of them keep trying to have a private (of sorts) conversation, but Old Boy won't be kept out.

Old Boy: 'They've never had it so good.' (This four-decade-old slogan is ignored, so he tries another tack.) 'Anyway, jolly good luck.'

Hamilton (retrieving his sincerity, he turns back to the Old Boy and touches his shoulder): 'Thank you very much. That's terrific.'

Old Boy (now he's got him): 'I must buy you a drink if you win that, that—'

Hamilton: 'Well, why not? There we are. I'll take a credit note now.'

Old Boy: 'No, no. You win, that's the thing. You get canvassing—'

Hamilton: 'Well, I am doing my best.'

Old Boy: 'And tell these people what they're missing. The best country in the world to live in, this is.'

Hamilton: 'That's right, it is.'

Old Boy: 'It won't be when the Labour government gets in, I'll tell ya.'

Hamilton: 'What do you mean, *when*? There's no *when* about it at all. They're not going to win, are they?'

A snapper asks Hamilton to kneel down next to the Old Boy for a picture. Basil hovers in the background.

Hamilton (to photographers): 'This isn't going to be presented as me kneeling for votes, I hope, is it?'

Old Boy (wagging an arthritic finger at Hamilton): 'He doesn't need to duck for me.'

Hamilton: 'The usual media misrepresentation.'

Old Boy: 'Listen, I know when I'm being well done to and when I live in a nice country.'

Hamilton (desperately trying not to look crestfallen): 'That's right.'

Old Boy: 'I've travelled all over the world and they want to come here and they want to see what's happening in the Pacific Basin and all the different places.'

Hamilton: 'Yes, absolutely.'

Old Boy: 'Never mind cheap labour.'

Hamilton (taking a swig of his pint): 'Yah. You're quite right.'

Old Boy: 'They work a bloody sight harder than we do, anyway.'

Hamilton: 'That's the secret of success.'

Old Boy (indignantly): 'Of course it is.' (Reaching for his pint.) 'There's too many free-loaders round here, I'll tell you.'

Hamilton (nodding): 'Yeah, yeah, yeah.'

Basil walks away.

Old Boy: 'And sort the Welfare State out, that's the first thing they ought to do.'

Hamilton: 'Well, we've made a lot of changes in that direction.'

Old Boy: 'Of course you have.'

Hamilton: 'And a lot more to come, too.'

Old Boy: 'And what are you going to do about all these lies they're saying, about you're going to stop the state pension?'

Hamilton: 'Yes, isn't it scandalous?'

Old Boy: 'Can't they understand that they want the young people to top it up?'

Hamilton: 'Yes, of course.'

Old Boy: 'That they'll get their state pension, save a few bob, and then they'll get more than their state pension when they retire?'

Hamilton: 'Well, it is actually a guarantee—'

Old Boy (pointing to his head): 'Common sense.'

Hamilton: '. . . it's a guarantee that we'll be able to pay the bills, isn't it?'

Old Boy: 'Yes, but the average bloody person dunt understand it.'

Hamilton: 'No, no. But, but, because we know in this country that there are going to be huge bills to be paid and the working population is going to be falling, whereas the retired population will be rising—'

Old Boy (high-pitched indignation): 'You don't have to tell me.'

Hamilton: 'So you have to make provision now, don't you?'

Old Boy: 'Of course you do.'

Hamilton: 'The taxpayers of the future won't be able to—'

Old Boy: 'These young people, they put a bit away and, as long as they get the state pension and this Labour government doesn't tell lies—'

Hamilton: 'That's too much to hope for. That they're not going to tell lies.'

Old Boy: 'Well, let them tell as many lies as they want to. It just depends how many unintelligent people want to believe them. That's the idea, in't it?'

Hamilton: 'Yup, yup. But I think most people have rumbled them on that.'

Old Boy: 'Do you think so?'

Hamilton: 'Well, I think it's such a fantastic story that they've been telling, that nobody's going to believe it.'

Old Boy: 'So you think I'm all right with this bet, do you?'

Hamilton: 'Oh, yes, I think so, rather.'

Old Boy: 'Me bank manager's worrying me, he sent for me this morning.'

Hamilton: 'Ha, ha. We need better odds, though. If we're going to retire on the proceeds, we need better odds.'

Old Boy: 'You were three to one on a fortnight ago.'

Hamilton: 'The trouble is, trouble is I'm too popular.'

Old Boy: 'No, you were six to five on until somebody from somewhere, they crawled under a stone and put £2000 on Bell. And then all your odds came down.'

Hamilton: 'Do you think that was in some Egyptian currency? It might have been an Egyptian currency.'

The cameras flashed.

Old Boy: 'It's a circus. I've never seen anything like it in Tatton in all the years I've lived here.'

Hamilton: 'No, that's right, that's right. It's turned the election into a bit of a farce, hasn't it?'

Old Boy: 'Well, they don't think about Prestbury and Alderley Edge and all that.' (As Hamilton stands up) 'You go and sort it all out.'

Hamilton: 'I'm going to have to get up off my knees, otherwise I'm going to seize up.'

Old Boy: 'That's right, that's right.'

Hamilton: 'Anyway, thank you for your support.'

Old Boy: 'Support?'

Hamilton (as he walks away): 'It's much appreciated.'

Old Boy: 'No problem there, mate.'

Christine has been chatting to yokels, explaining that they've
come to 'publicly not eat lunch' and the money they save is going
to the Save the Children Fund.

She turns to the camera: 'Haven't you got enough yet?'

Sharratt of the BBC: 'Mrs Hamilton! We can't get enough.'

Christine (blinking, or is it fluttering her eyelashes): 'Flattery
will get you nowhere.' Sitting on a chair next to ITN's Jim Nally,
she turns to him: 'Did you hear on the news this morning that
Living Marxism has positively endorsed Neil?'

Nally: 'Yes, I heard all about that.'

Christine: 'Were you there when it happened?'

Nally: 'I was there, yes.'

Christine: 'With *Living Marxism* and Miss Moneypenny, how
could we possibly fail?'

Julia Heartless-Bastard (who calls from behind Christine): 'And
are you attracted to John Sweeney now you've seen his piece?
Have you read his piece in the *Observer*?'

Christine (turning round and looking up . . . longingly?): 'I
never, ever, ever, I've never read the *Observer*, I've never read it, I
haven't read it for the last few weeks. Hang on. Am I . . . ?' (she
puts her hand to her breasts) '. . . supposed to be attracted to
him?' (The sun streams through the glass in the door behind her,
creating a halo effect around her blonde head.)

Heartless-Bastard: 'No, no. John Sweeney said something like
"She fixed me with a glare and I think she's attracted to
me. . . ." '

What I actually wrote was: 'Deep down, I think she liked me.'

Christine twitches, but maintains her smile.

Heartless-Bastard: 'Something like that.'

Christine (white slides holding blonde hair off her face, smile
displaying a set of perfectly straight white teeth, pink lipstick and
matching earrings): 'Ha, ha, ha. Well, he could not be more
wrong. He's not my type. Ha, ha.' (Changing her tone, as she
scents the opportunity for revenge): 'He has no sense of humour.

You see, I like people with a sense of humour, wit and fun, which is why Neil's so splendid. John Sweeney is, er. . . . No way.'

But she licked her lips.

The battle raged on.

The Hamiltons went to woo the voters of Mobberley. Stummer gave me a lift in his hire car. He recalls what happened:

Sweeney: 'It's probably best if we aren't seen together.'

I dropped him off round the corner, parked and made for the Hamiltons. It was too late. Christine had already spotted the two of us in the car.

Christine: 'You're not with your friend, are you?'

Stummer (nervously): 'No, haven't seen him. . . . Er . . . do you think your vote here will hold up?'

Christine (in another world): 'He's a nut, obsessive, a shit.'

Stummer: 'But are you hoping voters . . . ?'

Christine: 'Mad! Mad! Mad!'

Deep down, I think she liked me.

Scene VI: Knutsford Civic Centre

On Monday, 28 April Hamilton holds another public meeting in the Tatton Room at the Civic Centre in Knutsford.

Enter Hamilton, Christine, Panda Bear and General Jaruszelski.

The room is packed. Panda Bear, chairing the meeting, says there 'are strict limits on numbers because of fire regulations'.

Hamilton: 'Well, ladies and gentlemen, I am delighted to see such a large turn-out at a public meeting in an election campaign. I have always in the past made it my practice to make myself accessible to anybody who wanted to meet me in the course of the election campaign.'

This was a dig at Bell, who held no public meetings, although there had been a sudden and unlikely concentration of calls at the office enquiring whether there were going to be any. The calls almost certainly came from the Hamilton camp. Bell preferred to spend his time stomping the streets.

Hamilton: 'Of course, it's impossible for any candidate to—'

General Jaruszelski (from the back of the hall): 'Sorry, Neil, can I interrupt you? We've got constituents outside who want to come into the meeting and people here who are not constituents. Could they identify themselves, please?' (Pause. No one moves.) 'I mean, for instance, Kate Edgley. Are you a constituent?'

Only hours earlier, General Jaruszelski and K2, Bell's press officer, had been squabbling on Radio Five over the question of dirty tricks in the Tatton campaign. The general knew the answer to his question before he asked it.

K2 (submissively): 'No.'

General Jaruszelski: 'You are keeping constituents out of the meeting.'

K2 makes her excuses and leaves.

Christine (pointing to the other side of the hall): 'There's this gentleman from the *Observer*.'

General Jaruszelski: 'Yes, Mr Sweeney from the *Observer*.'

Sweeney (standing up): 'I understand that this is a public meeting. I am a member of the public.'

Mr Heavy approaches me and mutters inaudibly.

Sweeney (far from inaudible): 'Why am I being asked to leave?' (All heads are turned towards this scene. The audience becomes restless and joins in: 'Why is he being asked to leave?', 'Don't leave', 'Sit down.')

Mr Heavy: 'You're looking foolish.'

Panda Bear: 'Perhaps the members of the press could stand at the back? This is a public meeting, not a press conference. After the meeting you will have an opportunity to meet Neil . . . afterwards.'

Sweeney: 'It's a perfectly happy compromise for me to stand at the back and I will be delighted to do so, but I do not wish to be asked to leave.'

Heartless-Bastard of the *Evening Standard*: 'Perhaps the members of the local Conservative Party who already know what Mr Hamilton will have to say . . . perhaps they could leave and let other members of the public stay?'

Sweeney: 'It's a fine compromise. I'm happy to stand at the back.'

Panda Bear: 'OK. Thank you very much.' (I pick up my bag and go to the back of the hall and lean against the wall. The audience is very unsettled, lots of noisy chatter. It is becoming obvious that not everyone in the hall is a natural Hamilton supporter. On the contrary. . . .)

Panda Bear (banging his mallet on the table): 'Come on, ladies and gentlemen, we don't want to be here all night. Don't want to waste your time or anybody else's time.'

There is lots more kerfuffle as people, conducted by Panda Bear waving his mallet around, slot into empty seats.

Panda Bear: 'Can we fill the seats here, because we mustn't block that exit? Will some of you kindly come and sit down? We want to get on with the meeting.' (Pause.) 'OK. Now.' (Two bangs of mallet.) 'Can I have your attention, please? OK. All right. Are you all sitting comfy? Good. Let's begin. OK. There's another one here' (waving hand at an empty seat).

Voice from the audience: 'Two here' (prompts more chatter).

Panda Bear: 'OK.' (Pause.) 'Neil, shall we try again?'

Hamilton (rising to his feet): 'Well, ladies and gentlemen, once again I am delighted to see so many of you, indeed even more of you, here than when I last got to my feet. And that's, I think, a healthy sign in an election campaign. I've made it my practice over many years to have an extensive programme of public meetings, because I think it is important that candidates should make themselves accessible to the maximum number of constituents. There are 63,000 constituents in the Tatton constituency. Of course it's impossible for any candidate to knock on their doors individually, or at least all of them, and hence I think it's an important part of the democratic process that candidates should have public meetings. And it's regrettable I think that I'm the only candidate apparently who does.

'So I'm delighted to see you here this evening and, indeed, to welcome members of the press. Indeed, some who hang on every word that falls from my lips because, like Mr Sweeney at the back of the hall, he turns up at all my meetings.' (This crack occasions a short burst of machine-gun laughter from Heartless-Bastard.) 'And I'm also delighted that the London *Evening Standard* is here this evening and to know that the burghers of our capital city are taking so much interest in what happens in the provinces.

'Well, my speeches in this campaign have introduced a novel element into the election because I talk about politics. And at least one of my opponents who is standing as a candidate in this election, Martin Bell, is of course making a virtue of his own inexperience in politics. At the beginning of this campaign, when he made an opening statement which was reported in the columns of the *Sun* newspaper, he said that he had no wish to become an MP. And he had no wish to make a political career. Well, my aim in this campaign is to make his wish come true. . . .'

He went on, blah, blah, blah.

The first question came from a Hamilton supporter, needling away at the role of the press in Tatton.

Hamilton: 'If the wells of public information are poisoned, then the whole of the democratic process itself is poisoned with it. . . . And so, although of course I am carrying on a personal fight to salvage my career and my reputation, I am also carrying on a fight to cleanse public life in this country of this cancer which is eating away at the very heart of democracy itself.'

This was powerful talk, reminiscent of Jonathan Aitken's 'simple sword of truth' speech when he started his not entirely successful libel action against the Evil Empire.

Sebastian Doggart (Bell camp and the man who solicited Obi Wan Kenobi): 'Mr Hamilton, I share your position that you're innocent until proven guilty, and I share your regret that the

Downey Report has not been published because we would all have been able to make a better decision if it had been. Now you stated that you've offered four times to Mr Bell access to the documents you presented to the Downey Commission, and particularly the financial information, your full tax returns. Would you not also be prepared to extend that invitation to the people of this constituency, perhaps through an independent audit, so that they can make up their minds through those full tax returns? Would you be prepared to make them available to the constituency in Tatton?'

Hamilton talks fluently about his evidence to Godot but he does not answer the question.

Sweeney (trying to interrupt): 'And so——?'

Hamilton (holding his hand up): 'Please don't interrupt me.'

Sweeney (persisting): 'And so——'

Hamilton: 'Please don't interrupt me.' (Jeering from audience.)

Panda Bear: 'You have time afterwards.'

Sweeney: 'I would very much like to ask a question.'

Hamilton: 'Mr Sweeney of the *Observer* newspaper has dogged all my meetings in the course of this campaign, and sought to fling questions from me at the back of the hall.' (Tory lady at the front shakes her head in irritation.) 'I prefer to give priority to my constituents.'

Sweeney (sounding unctuously reasonable): 'If it's possible, I would like to ask a question.'

Hamilton: 'Which does not include him.' (Tory lady nods and smiles smugly.) 'Particularly as it isn't necessary for him to actually witness events in order to write about them in disparaging terms.' (Tory lady, her neighbour and Christine at the back clap vigorously.) 'And although I have not read the insulting articles which he has written about my wife in his newspaper, I have been told about them and I am not disposed therefore to give him any credence or any room in this meeting.' (More clapping from Tory trio.)

Sweeney (shouting): 'Sir, this is a public meeting. I am a public citizen, I am entitled to ask questions.' (Tory two at the front mutters 'Shut up' and 'We don't want to hear'.)

Hamilton: 'Can I remind you that under the Representation of the People Act, it is an offence to disrupt a public meeting?'

Mr Heavy now moves and stands in front of me.

Sweeney (trying to peer round Mr Heavy): 'Hold on a second, I'm trying to listen to two people at once.' To the meeting: 'I would like to ask a question, if that is possible. I would like to ask one simple question and then I will be quiet.'

Panda Bear: 'You will have an opportunity later.'

Sweeney: 'Very good. But I would like to ask this question before the meeting is over.'

Panda Bear: 'There are more important people here and I'm going to give them the time first. You've had many opportunities as a member of the press to ask questions, so be quiet, please.'

Hamilton continues with his innocent-until-proved-guilty answer.

Sue Addison (Bell camp, supplier of two photocopiers, two telephones, kettles, mugs, heaters, extension leads, a computer and radio to the old electricity showroom): 'I am a constituent and I've lived here twelve years and I was wondering, in view of what you were saying of what a pain and a burden it has been, everything that's been said about you, and all the press here, all the media here, why don't you seem to have support from the Prime Minister and other major politicians here, representing you, saying what a decent chap you are and how they should vote for you? You seem to be standing by yourself, and they seem to have rather abandoned you.'

Hamilton claims that Major has voiced support for him publicly, in the House of Commons. He adds it's not unusual for senior politicians not to come to Tatton. It has never happened in the past.

Panda Bear tries to pick out a friendly-looking questioner. He avoids man with cropped hair, beard and lumberjack shirt who has his hand up, and points to smart chap in suit and tie.

Smart chap: 'I too am a constituent, I've lived here for eleven years now.' (Questioners now feel obliged to provide evidence of their suitability to ask questions.) 'And I understand that you'd only be prepared to resign if the whip were permanently taken away from you. Could you let me know the last time the whip was permanently taken away from a Tory MP?'

Hamilton replies that the man has fallen victim to Bell's propaganda, and that he has said he would resign if Godot finds against him.

Panda Bear scans the room like the radar at Manchester Airport, seeking a friendly questioner, before settling on a smart young man in the corner.

Mark Whittle (Bell camp): 'I've been a Knutsford resident for the last ten years. And I'm a first-time voter and I was wondering why is it that leading Tatton Conservatives are only prepared to support you if you are prepared to resign?'

Hamilton looks at Panda Bear. His voice says nothing but his face says: 'What the fuck is going on here?'

Panda Bear: 'Well, I'm a leading Conservative and I can tell you, I'm totally behind him.'

Whittle: 'What about Derek Squirrel?'

Panda Bear: 'What about Derek Squirrel?'

Hamilton replied that Squirrel Nutsford was incensed that his private letter had been published and said he had his support.

Panda Bear looked around for the next question.

Punter (not Bell camp but might as well have been): 'To be honest, I've learnt more about Mr Bell's policies than actually your own because I've not – I made a note – because I've not really heard anything about the health service, education, pensions, any matters affecting young people, middled-aged or old people.'

Hamilton puts his hand pensively to his mouth, fiddles with his pen, writes things down, blinks as the hall resounds to clapping.

Next question?

Anthony Crean (Bell camp lawyer): 'You are, if I may say so, a clearly eloquent and skilled debater . . .' Hamilton takes a gulp of water from his glass and holds it in his mouth in anticipation. '. . . and you've made a number of points against Martin Bell. If you thought, genuinely, that there was the remotest substance in any of those points, then could you explain to your constituents why it is that you refused to appear and debate those points with him at the Charter 88 meeting last Tuesday in this constituency? And nationally on the *Newsnight* programme with Mr Paxman? Are you able to explain why you refused to attend on either occasion?'

Hamilton: 'Well, I will ask why Mr Bell is not having any public meetings in the course of this election campaign.'

Crean: 'That isn't an answer to the question.'

Panda Bear: 'Give him a chance to answer the question. You've given the question. Wait for the answer.'

Hamilton: 'I'm delighted that there are so many Martin Bell campaign team members here this evening, because I'm very happy to answer the questions that they've been prompted to put. But it is not for me to organise Mr Bell's campaign and not for me to provide him with particular platforms. I am a candidate in this election. I am making myself available to all and sundry who want to come to these meetings as far as the room will permit them to get inside. And I am prepared to answer questions from you and others. It's very difficult to find Mr Bell in circumstances where questions can be addressed to him. And we must all fight election campaigns in our own way. Mr Bell could have come to my meeting here this evening, in the same way as I attended his first press conference on the Heath. And we could see what the comparison between the two is. And so . . .' (cries of 'Answer the question' from the floor) '. . . we could have had a debate of that kind.'

'Answer the question!'

'Answer the question!'

'Answer the question!'

Panda Bear bangs his mallet on the table: 'Listen, please.'

Hamilton: 'I have my own programme for this election and I've organised my campaign to suit the convenience of my campaign team, not the campaign of other candidates who are unwilling to place themselves at the disposal of the electorate in the way that I do. As for the television programme, then once again, it's not for me to justify the way in which I fight my campaign. But there were, as my agent informed me, legal considerations arising out of that.'

Panda Bear, mallet in hand, indicates that General Jaruszelski wants to make a point.

General Jaruszelski (from the back of the room): 'Yes. In case the gentleman still doesn't feel his question has been answered, I can advise him, as a qualified election agent – I think the only one in this campaign – that both the Charter 88 meeting and the debate on *Newsnight* would have been illegal under the Representation of the People Act.'

Panda Bear is poised, motionless, mouth open, clenching the mallet to his chest as if it were a bamboo shoot.

Crean: 'Could you explain why? Could you explain why? And if your point is that there were other candidates in this election who ought to have been included, could you indicate to these constituents that each of them signed a waiver so that they wouldn't have to be invited. Is that the case?'

General Jaruszelski: 'Which of the meetings are we talking about?'

Crean: '*Newsnight.*'

General Jaruszelski: '*Newsnight* told us that they were trying to get waivers. We never saw those waivers.'

Crean: 'Was that your point about the meeting being illegal?'

General Jaruszelski: 'Yes. If a meeting is held, or a broadcast is made, there are two separate issues. A broadcast . . . under the RPA, all candidates must be given the opportunity to take part in the broadcast, or they must sign a waiver in order to show that they don't wish to take part.'

Crean: 'And are you telling the constituents that the other

potential participants in that debate didn't sign a waiver? Is that your point?'

General Jaruszelski: 'We never saw any waivers from any other candidate.'

Crean: 'Are you telling your constituents that they didn't sign a waiver?'

General Jaruszelski: 'It's perfectly all right for other candidates in this constituency to break the law.'

Crean: 'That's not an answer to my question.'

General Jaruszelski: 'I'm trying to answer your question, if you'll let me finish. It's perfectly all right for other candidates in this constituency to break the law, Martin Bell, all the fringe candidates, because it doesn't matter to them what the result is. But it matters to us because we have to represent this constituency.'

Crean: 'How is that an answer?'

Gillian Cadwallader (Bell camp): 'Would you answer the question, please? I'm a Conservative voter.'

Panda Bear: 'OK. Finish with that question. Any more questions, please?'

Sweeney (hand shooting up from the back of the class): 'I have a question.'

The hall rings with peals of laughter.

Several questions later. . . .

Sweeney (Mr Heavy still standing next to and slightly in front of me): 'I would like to say first of all that I am a foreign correspondent and I am used to physical intimidation from secret policemen, like the person standing next to me. This last happened to me about a month ago when I was in Albania. . . .

'Mr Hamilton, on tax. First of all, one, do you believe that those who vote for tax should pay tax in full? And secondly, do you believe that the Special Compliance Unit of the Inland Revenue, which targets those people in public life who may have been cheating in their tax, should be closed down?'

Hamilton: 'Well, I've never heard any proposal that it should be closed down. I know nothing about the Special Compliance Unit but, er, no I don't think that it should be closed down. I certainly believe that taxpayers should pay all the tax which is duly owed from them under law, and I have acted in my own case on professional advice throughout. All my tax computations have been made by my accountant and I have signed the declarations accordingly.'

Crop-haired bloke in lumberjack shirt: 'On that I'd better be off.' He exits, smiling and waving to the laughing crowd.

Sweeney: 'He's not standing for Parliament, then, is he?'

Hamilton: 'Well, it's very difficult to follow that.'

Panda Bear: 'I didn't think we'd have such sensitive consciences here tonight.'

Hamilton: 'Of course one negotiates with the Inland Revenue and argues points of law with them, but I'm perfectly certain that in my own case I have no fears whatever in respect of any allegation that might be made against me of dishonesty or impropriety in respect of my tax returns, and any imputation of you, your newspaper or its scurrilous confederate I wholly reject.'

He sat down triumphantly. He never lost his cool, never cracked under pressure. Like him or loathe him – and I loathed him – he was a formidable enemy.

On the way out the Hamiltons were greeted by Lord Byro, refreshed from a couple of hours in the Cross Keys, carrying his election banner. It consisted of a large cardboard cut-out of an outsize Christine with Hamilton on her knee. He had got the idea from the Tories' national advert, showing an outsize Chancellor Kohl with Tony Blair on his knee.

Lord Byro's diary records what happened next:

His supporters start to emerge. An old woman screams at me 'You're the most despicable person I've ever met.'

'Why should the Tories have a monopoly on despicability?' I reply.

A cameraman laughs. The Tories give me more abuse.

'I take it I haven't got your vote, then,' I answer back.

Hamilton and his wife appear. I show him the banner. He won't look.

'Is it true, Mr Hamilton, you're being manipulated by your wife? You wanted to stand down but she wouldn't let you?'

'Of course it's not true,' replies Hamilton.

One of his sidekicks starts shoving me around, a man with bloodshot eyes and a face like a clapped out bulldog [this appears to be a description of Mr Heavy the Bouncer].

Christine's right eye is twitching heavily. 'It's no good winking at me – that won't get you anywhere.' She looks outraged.

Hamilton walks past me. 'I've left my raincoat in the hall,' he says.

I head for the pub.

Scene VII: Banquet, Great Budworth

The Hamilton camp had yet more exciting tricks up its sleeve.

'Bell admits Fayed link' was the headline on a Hamilton press release dated 29 April. It read in bold black type: 'At a meeting in Great Budworth last night, Martin Bell admitted that he is a great friend of Mr Michael Cole, Public Relations Officer to Mohammed Fayed, and that he is planning to have dinner after the campaign with them.'

And underneath, in smaller type, it continued: 'Commenting, Peter McDowell, Election Agent for Neil Hamilton, said: "This shows who is really behind the Martin Bell campaign. It is just an extension of the long-running campaign run by Fayed and the *Guardian* against the Conservative Government and against democratic choice in Tatton." '

The Hamiltons' Fayed–Bell smear came about thanks to a bit of a do at Great Budworth, a pretty little village in the constituency.

Bell supporters had arranged a drinks reception for sympathetic Tories at a private house there. Geen didn't like the idea. He decided to veto the arrangement, though Melissa could go and, an additional palliative, so could Soul. It was more important for Bell to canvass the streets of Lacey Green. But the message that Bell himself would not be attending had not percolated down to the broad masses of Great Budworth. They were still expecting the Man in the White Suit.

At 7p.m. Melissa and Peter Bracken, a capable and hard-working army officer who was a late addition to the team, drove to Great Budworth, leaving instructions at the old electricity showroom that Soul should follow without delay. Melissa was on edge. She had asked her father privately – that is, beyond earshot of Geen – to make every effort to attend the event, and Bell said he would. But there was no guarantee. The weather had deteriorated, too, and the chances were that Bell, tired and probably drenched, would knock campaigning on the head and go home early. The fact that his mobile phone was switched off added tease to uncertainty.

Melissa and Bracken walked into the converted school-house to a mingling of seventy-plus pinstripes and florals. The event was clearly grander and more serious than anyone at HQ had predicted. If nothing else these were Tatton Tattlers, opinion formers *par excellence* and the bedrock of the constituency's conservatism. Melissa's entrance caused a *frisson* of anticipation. But they were still expecting Bell. Hobday, the Tory councillor who had quit the party to nominate Bell, was there.

Soul turned up, but still no Bell. Melissa was now palpably worried and nervous. The impropriety of Bell's lateness was on the verge of causing offence. Hobday was briefed on the problem and agreed that things should start without Bell, if only to settle the shuffling and murmurs of disquiet that the delay was causing. Hobday would open by explaining his decision to endorse Bell, Soul would schmooze – though this wasn't the venue for a quick burst of 'Don't Give Up on Us, Baby' – and Bracken would give the latest canvass returns. If necessary, Melissa would mop up with a brief question-and-answer session.

The speeches went off and everything seemed to be going fine when someone among the assembled piped up and asked rhetorically if Bell's lateness – by now he was forty minutes late – was not little short of rude. The ripple of agreement was tangible, if restrained. Now the Bell campaign was facing a gathering the mood of which could only become more aggressive. The opportunity of engaging influential Tatton Tories was about to be squandered.

And then, on cue, in hobbled Bell. Dishevelled, damp yet dignified. He made his way to the front and began his address. He spoke for fifteen minutes. It was a bravura performance. The nascent aggression metamorphosed into a warm enthusiasm. Some of the grandees had not been overcome, but their hostility had been lessened.

But one of the Hamilton die-hards had picked up a scent that Bell had known Cole from their time together at the BBC. And now Cole was the press officer of Hamilton's great accuser, Al Fayed.

The Bell campaign whacked out an immediate rebuttal:

Any suggestion that the Martin Bell campaign is 'run' by Mohammed Al Fayed or the *Guardian* newspaper is entirely ludicrous. Martin Bell has never met or spoken to Al Fayed. He has responded to a public need. It is very well known that his campaign is staffed by volunteers and funded by small contributions from people in Tatton and all around the country, and none of these contributions exceeds £100. Peter McDowell's comments are those of a desperate man.

As the hours ticked by to polling day, the mood in both camps grew tense. Whatever happened, everyone though it was going to be close. A few votes here or there might tilt it either way. The Bell camp had enthusiasm, youth, the support of Obi Wan Kenobi. The Hamilton camp had 32,000 votes.

One morning I walked out of the old electricity showroom. Coming along Princess Street was a red Ferrari. The driver gunned his engine aggressively as he passed the Bell HQ. Across the road a postman glared at the Ferrari. Our eyes met; we scowled in unison. I walked across to him and asked whether he might be voting for Bell. 'I most certainly am,' he said, and drove off in his van.

Bracken hit the campaign with a touch of the Billy Grahams. He addressed the Bell canvassers in the run-up to the closing stages of the campaign: 'We've got forty-eight hours before polling day. Martin has a high presence in the constituency. We want to have a high presence as well in terms of posters in the windows in houses, in cars. So, if you see a house which doesn't have a sticker on, then feed through a Martin Bell poster, because we have to get that message across.'

The response on the stump was varied. Some people swore their allegiance to Bell, others simply swore at the Bell canvassers. Laura Gillan, the seventy-year-old Bell's Belle, recalled one touching encounter on the campaign trail. With another volunteer, Charles Tanner, she was sent to an upmarket newish private estate on the edge of Knutsford with three or four cars to every home. On the other side of the road lay an old farm. She recalls:

'We went through the gate, noting a couple of particularly large sheep ambling round the garden. The elderly owner appeared, closely followed by a man who emerged from a posh car. He was an enormous flabby man in a pin-striped suit, carrying a briefcase. He proceeded to berate all the national leaders, particularly Paddy Ashdown for his lack of support for the business community and his "ridiculous" attention to the less well off.

'At this point one of the sheep approached him, took a small run and butted him in the stomach, sending him flying, briefcase and all, to fall heavily in the mud. We made our excuses and left.'

That night a group of kids came into the old electricity showroom and took a load of 'Martin Bell For You' posters. Just before bedding down, Bateson got a bad feeling about those kids. He decided to have a prowl around Knutsford. In the square around the Brick Red Lubyanka, every space big enough was now adorned with a 'Martin Bell For You' poster. Hamilton's offices, the Rolls Royce car showroom, cars parked on the roads, lamp-posts – the entire area was plastered with around forty posters. Bateson phoned the police. When the copper arrived, he was chuckling. Even his patrol car had had one stuck on it. The two of them dismantled the display.

'It could have cost us a lot of votes,' said Bateson, later.

Wednesday, 30 April, was the day before polling day. With former Tory dissidents like Keegan and Squirrel Nutsford scampering back to Hamilton, it was vital for Bell to get out and meet the constituents. The vote was going to be close, very close. Bell had been doing well, but one could feel the confidence returning to the   Hamilton camp.

That morning   David Geen had
organised something
rather special for Bell.

They came from
Tajikistan – the
land of Genghis
Khan.

Stone faces in designer suits, they listened to an intense translator rephrase in Russian why Bell was standing for Tatton. The anti-corruption candidate stood outside the Alderley Edge Assembly Rooms talking, then being translated, to a group of 'parliamentarians' from what used to be known as Soviet Central Asia. They were on a fact-finding trip. Where better than to discover the reality of British democracy and how to get into the Mother of Parliaments than in Tatton?

Bell patiently explained why the fight in Tatton was different from what was going on in the rest of the country. His thoughts were translated into Russian.

The stone faces listened, mpassive.

'I'm not really a politician. . . .'

From the cut of their suits and the way they handled their bodies, they looked like central Asian Tories: Genghis Khan for Neil Hamilton.

'If the voters vote for Hamilton, then I shall shake him by the hand. . . .'

The interpreter droned on in Russian.

'BUT MARTIN,' I felt like screaming, 'THERE ARE NO FUCKING VOTES IN TAJIKISTAN!'

I hopped up and down, banged my watch with my finger, rolled my eyeballs around my head and hopped up and down some more.

Bell slowly came to a close.

Then everyone said thank you.

And shook his hand.

Then he nodded to them all, and limped into a charity do for the Guide Dogs for the Blind in the Assembly Hall.

And then limped out again.

Someone inside had objected to the idea of the charity being tainted by politics. The Clean Machine had not properly squared off the Guide Dogs for the Blind, so Bell, very politely, had been asked to leave.

Bell came out and stood in the sunshine, blinking.

The stones faces from Tajikistan twitched. Here was the candidate again.

NO! NO! NO!

Bell started talking to them again.

He was translated.

Had there been any point to it, I would have got down on to the ground and head-butted the tarmac. But there was no point. Bell is the soul of courtesy.

After an aeon of time, Bell said one last goodbye and what he called his contraption – it never quite became a machine – shuffled off into a rare council estate in Alderley Edge. It was around ten o'clock in the morning and everybody was either at work or shopping or running errands. Most people were not in.

That night, Hamilton had got his confidence back. He was on top form at his last public meeting of Tories, semolina pudding with a hint of arsenic.

I asked him: 'Sir, you've been an MP for fourteen years and you're sitting on a 22,000 majority. Do you heed Lord Acton's warning, "Power corrupts, absolute power corrupts absolutely"?'

'You could quote it accurately: "Power tends to corrupt and absolute power corrupts absolutely. . . ." '

He squashed me flat. Mr Heavy didn't have to get up from his seat. Afterwards, a Tory couple drilled him on cash for questions. He spent time working on them. I caught up with them in the car park. Were they convinced?

The woman looked diffident, the man damned the press. I told them how once in Bosnia Bell had saved my dignity, how he had prevented me from losing my courage in front of my colleagues. They didn't seem to care.

General Jaruszelski came over and paid me a compliment. 'I admire your tenacity, Mr Sweeney.'

I had a 100 per cent attendance record at all Hamilton meetings.

'Shall we have a bet on the result?' He agreed on a pound. We shook hands. Secretly, I rather liked Jaruszelski.

Sharratt, the BBC's fly-on-the-wall cameraman, asked Bell what was going through his mind. The conversation took place in the old electricity showroom.

Sharratt: 'The day before polling, Martin?'

Bell: 'Yeah. Alone on the burning deck. I should be canvassing, but there's nobody here. I guess they'll come. I think it's all right. I think it's two thousand either way. But either we win or we win. I mean we win on the vote and I become the first independent MP for sixty years, or we narrowly lose but with such a large vote that I think we can claim to have made a difference here. It would be easier for me to go back to private life, but I'd prefer to win.'

That night Soul, K2, Ben Fenton of the *Daily Telegraph*, Julia Heartless-Bastard and I got drunk in the dive bar of the Longview.

It was Hamilton's confidence at his last meeting which had been so disturbing. He was so sure of himself. He must know something, must have had calls telling him that Tatton's natural Tories were swinging back to him. All of us remembered the last election, when the groundswell of support for Kinnock disappeared into the sand and all the silent people voted Tory in droves. Bell had tried very hard, but it was always going to be an impossible job to get on top of Hamilton's 32,000 votes.

We drank in silence and thought it certain that Bell would lose and Jaruszelski would win the pound.

ACT FIVE

. . . lay on, Macduff;
And damn'd be him that first cries, '*Hold, enough!*'

Scene I: *A polling station at Nether Alderley*

The sun had got his hat on and had come out to shine on the great British electorate as they went to vote on May Day. In Nether Alderley, the church daffodils had read their Philip Larkin's 'Dockery and Son':

> Life is first boredom, then fear.
> Whether or not we use it, it goes,
> And leaves what something hidden from us chose,
> And age, and then the only end of age.

Past the dying stalks Hamilton and Christine marched to the sandstone polling station, just on the far side of Nether Alderley church, bracing the usual witchcraft of journalists. We monstered them a little, but as they approached the polling station our jabber thinned out and died. There is something holy about the vote; something that must not be mocked.

They reappeared and posed for the TV cameras and the snappers, their faces basking in the spring sunshine. This being Planet Tatton, of course, not everything was as it seemed. Although they had gone to the polling station, their journey had been a make-believe. Like President Marshal Mobuto Sese Seko Wa Za Banga of what was Zaire (official translation: 'The All Powerful Warrior Who Because of his Endurance and Inflexible Will to Win Will Go from Conquest to Conquest leaving Fire in his Wake') they had already exercised a postal vote, so they needn't have gone to the polling station. The only purpose of the visit was to impress the witches from the media. By polling day the transparency of their contempt for the 'reptiles' was absolute; a contempt which was returned in full measure.

As they left the polling station, they paused for questions beneath a flight-path of dead coypus.

'Who did you vote for?' I asked, to annoy them.

If eyes can sashay round eye-sockets, then Christine's did.

'Miss Moneypenny, of course! Of all the stupid questions in this campaign, that, Sweeney, was the most stupid!'

Lady Macbeth – sorry, Christine – could not resist me.

They started to march back home to a clatter-clatter of motor-drives.

'What are you doing today?' asked another hack.

'Giving an exclusive interview to Mr Sweeney of the *Observer*,' snapped Hamilton.

'What happens if you lose?'

He stopped, spun 180 degrees on his heel and spat out the reply: 'I will never become a reptile.' He paused: 'Wring your necks. . . .'

'Whose neck will you wring first?' I asked, suspecting the answer to the question.

But they were gone, padding down the drive of the Old Rectory.

As happy-clappy PR photocalls go, that one went as sweetly as a communication between North and South Korea.

They turned up again at the Tory supporter's house in Knutsford, their Rover limo pulling to a harsh stop. The Hamiltons darted into a large house, to the evident frustration of Peter Macdiarmid, a photographer from the *Independent*. He had wanted a decent snap of the Hamiltons, but they shot past him into the house, waited, then stepped smartly out, dived into their car and zoomed off, Christine at the wheel.

Macdiarmid and I had been together in the eastern Slavonian town of Osijek in the autumn of 1991, when the Serbs had blasted the place with a steady rain of mortars and tank-fire and the front line was the wild goat enclosure of the town zoo. Osijek was our Da Nang. A friend of ours, photographer Paul Jenks, had been murdered there a few months later. Jenks was irritatingly handsome – he looked like Terence Stamp – funny and perceptive. He would have loved Tatton.

We looked at each other, nodded and both dived into Macdiarmid's Land Rover. The Hamiltons' limo had speed, but Macdiarmid had clearly been on the Former Yugoslavia advanced driving course.

We gave chase.

What happened next was yet another surreal episode in the daily life of Planet Tatton, and my memory may be at fault as to the exact details.

At the first junction the limo shot across. Macdiarmid followed, nervelessly. They were 250 yards ahead; worse, the road was constricted to one lane because the street was being dug up to put down Porn TV cables. Christine had shot through and now a car was coming the other way. If we waited for it to pass, they would have lost us. The Land Rover hit the kerb at 40 mph, causing it to fly through the air like a half-ton bat. Not flying exactly, but, as Buzz Lightyear says in *Toy Story*, 'falling with style'. Inside the Land Rover cab, Macdiarmid's stereo, fitted to a curious metal arm above our heads, lurched crazily into my hat and socked my head. I used that pain.

He accelerated up the road, two wheels on the pavement, two wheels off. No pedestrians were in sight. Christine indicated left but zoomed sharp right. The Land Rover curved round on two wheels, still accelerating, the stereo system smashing into my hat and head again. It was *Starsky and Hutch, Hawaii Five-O* and *Return to Osijek* all rolled up together in real time, in real life.

For twenty minutes or so the Hamiltons zoomed around Knutsford, our Land Rover's diesel engine squealing to keep up. Christine drove like someone possessed, accelerating hard, standing on the brakes, doing a U-turn on a busy main road. . . .

She dived into the Knutsford council estate where Bell, his Belles, Melissa and all had been canvassing an hour or two before. The estate was littered with BELL posters.

At a junction, she stopped dead.

Silence.

As a method of getting the Tory vote out, what they were up to clearly left something to be desired.

It was worse than that, for them. She was driving like someone who had lost possession of her senses. Mad. Mad. Mad.

Then she indicated right, turned right and drove, sedately now, to the home of a Tory supporter. They scurried in. Macdiarmid raced out of the Land Rover, but – not his day – he had missed the shot again.

As they disappeared into the house, I felt a sudden pang. They were losing. The spell of last night's pessimism, the unbearable confidence of Hamilton at his last public meeting, had been broken. Our quarry, in the space of that pathetic car chase around Knutsford, had ceased to be a merciless enemy. They had become objects of pity.

General Jaruszelski arrived, a pained look on his face. I told him that we were just after a photograph, then we would go. After a short pause, they reappeared.

'Someone wants to take a photograph?' asked Hamilton.

Macdiarmid did his stuff and then we left them alone.

Scene II: A street in Wilmslow

I got a lift to Wilmslow, where the Bell Contraption was getting out the vote. On the way, we had to stop at a road census survey. A bloke in a safety hat and an emetic lime-green jacket asked us some drivel about the purpose of our journey, business, pleasure, blah, blah. When he had finished, I leaned over.

Sweeney: 'Have you voted?'

Bloke: 'Yeah.'

Sweeney: 'Who did you vote for?'

Bloke: 'I voted for Martin.'

Sweeney: 'Why?'

Bloke: 'Because I fancy his daughter.'

The Clean Machine had started the day by working the council estates in Knutsford. They knew that the key to the election was within the minds of the Tory voters, but it made sense, at least, to maximise Bell's natural supporters. The reception had been unbelievable.

'Oh, yes, we've voted for you, Martin.'

'Don't bother with us, love. We've voted for him.'

By the time I had caught up with them, the mood was euphoric. It felt like a victory parade. Nearly everyone was there – Bell, Melissa, Bateson, the Belles, Mark Whittle, Doggart, Soul. People were coming out on to their doorsteps, clapping, waving their hands, giving their thumbs up. Passersby in their cars would screech to a halt, get out and shake Bell by his hand.

Voter: 'Well, we've voted for Martin, yes.'

Soul: 'Yeah, great. We're just making sure that everybody has voted who can vote.'

Bell (unnecessarily): 'I'm Martin Bell.'

Voter: 'Yes, I know you are Martin. My son knows you very well, actually. He's spoken to you in Croatia when you were a war correspondent.'

Bell: 'Was he a soldier?'

Voter: 'He was in the Croatian army.'

Bell: 'Good heavens.'

We ended up in a pub and sat out in the garden. There was no urgency, no panic. Just beer and sandwiches and silly jokes. There is a line in David Hare's book on his true play about Fleet Street, *Pravda*, in which, before the curtain opens on the first night, a wave of laughter ripples through the audience. That was how it felt in the pub.

For Soul's benefit we mimed the *Hawaii Five-O* theme tune all over again, complete with the canoe-paddling action which opens the title sequence. A drunk who had been nasty to Soul the night before came up to him to apologise. He accepted the apology graciously.

Bell was sipping his beer on his own, under the shade of a willow. I joined him for a bit, gossiped, told him about the car chase. He grunted. I felt like Mr Toad confessing to Badger in *The Wind in the Willows*. But his face was only a little grumpy. He was, I think, in a good mood, though you can never quite tell.

That afternoon I returned to Knutsford to do some psephological studies. In the Longview, Basil and his staff had voted for Bell. 'I am a Tory, really,' said Basil, 'but I voted for Martin. He's a good man.' One of the barmen said: 'My father's on the committee of the golf club. They're all Tories, but they're all voting for Martin.' Two old ladies, dyed-in-the-wool Thatcherites, had told Sybil, just before they had left to go abroad, that they had used postal votes. Who for? 'For Bell, of course.'

That evening I popped into the Freemasons' for perhaps the last time. I got the customary abuse. But virtually everyone had voted for Bell, including the landlord.

With a lot of painstaking detective work, we identified one Hamilton voter: the landlady. And to think of all the money I had spent in that pub.

Bovver, the chap who had walked out of Hamilton's meeting at Knutsford Civic Centre when the subject of the Inland Revenue Special Compliance Unit had come up, was sitting around, twiddling his thumbs. I wanted to see how the Bell campaign was doing in the last few hours of polling. He offered to give me a lift in the Freemasons' van. We raced over to Barnton on the western extremity of the constituency, me bawling 'Freemasons for Bell' out of the window as we went. I am not sure how many votes Bell lost by this trick, but it must have been a few.

The van lurched to a stop. Barnton, a run-down, working-class neighbourhood, is not typical of Tatton. Many of its inhabitants had not voted in years, knowing that there was no point. The local economy is in bad shape, the ICI factory which used to provide employment all but a hulk, the pub opposite closed up. But the atmosphere on the streets that evening was amazing, like Bucharest on Christmas Day 1989.

We were witnessing an English revolution.

Bell posters in stark black and white were everywhere, rapping out their message like gunfire. Cars whizzed by, trailing white streamers, tooting for Bell. The man himself limped on, 'grimmer than before, but no less determined. . . .'

At the age of fifty-eight he had walked and walked and walked the constituency, coming up to the same people, again and again, shaking them by the hand. He had walked – despite the pain from his Sarajevo injury – so far that he had worn out the soles of his shoes. Earlier on polling day he had taken a breather, getting his shoes repaired. As the national election campaign had taken off, the media focus had drifted away from Tatton. The paralysing effect of the Representation of the People Act and media fickleness had meant that the broadcasters had switched off; print journalists, too, had become somewhat less interested in the battle. So the so-called 'media candidate' had, in the end, to fight a very old-fashioned campaign. That suited him down to the ground, because he is an old-fashioned man. After nomination day, he spent less and less time in the Back Room and more and more time pounding the streets:

'Hello, I'm Martin Bell.'

He worked so hard that he met people for a second, a third and sometimes a fourth time. Jon Kelly, the Labour Party candidate who stood down for Bell, recalls the time when he took him to visit Lindow Park caravan site, one of many locations where people could not remember having glimpsed the sitting member, in the last few days before polling day.

'The weather was appalling so we held an impromptu umbrella party. But, understandably, people were rather reluctant to come outside. We knocked on a few vans and I introduced Martin.

' "Yes, I know," said one caravan-dweller, clearly under-whelmed. "He met my granddaughter at Lacey Green School last week, my daughter in the Wilmslow Flyer, and I shook his hand in Grove Street on Saturday." '

There was something humble and humbling about how hard he had worked to win votes. The Bell campaign had many things going for it: idealism, conviction, clever people, beauti-ful people, mad people, a deeply flawed enemy with his loyal but pitiable wife, a sea-change in the mood of the nation. But these components were not enough, on their own, to smash through that mountain of 32,000 votes. He did it by wearing out his own shoe leather, by personal contact, through word of mouth.

By his side Bateson lolloped along, barrel-chested, scenting victory, making the pavements wince. Further down the street, Melissa, wooing votes. On the other side, dozens of Bell's Beautiful People, knocking on doors, smiling at sticky-faced tots or grandads in their Albert Tatlock slippers.

Outside the sweetshop stood Soul – 'Ooooh, look it's that bloke, you know, from *Startsky and Hutchinson*' – haranguing an oik in a shell–suit to vote for Bell. You got the feeling that if he had to jump over a car bonnet for Bell, he'd do it.

The oik was proving stubborn.

'On 8 October 1972,' I started, 'the *Sunday Telegraph* printed a story entitled "Tory trio meets fascists". One of the three. . . .'

The oik moved off, towards the polling station.

I went up to two ladies wheeling their kids along in pushchairs and smiled at them and their children. I like kids. I had forgotten I was wearing my Hamilton attack uniform – black suit, black hat, white T–shirt. The effect, people said, was to make me look terrifying and sinister. Soul grinned: 'Hey, it's Freddy Krueger for Neil Hamilton.' It was his revenge for all the *Hawaii Five-O* jokes.

One woman appeared at her door in a nightgown.

'Oooooh, I'd love to meet Martin Bell. Just let me go in and get me teeth.'

Bell came up to the door when she reappeared.

'Hello, I'm Martin Bell. I've been in your living room many times before.'

'Ooooh, Mr Bell. You can come in my living room whenever you like.'

'Thank you. Now have you voted yet?'

'I'm just on me way. But I will be voting for you. Oh, would you mind if I gave you a kiss?'

'Not at all,' said Bell graciously, and moved to kiss her on the cheek. But she headed straight for his lips and planted a lengthy smacker on his mouth. It was, recalled Doggart, 'the first time I have seen him flustered. As he walked away, he muttered: "Well, if that's not sexual harassment, I don't know what is." '

I wandered into the polling station in Barnton. Inside, the atmosphere was different, cathedral-quiet, the still dignity of democracy in action. People died for the right to vote. The people of Tatton, that day, made sure they did not do so in vain.

Scene III: Macclesfield Leisure Centre

The count was held in a vast hangar, the kind of place where bank managers play badminton. There were two counts going on that night. The Macclesfield count, where everyone expected Nicholas Winterton, the sitting Tory, to get back in though with a reduced majority, and the Tatton count, where everyone wondered what on earth was going to happen next.

We waited in the cold for the main players to arrive. Clarence Mitchell from the BBC had a radio ear-piece jammed into his head: his brain was wired directly into the BBC ring-main. We heard reports from the rest of the war – noises off – from him. Clarence and I had been to Mostar together in the spring of 1993, shortly before the graceful bridge across the river was blasted by Croat extremists. We share a taste for high drama.

Clarence heard something, motioned for silence.

'Mellor's gone.'

My MP. Goodbye, Mr Mellor.

Clarence gave the news from Putney, blow by blow: 'As Mellor's speaking, he's being heckled by Sir James Goldsmith. He's leading the chant: "Out, out, out". Mellor's speaking now: "I would like to say this to Sir James Goldsmith, who's got nothing to be smug about, and I would like to say, I would like to say, that fifteen hundred votes is a derisory total and we have shown tonight that the Referendum Party is dead in the water. And Sir James, you can get off back to Mexico knowing your attempt to buy the British political system has failed. . . ." '

We listened in awe. Putney was a safe-ish Tory seat. If it had gone, what might happen in Tatton? Clarence shushed us: 'Mellor's saying: "I think it's important to explain that all that rowdiness was not due to the major parties, it had nothing to do with the Labour party, nothing to do with the Liberals. It had to do with a small bunch of gun fanatics who stood against me because I led the fight on the Conservative benches to ban handguns. And also from the Referendum Party. I think one thing needs to be made absolutely clear. We lost fair and square tonight to the Labour Party, and I may regret that but I don't begrudge it. It's part of the inevitable part of politics. What I'm very delighted has happened is that Goldsmith has been stopped dead in his tracks. His fifteen hundred votes is a derisory vote. You know, I'm afraid that Putney said 'Up your hacienda, Jimmy.' And as far as he's concerned, he can't buy the British political process. . . ." '

Clarence stopped as the word spread: 'They're coming, they're coming.'

Enter Hamilton and Christine.

I shall never forget the colour of his face. It was the same shade as a full ashtray. She was tougher, her eyes blazing in the firefight of the cameras, the roar of questions.

A security man asked for her pass. 'I haven't got my pass, but everyone knows who I am.'

They disappeared through the media and entered the hall, prowling round the long tables, looking at the heaps of votes as they slowly piled up. The three witches – Press, TV and Radio – were banned from the counting floor and held in quarantine on a mezzanine, their noses pressed to the plexi-glass.

I looked up from the counting floor. I recognised Jojo from the *Indy*, who had had a crush on Soul when she was seven. In the broadcasting gallery was Clarence, burbling into a mike.

On the floor the Hamiltons had their whole army gathered together: their high command, General Jaruszelski, Panda Bear, Mr Heavy and Bouncer, and whole regiments of Blonde Group-ies, Blue Blazers and Pink Chins.

The Bell people were there too, though not the candidate. The moment Christine caught sight of me on the floor I could see her eyes blaze, her nostrils flare. She stormed – there is no other verb for it – over to Longden, the returning officer with a face like Mildred's George. She remonstrated with him, pointed to me. He stared at me.

Longden came over, accompanied by two toughs – or as tough as any local government officers in Macclesfield can get – and addressed me.

'I understand you are a journalist. As such, I must ask you to leave the counting floor.' He was polite, but firm.

I was no less polite and no less firm.

'Sir,' I said, 'I am on the floor in my capacity as counting agent for the Lord Byro Against Scallywag Tories Party. It is my right to be here under the Representation of the People Act.'

It was a truth delivered with due solemnity. Mildred's George and his muscle retreated in disorder. One should never wear one's best trousers, wrote Ibsen, to go out and battle for freedom and truth.

For the hell of it, in my official capacity as counting agent for the Lord Byro Against Scallywag Tories Party, I lodged a formal protest against Christine being allowed on the counting floor if she did not have a pass. My objection was not sustained, but it was noted. By her.

The votes piled up in boxes. Without counting a pile, you could see how things were going in the faces of the two camps. (This is the only tip I would ever give a young reporter: what counts is not what a person says, but what is written on his face. Nietzsche says it better: 'One may sometimes tell a lie, but the grimace with which one accompanies it tells the truth.')

Hamilton and Christine, shades of grey; General Jaruszelski even more Sphinx-like than usual; Mr Heavy the Bouncer refusing to meet my eye; Panda Bear, his last shoot long gone, studying the leisure centre for signs of fresh bamboo and finding it barren.

And in the faces of the Bell contraption: Ks 1 and 2, their eyes on fire; Kamm, in a too-white suit, looking like the dead private eye in *Randall and Hopkirk, Deceased*; the Belles, ogling the cameras; Crean; Doggart; Geen; Pullen; Soul; Whittle; all beaming.

And secret smiles on the faces of those Conservatives who

thought not so much of Hamilton: Cussons, still giggling at the memory of the candidates' debate, a lady with a cut-glass accent, a Crusty Major.

Yet still the tension was unbearable. For days I had suppressed the thought that Bell might win. Again and again I had considered the numbers – Hamilton's 32,000 votes which he had to smash through – and thought it impossible. But the evidence was overwhelming.

Whittle had counted the first 50 votes that came in. He noted in his diary: 'They were from Mobberley, a true blue area. They read 43 for Bell, 6 for Hamilton and 1 for other. At that moment I knew for sure that Martin had won.'

Kamm recalls: 'It was obvious from the moment that the boxes were opened that we had won. The high Tory areas were dividing 50–50, while the Labour areas were about 80–90 per cent for Martin. At a strategic moment Kate Jones and I had gone outside to phone Martin and Melissa. Kate, being superstitious, told them merely that we were ahead at this stage. I, being rational, told them that we had won. Nigel [Bateson], being practical, said he would rearrange the position of my head relative to my shoulders. But I was right.'

K2 recalled: 'It was, before Martin arrived, perfectly obvious what the outcome was going to be. In the early part of the evening, we collected sample results by looking over the work of the counting agents. The results were so favourable as to be worrying. Complacency was reined in. Le Breton ordered everyone not to give anything away to the press, who were, with the odd exception, not allowed on to the counting floor but were shut away in the bar. The broadcasting press got the nearest, peering down into the hall from the viewing gallery. As the night wore on, the result could not remain a secret. The piles of votes, labelled "Bell" and "Hamilton", built up on the tables of the counting floor for all the cameras to see. The Bell pile hinted landslide; the Hamilton pile hinted vasectomy.'

The vote from Labour and Liberal areas was phenomenal. In

Barnton, it had hit 90 per cent. The Clean Machine had actually fucking worked. No one could quite believe it.

Bill Le Breton called me over, ignoring his earlier instruction for no one to talk to the media, for one final piece of plotting. When it was finished, he looked left and right. We were not overheard.

'Eight thousand majority.'

'No.'

I didn't believe him. It could not be possible.

Enter Miss Moneypenny with Flashing Nipples.

They flashed on and off at the end of two-foot-long pendulous breasts, with the same beat as the Channel Light Vessel Automatic: 'rising more slowly'.

Surpassing – transforming even – her shock-shlock dress chic thus far, on the evening of the count the diplodocus-necked transvestite was attired in a velvet creation with a fur train at least the length of a parish church aisle. On top of her head she sported not a birdcage but a curious fan construction. Matching objects splayed out either side of her dress behind her back. She was shod – less tastefully, some might say – with shoes adorned with skulls. Her face was a mask of purple lipstick and eye shadow, false eyelashes, a row of glittering studs along her eyebrows, yellow foundation, black eyeliner around her jawline and down her manly cheekbones.

But, for once, the entry of Planet Tatton's most gorgeous creature was eclipsed by that of another, shyer, human being.

Enter Martin Bell.

When Bell walked on to the counting floor, something amazing happened. People – not just the Bell supporters – started to clap and cheer. Then there was a scraping of chairs and the counters (civil servants, bank clerks – the accountants of our democracy) stood up and gave him a standing ovation.

I was clapping hard when Heartless-Bastard, another counting agent for Lord Byro, came up and seized my hands: 'No, you shouldn't do that.' Her motive was caring – she thought I might get in trouble with the *Observer* for appearing so blatantly partisan.

Puh-lease.

I shook myself free and carried on clapping.

I am a reporter, but I am a citizen first.

Bell looked pained, slightly embarrassed, as he and Melissa, Bateson lolloping behind, walked through the cheers to the front of the hall.

As Michael Solomon was applauding Bell when he arrived, one of Hamilton's blue-rinsers turned to her friends: 'This is the kind of yob we've had to put up with.' Solomon is a chartered accountant. He has a fine, domed forehead. He wears spectacles. He plays the violin. He cleared his throat: 'If you'll excuse me, madam, that's the first time in my life I've been called a yob.'

The Macclesfield count was announced first. Winterton had got in again. He is a decent MP, with a strong streak of individualism. As he walked to the podium, he passed within a yard of Hamilton. Winterton looked through him as if he wasn't there.

Before the Tatton result was announced publicly, the Returning Officer gathered the candidates together in a huddle to tell them in private. Bell and Hamilton – as ever, their faithful women by their sides – were five feet away from one another, probably the closest they had been physically during the entire campaign since the Battle of Knutsford Heath.

Then the Returning Officer turned to Hamilton and said: 'We don't usually consider a recount under these circumstances.' This was, it struck the others, just in case Hamilton was about to ask for one.

Hamilton had aged in the course of the night. He looked like a man tortured beyond endurance – his formerly pink skin dishcloth-grey, his handsome face creased with worry, illness even. He stood hunched, smile-less. His hand was across his mouth; he chewed his forefinger. It was difficult not to feel sorry for him, not because of the outcome but just because of his diminished stature at that moment. Not to have felt moved, to have felt triumphant, as a reaction to his troubled expression would have been like an insult to one's common humanity. Bell expressed this himself several times after the election. He admitted he felt sorry for Hamilton. But, as he pointed out, it was, ultimately, a situation of his own making, born of his greed. Hamilton had been the master of his own undoing.

It was time for the candidates to shuffle on to the podium. Bell, Melissa, K1 – an immovable grin plastered to her face, and why not? – walked on to the stage to more thunderous applause. She was followed by the top-hatted Lord Byro who, helpfully, carried Miss Moneypenny's train, although that may just have been to stop himself and others tripping over it. Other candidates followed, less conspicuously. The Alien from the Natural Law Party would have shut up the sceptics had he floated to the podium. He did not.

Miss Moneypenny took – as she would – centre stage, directly behind the podium. Her head-dress stood twice as high off the ground as the heads of everyone else. Her nipples flashed off and on.

The returning officer: 'The number of votes recorded for each candidate at the election is as follows. Martin Bell . . .'

Scene IV: Knutsford Heath

Dead coypus levitated as three witches came to Knutsford Heath to watch the murder of a day-old politician called Martin Bell. The witches coiled and slithered. . . .

Enter Hamilton, Christine, Blonde Groupie.

Enter Bell, limping.

Christine: 'Do you accept that a man is innocent unless proved guilty?'

Bell: 'Yes, of course I do . . . but that's not an issue—'

Christine: 'So you accept that my husband is innocent.'

Bell: 'I think there's a lot—'

Christine: 'Do you accept that my husband is innocent?'

Bell: 'Look, I'm not going to be facing an ambush here. Let's just see, let's just see, let's just see what comes out . . . I, I don't know . . . I don't know. I'm standing here—'

Christine: '—because you're not prepared to wait for Gordon Downey?'

Bell: '. . . because a lot of local people have asked me to stand here. The impetus comes from local people. And let them just choose between us.'

Christine: 'I thought it came from a dinner party. In London.'

Hamilton: 'I . . . I . . . I would just like to say, then, that you are prepared to give me the benefit of the doubt on the allegations that have been made against me?'

Bell: 'Absolutely. Absolutely.'

Hamilton: 'Good.'

It was a deadly moment.

They lost the election there and then, for themselves, and for the Conservative Party across the nation. None of us realised that at the time. But the truth was that the Hamiltons were the losers, not the victors, of the Battle of Knutsford Heath. The most successful political ambush in recent history provided the defining moment of the 1997 election campaign, but not the way it had been planned. It rebounded in the faces of the ambushers; the people saw and felt and voted for the underdog, the good man who had been unfairly tricked. It was the full stop for eighteen years of one-party rule in Britain, and they typed it.

Scene V: Macclesfield Leisure Centre

The returning officer: 'The number of votes recorded for each candidate at the election is as follows. Martin Bell: twenty-nine thousand, three hundred. . . .'

Bell takes a modest bow, put his hands in his pockets and looks down at the floor, a controlled smile on his lips as the screams, claps, floor-stamping and table-thumping silence the returning officer. K1 shakes her fists above her head in victory, her face contorted with joy: the female publisher as prize fighter. Bell blinks. Hamilton's face is a puddle of ashes, Christine is speechless.

The returning officer continues: '. . . twenty-nine thousand, three hundred and fifty-four votes.'

'David Lawrence Bishop:' – Lord Byro – 'one hundred and sixteen votes'. To celebrate this achievement, Lord Byro spits shredded brown envelopes on to Miss Moneypenny's train. This gesture is missed by most onlookers, except a white-haired woman in a lilac jacket on the stage next to the Alien. His mother? She frowns at Lord Byro.

'Mostyn Neil Hamilton: eighteen thousand' – Hamilton pulls his tightly closed mouth back in an attempt to smile at the tempered applause – 'eighteen thousand, two hundred and seventy-seven votes.'

Hamilton is dead, then. Purple homicide.

'Sam Hill: two hundred and ninety-five; Michael Paul Kennedy:' – the Alien – 'one hundred and twenty-three; Simon Ludo Kinsey: one hundred and eighty-seven; John Richard Muir:' – Mr Eerily Normal – 'one hundred and twenty-six; Ralf Nicholas:' – the Alien Abductee – 'one hundred and thirteen; Burnel Penhaul, otherwise known as Miss Moneypenny Transformer:' – more cheers, she waves lavishly and dishes out kisses to the air, one mammary wobbles dangerously close to the lilac jacket, the other is grabbed and kissed by Lord Byro – 'one hundred and twenty-eight votes; Julian Matthew Price, seventy-three votes. I do hereby declare the said Martin Bell is duly elected a Member of Parliament for the Tatton constituency.'

The sports hall resounds with applause fit for a Michael Jordan slam dunk.

Bell limps to the podium and takes the microphone, his clipped syllables familiarly unextravagant. His speech was almost a parody of himself.

'Ladies and gentlemen, Mr Longden. I believe this is a proud moment for the people of Tatton, though I have to say a rather humbling one for me. I did not do this; you did it. It was not my victory, it was your victory. Though maybe it was the time when I received the endorsement of Sir Alec Guinness that I knew the Force was with us.'

A ripple of warm laughter envelops the hall.

'I believe you have lit a beacon which will shed light in some dark corners and illuminate the Mother of Parliaments itself. It's a strong signal to the rest of the country which will be heeded. My thanks go to the returning officer and his staff, to the police, of course to my own staff, Kate Jones, my publisher and agent; Melissa, my daughter and spin doctor; Nigel Bateson, my former cameraman and close friend; to Kate Edgley, Dave Geen and many others.

'What you have accomplished here has been to me some kind of political miracle. I shall be, and shall remain, independent. I shall take no party whip, I shall serve for one term only. I am deeply grateful to all of you, and may I just repeat, for the last time, a couple of lines from G.K. Chesterton that I used during the campaign.

Smile at us, pay us, pass us; but do not quite forget,
For we are the people of England, that
    never have spoken yet.

'You have spoken tonight, magnificently, and I thank you from the bottom of my heart.'

Hamilton edges towards the microphone. His clothes, hair and face are a symphony in sad grey.

He ignores the applause for Bell
and unfolds a piece of
paper. A loud 'boo'
sounds through
the applause.
Someone shouts,
'Well done,
Martin'.

Nothing in Hamilton's political life ill-becomes him like the leaving it. He makes his loser's speech from between the flashing purple synthetic nipples of Miss Moneypenny. It is, as the victim of the Dinsdale Brothers would say, a 'cruel but fair' way to go for someone who has always treated parliamentary democracy as a bit of a joke.

Hamilton has to grip the microphone with two hands because he is shaking so much.

'Mr Longden, ladies and gentlemen. First of all I would like to thank you, Mr Longden, for the exemplary way in which you customarily have carried out your functions this evening, and to the police and all those who have been responsible for maintaining the security of this building to enable this democratic process to be carried out to the full. And to all those who have been responsible for counting the votes and delivering them here this evening.

'I have been proud to represent the Tatton constituency for the last fourteen years and, of course, am devastated at the result here this evening. I know it will come as a great disappointment to all those who have worked so hard to attempt to elect me for the fourth time as the Member of Parliament for this constituency. Foremost amongst those, of course, are my wife, Christine, my chairman, Alan Barnes, my agent, Peter McDowell, and many others here this evening and outside the building.

'We've worked very hard. We have fought the decent and dignified campaign which' – jeers drown him out – 'which Mr Bell expressed a hope at the beginning that he would also fight.

'Alas, it seems that the results in the rest of the country have gone the way of the result in the Tatton constituency. In 1945, when there was the last Labour landslide, Mrs Churchill said to Mr Churchill, "It may be a blessing in disguise", to which he replied, "At the moment it seems pretty effectively disguised." That is the way it appears to me at the moment, but, although this is undoubtedly a setback of course for me personally, I believe also – I'm bound to say this – a setback for the Tatton constituency.'

Jeers, more jeers and heckling. K1 studies Hamilton, her eyes dull with contempt. Bell and Melissa take the family option and look down at the ground, sad at Hamilton's lack of dignity.

'This is not the end of the road. This is not the end of my political career.'

Bell looks up, incredulous, and around at K1. They exchange the tiniest of smiles.

'There's another truism which Winston Churchill also said was that politics is far more interesting than war, because in war you can be killed only once, but in politics many times. And so, we will be back as a party, I will be back as a man. I would like to thank you all, my supporters and constituents, for the loyalty which you have shown me during the last fourteen years, a loyalty which I have sought to repay and in spite of the grave slurs and false allegations to which I have been subjected' – renewed boos and jeers – 'not least during this election campaign.

'I know that I shall be vindicated when Sir Gordon Downey's report is published very shortly'– shouts of "Oh, come on" and "Leave it to the report" – 'and then the full confidence of my supporters in me will be fully repaid and justified. Thank you.'

The clapping is sparse and short, the boos heartfelt. Hamilton walks back to Christine, who, with her first smile of the evening, just to cheer him, firmly sinks her fingers into his shoulders and kisses each cheek. They leave the stage.

As they head towards their car, the media scrum is at its most malevolent. I hear a cry: 'Is John Sweeney there? John Sweeney?'

A fist punches through the melee. In it, a £1 coin, from General Jaruszelski. I admire his tenacity, too.

I run upstairs for a drink. As I do, I pass a television monitor and stop dead.

Jeremy Paxman: 'How can the party unite around the present policy on the single currency?'

Michael Portillo: 'Well, I'm now a man outside the House of Commons so I don't have to bother with questions like that.'

Paxman: 'I thought you just told the people at your declaration that you were going to work in any capacity you could to further the party.'

Portillo (smiling): 'Jeremy, I'm taking an evening off. . . .'

Paxman: 'Is the present policy the right policy?'

Portillo: 'Oh, Jeremy, do stop this nonsense.'

It is only then that what has happened in the rest of the country begins to sink in. Portillo has lost at Enfield–Southgate. Across the nation the Tories have been massacred. A wipe-out in Wales and Scotland. Seven Cabinet ministers out. How many seats have they lost thanks to Hamilton? Someone says fifty. Maybe more.

Bell is smuggled out of the back door of the count because of the police inspector's fears that the greens might get him.

Stummer gives me a lift to Bell's victory party in Knutsford. We drive past a Hamilton placard in a field. He skids to a halt, reverses, and I get out and tug it out of the earth and walk into the party with 'Vote Hamilton' on my shoulder.

'Pray silence for the Honourable Member for Tatton.'

Cheers.

Bell: 'Friends, colleagues, what can I say? I'm absolutely overwhelmed. We never had a machine, but we had a contraption.'

The crowd (singing): 'For he's a jolly good fellow, for he's a jolly good fellow, for he's a jolly good fellow. . . .'

Bell: 'All I'm going to say is that I'm going to work as hard as I can and do as well as I can and, is it ungracious to say "I think I've got an easy act to follow"?'

The crowd: 'No!'

Bell: 'I think I've got an easy act to follow.'

I go to bed. As my head hits the pillow, Hamilton's bleak pay-off from *Terminator* buzzes in my ear:

'I will be back.'

Oh, no, he won't.

Oh, yes, he will. . . .

EPILOGUE

Scene I: The set of Have I Got News for You,
London Television Centre

She saw me first. Our eyes met across a crowded studio. Two
strangers with so much to say, so little time. . . . Could it only
have been a week earlier that we had both stood at the Tatton
count, waiting for the returning officer? She winked at me, it
seemed longingly, though Lord Byro said she does that to
everybody.

Christine looked ravishing in a black blouse splattered with
guano-sized blobs of every hue: Hamilton was there too: a used-
vote salesman with a queasy grin, a vampire bat bow-tie snacking
off his carotid artery.

England's most talked about couple since Fred and Rose
walked on to the set of *Have I Got News for You* to an affectionate
hiss from the audience, like the sound of air being let out from a
lilo.

It was their third and strangest appearance together on the
nation's airwaves since the Man in the White Suit polled 29,354
votes to Neil's 18,277.

At the beginning of that first week after polling day, the
Macbeths of Knutsford Heath appeared on *Kilroy* and received

as gruelling a going-over as you get on daytime television: 'How
is unemployment for you?' . . . answer. . . . 'Everybody clap . . .
and, after the break, the car that runs on marmalade, Donny the
Donkey takes the orgasm pill and what you think about quantum
mechanics. . . .'

I hadn't watched it, but there was something that made
me uneasy at the prospect of the Hamilton making new fame
and fortune for themselves on the back of appearance fees.
The conventions of daytime television – 'Thank you for
coming, the cheque is in this envelope, the hospitality room
is this way, there is a car waiting to take you to the next
venue' – do not sit well with a forensic examination of the
life of a controversial public figure. There are too many
comfy chairs.

The Hamiltons were certainly pleading poverty. Their exit
from the House of Commons meant that they lost not just his
salary, but hers too: taken together, an MP and his secretary
would expect to earn more than £80,000 a year, plus perks like
first-class travel, nights in lush hotels, etc. Christine told Chris
Boffey of the *Sunday Telegraph* immediately after their fall that
they would have to sell the Old Rectory, though Hamilton later
wrote a letter to the *Daily Telegraph* denying it. A lifetime of
appearances on daytime television would never make good that
lost parliamentary income.

They popped up next getting lost inside Radio Four's *The
Moral Maze*.

The exchanges were surreal. Hamilton was asked: 'You don't
believe in truth as an absolute?'

Hamilton: 'I certainly think that truth is . . .' (painful hesita-
tion) '. . . nearly' (cough) 'an absolute . . . of course every human
being that is not a saint is likely to shave away at the edges of truth.
Nobody in this world can put his hand on his heart and say that he
has never told a lie, never dissembled. . . .'

As he disappeared into the Maze, pursued by panellist
Michael Mansfield, QC, one could almost hear Christine

throw a ball of string to her man. She entered the conversation in the same eirenic spirit as the men in grey crossed the Vistula in 1939:

Christine: 'Michael Mansfield is being incredibly sanctimonious when he accuses my husband of moral bankruptcy. . . .'

Mansfield (icily): 'Funnily enough, I haven't done that yet . . .'

But fellow panellist David Starkey prompted the best line in the show from the former sitting member of Tatton:

Hamilton: 'I would be against political prostitution', implying, somehow, that others at Westminster might be in favour.

To go on a daytime chatshow and *The Moral Maze* to defend your corner was almost admirable in its effrontery, but to appear on Britain's most savage satire show having been kicked out by the electorate was the act of a couple who might, some say, be in need of psychiatric counselling.

The *Have I Got News for You* team attacked from the word go: Angus Deayton wore a white suit, just like Martin Bell. Paul Merton sneered at his fellow team members: 'I'm not brimming with optimism', and Ian Hislop, a garden gnome on acid, never stopped.

On and on it went, Neil's attempts at making fun of himself pathetic, his punchlines bathetic.

'This is Neil Hamilton, England's number one hen-pecked husband. . . . It's much better telling political jokes than being one. . . .'

Worst of all was his crack at the expense of Neil Kinnock, John Prescott, Robin Cook and Peter Mandelson jiving to the beat at Labour's victory party at the South Bank: 'I didn't know they had Parkinson's. . . .' The groan from the audience at Hamilton mocking victims of that disease hung in the air like low cloud. The crack was not broadcast. It was just too distasteful.

By contrast, Christine was almost noble in her garrulous defence of her husband. She did not stop smiling, did not lose her sense of herself as someone who is, at all times, a 'good sport'. I sat on the back row of the studio audience, imagining

her as Joan of Arc, being burnt as a witch: 'Gosh, it's getting a
bit hot, eh?'

At the kill, the Hamiltons and Merton lost and Deayton handed
over two thick brown envelopes. Despite himself, despite being
filmed on national television, Hamilton could not stop himself
from opening the envelope and taking a peek.

Scene II: The El Djazair Hotel, Algiers

I was in Algeria – well, someone has to go there on holiday –
worrying. The exciting New Labour government, whose values I
believe in, seemed to have the same practical view on the sale of
British defence equipment to horrible regimes as the Old Tory
one. Leastways, a couple of weeks after the general election the
only other Brit on the plane to Algiers from Heathrow had been a
salesman, flogging flak jackets to the Algerian *pouvoir*. He went
first-class and had a proper drink; I flew economy and sipped
Coca Cola.

Britain trades arms with Algeria.

Readers: don't worry, this train of thought eventually gets to
the importance of the Battle of Knutsford Heath, albeit by way of
Tamanrasset and the Grand Erg Oriental.

Our defence manufacturers, trying to catch up with the French
and the Italians, flog the military regime lots of stuff.

Oh, no, they don't, says His Excellency Ahmed Benyamina,
the Algerian ambassador to Britain. He is on record as saying:
'Algeria does not import arms from Britain.' Nearly right.
According to Safeworld's latest report, the UK government
granted seventeen licences to export arms to Algeria in the first
six months of 1996. Licences were granted under categories
covering small arms, machine-guns, smooth-bore weapons,
bombs, torpedoes, rockets, missiles, mines, tanks and armoured
cars.

No arms there, then.

'When I use a word,' Humpty Dumpty said in a rather scornful tone, 'it means just what I choose it to mean – neither more nor less.' But then Humpty was just a fat egg who broke only himself, not the backs of other people.

The big money is in oil and gas. Our oil majors, in particular BP, are sucking Algeria's petroleum riches out from underneath the Sahara and spiriting them to Europe.

Human rights? Don't be silly. The regime uses blowtorches in the Château Neuf detention centre in downtown Algiers and elsewhere; I've met someone – let's call him Peter – who was blowtorched, but was so cruelly tortured that that was not the worst; sixty thousand people have been murdered since the military coup in 1992 – many of them killed by the forces of the government which the West backs; one hundred foreigners and fifty-eight journalists have been killed.

So I was sitting in my hotel room in Algiers, knowing all this horrible stuff, and worrying that I would be happier and richer and less tortured were I a royal reporter with a piece of Balmoral heather sticking out of my plus-fours. Because no one gives a damn, and no one cares.

I picked up the phone: it was K2. Bell had made his maiden speech in the House of Commons.

'It was about the evil of land mines. How they are no respecter of ceasefires. It was brilliant. He was on the news, everywhere.'

Hamilton had always said that, in the unlikely event of Bell being elected, he would make no impact in the House of Commons.

The Labour government announced in the course of the debate that they would indeed ban the manufacture of land mines.

I put down the phone and went for a beer and I raised my glass, in one of the worst places on earth, to Martin Bell, MP, and to the idea that decent people can make a difference and that, despite all the misery and selfishness in the world, there is such a thing as the power of good.

Scene III: The House of Commons

We had waited for Godot for so long we had almost given up. In the last few days before he was due to appear, we had the feeling that Hamilton was going to get away with it.

Again.

The report was due to be released at four o'clock on 3 July 1997. Those former parliamentarians judged in the report – including Hamilton – had the right to read it beforehand.

The fear was that Hamilton would do another Battle of Knutsford Heath – would emerge at five minutes after four and strike first, giving his pre-emptive gloss. By the time we had digested the report and found the right questions to ask, Hamilton would be miles ahead.

Bell was – absolutely typically – picking up an honorary degree at the University of East Anglia that day. BUT MARTIN! WHAT IF GODOT GOES AGAINST YOU?

The night before, I had questioned the wisdom of his disappearing off to the Fens when Hamilton could still cause damage. But Bell was determined to pick up his degree – his father had never had the opportunity to go to college – on this, the most important day of his new political career. I ripped my head off, realised there was no point, and stuck it back on again.

I phoned someone who might conceivably know what was in Godot's mind.

'What's in the report?'

'That's an improper question.'

'I know Neil Hamilton. He'll walk out of the door five minutes after it's published, protesting he's innocent, and by the time any of us have studied the fine detail he'll have gone.'

In my mind was an echo of Harold Wilson: by the time the truth has got his boots on, the lie has gone round half the world.

My interlocutor said: 'Let him' and put the phone down.

And I began to wonder.

At one minute past four Adam Boulton, political editor of Sky News, zoomed out of Westminster's Central Lobby, muttering to himself. We have a bond. We both do not admire Hamilton's friend, Kelvin Mackenzie.

Boulton, a plumpish figure, headed for the camera crew waiting on St Stephen's Green, leaving me puffing behind. Moving like a pastrycook on steroids, he skidded to a halt at his camera point, wired his brain into Sky Centre and started muttering.

Sky Centre was broadcasting an anchorman, intoning from a Press Association report about another dodgy Tory, one called Tim Smith. But he had confessed his guilt and had not stood at the general election – unlike Hamilton. Godot's verdict on Hamilton was the better story. Boulton jumped up and down, screaming into his mike: 'Come to me, come to me, come to me.'

And then they switched to St Stephen's Green and Boulton read out Godot's words to the nation and, because I was standing behind his cameraman, me:

'The evidence that Mr Hamilton received cash payments directly from Mr Al Fayed. . . .'

Scene IV: Mere Bowling Green hall

He had been fluent, precise, articulate.

'We shall know in a very short time what the outcome of the Downey inquiry is, within a very few weeks of Parliament resuming. It is already complete and sitting in a safe – unfortunately for me. Nobody would like more than me to have this report published. This election would have been much easier to fight if his conclusions had been made public before Parliament was prorogued. So I'm actually the principal victim in all this.'

Godot had not agreed.

'The evidence that Mr Hamilton received cash payments

directly from Mr Al Fayed in return for lobbying services is compelling; and I so conclude.'

Hamilton was not the principal victim; he was the principal villain.

Hamilton was dead, then. This time for good.

Scene V: Inside Bill Le Breton's head

Hamilton had been – once – dangerous. After Bell's failure at the Battle of Knutsford Heath the Labour and Liberal party machines had been scared that Hamilton was in danger of turning sleaze around and making it work for him. For the first time – after the election – one of the Back Room people opened up to me about what was really going through his mind.

Bill Le Breton, the Liberal wizz-kid, sent me this email:

I know you thought the campaign too dove-like. But the Battle of Knutsford Heath and the coverage of the first walkabout in the town made Martin incredibly vulnerable at the outset. A barrage of writs could so easily have confirmed the impression that Martin was a well-meaning but bumbling, error-prone, unreliable ex-BBC correspondent.

The white suit could convey either of two images – the clean-cut, dependable, amateur, trustworthy white knight or the eccentric, intruding, theatrical, Hampstead no-hoper. This is why, when at the London press launch of his campaign Martin was embarrassed by the revelation that Labour had paid for the hire of the room, and when at his first press conference in the constituency, held under the full glare of the TV cameras on the bearpit of the Heath, the Hamiltons forced him to relinquish the key campaigning issues, alarm bells sounded in Millbank Tower [Labour] and Cowley Street [Liberal] command and control centres. The prospect suddenly formed of Martin, out of his depth and floundering about, actually giving the Tories the chance to turn the story to their advantage, accusing opponents of party political manipulation and the media of bias – making Hamilton the victim and deflecting sleaze back on to politicians of all parties.

Back in Room Seven of the Longview Hotel, did Bell also glimpse the abyss? I think he did. I think, though, that it only made him fight harder. Forget the nonsense of him wanting to have the shortest political career in history. That was a line for the public and a self-defence mechanism. The first question I asked him in Room 7 on the Wednesday evening when I met him was: 'Do you want to win?'

He replied. 'I have to win.'

It was within hours of him being forced to resign from the BBC. He wanted to win. His relatives and friends, who knew his front-line career in journalism was ending and saw how appropriate was this unexpected opportunity to become an MP, wanted him to win. Most of the people of Tatton wanted to believe he could win. And Labour and the Liberal Democrats wanted him to win. Martin's total commitment to becoming Tatton's next MP was all I needed to know to confirm, within minutes of arriving in Knutsford, that we would win.

I'd cut my campaigning teeth in the Isle of Wight where in the February 1974 general election the Liberal Stephen Ross had come from third place to topple the 14,000 majority of a sleaze-mired Tory MP and win by 7000 votes – a 20 per cent swing. I knew how people reacted when the trust they have placed in an MP is shattered by the suspicion of corruption. I knew to what kind of person they would instinctively turn. It had taken Ross seven years to convince the people of the Isle of Wight that their MP had abused their trust. When Martin arrived, the people of Tatton already knew Hamilton could not be trusted. They were crying out for a champion.

Our task was to give the people of Tatton the confidence that they could trust Martin and that he could win. Certainly those were the two themes of the leaflets.

And then there is another myth: that of the Heath Robinson campaign. People in the constituency received five or six leaflets in the last eleven days leading up to 1 May. The barrage reached its crescendo on election day. That is up to the standards of a full-monty by-election assault.

The assessment I made very quickly in Knutsford (and Alan Olive came to similar conclusions) was that, as soon as the Representation of the People Act kicked in, the TV coverage would dry up. Martin could be made to see a great number of people, but even then he would only meet a fraction of the electorate. There was no escaping the mainline political campaign route of leaflets through doors. There would be help, but inexperienced help. At that stage it looked like the most certain way of delivering the message would have to be the GPO, via the free election communication that all candidates can have delivered to every house (if unaddressed) or to every elector addressed individually. Alan provided two sets of labels, one to the first-named on the electoral register at an address and a second addressed to all other names at an address (33,000 and 30,000 labels respectively).

Three or four other leaflets were delivered by hand. Whose hand? Volunteers, yes, but in the main (i.e. two-thirds) by local activists from the two political parties. At the start of the campaign it was not known how helpful these people would be. But, led by John Kelly and Roger Barlow, these people worked tirelessly.

Only someone involved in party political campaigning will know what this entailed. General elections are the highlight. They come once every four or five years. Four years planning, fund-raising, leafleting, casework and sacrifice lead up to the big event. For most people fighting a GE as a candidate for their party is a privilege and an honour. To do all the groundwork and then twenty-three days before the off to stand down and throw yourself into someone else's campaign is a very selfless act.

Hamilton, in contrast, put out one leaflet through the GPO and partially delivered another. As a Tory in a normally safe seat, and with most of his Association resenting his candidature, he had no means of conducting any kind of campaign. Once we realised this, we knew he was dead in the water. I think, therefore, that the campaign was won (or more accurately prevented from failing) in the few days after the Battle of Knutsford Heath.

At the weekend after the battle, there had been some pressure on Martin to return to London and sort out his laundry, both real and political. Le Breton continued:

To my great satisfaction and assurance Martin was determined to stay where he was and to fight his ground. I am sure that if anyone had got wind, in those early days, that Martin had left the constituency, even for a fresh white suit, he would have been doomed. The decision to tough it out, camped in a hotel room with a dwindling supply of laundry, was crucial, and was typical of the man. On every subsequent big decision that a candidate must make in an election, Martin showed similar steel, resolve and good judgement.

Kate Jones was a key recruitment. I warned him to expect a flurry of lawyers' letters and perhaps writs. We knew that scrupulous attention would need to be paid to money coming in and expenditure to safeguard his probity. It had to be someone whom he could trust implicitly, and whom Alan and I could rely on for a safe pair of hands. The political parties have people they depend on to take this role, who do it over and over again as the by-election circus travels the country. Kate within days, literally, was as good as any of them. If Pooh Bear had had a Kate rather than a Christopher Robin he would never have experienced the inside of a heffalump trap.

What were my thoughts as I travelled to Knutsford? I was going to be in on the campaign that might finally drive a stake

into the heart of a period of British history typified by greed,
selfishness and the I'm-all-right-Jack attitude let loose by
Thatcherism. I knew the campaign could wreak huge damage
on the Tories, and my mind was on the many friends I had
defending their seats or campaigning to be MPs for the first
time. I was confident from my experience in the Isle of Wight
that a 20,000 Tory majority was as stable as quicksand once an
MP loses the trust of the public, but I sensed, as I passed
Knutsford Heath, that those two impostors, triumph and
disaster, were close at hand.

And I wondered how the hell I'd find the Longview Hotel
and Martin Bell. I need not have worried on any account,
especially the last. As I drove beside the blasted heath I saw,
against a backdrop of satellite dishes and outside broadcasting
vans, a small figure in a white suit. His hand scratched a
furrowed brow. He walked alone, collecting his thoughts. It
looked for all the world as if he was gazing into an abyss.

He wasn't, of course.

Scene VI: Number Four Millbank, Westminster

He wore dark grey, she a stripey ice-cream seller's jacket. 'I'll have
a 99, please, Christine' – I was tempted by the joke, but decided
against it.

They walked into the make-up room at Sky's offices in
Westminster, passing within a few feet of me, around twenty
minutes past four that afternoon. His make-up on, they re-
emerged and were ushered into the studio.

I could see him through a peep-hole, smooth as ever,
arguing his case. A studio hand called me away from the
peep-hole and pointed to a television set. Hamilton burbled
on, discounting disgrace, to Sky and everyone else. Hamilton
stood Godot on his head, arguing that Godot had relied on the

uncorroborated testimony of former employees of Al Fayed. Godot was wrong.

That particular interview over, they left Sky and moved round Number Four Millbank – a tart's boudoir of over-heated air conditioning, gold-effect hand-rails and neo-oak panelling which houses Westminster's broadcasting studios – to be done by one of the many sections of the BBC.

His face was dirty grey, but his manner was unbending, controlled. It was not he who was in the wrong, but Sir Gordon; Hamilton continued to protest his absolute innocence.

Every now and then he popped out of one studio into another, from PM to Radio Five, giving 'the pack of animals' – Christine's loving phrase – a few seconds to challenge him. Cameras flashed, spools coiled inside Betacams, tape recorders faithfully noted our mocking:

'Mr Hamilton, Sir Gordon says you took cash. "And I so conclude." What's your response?'

'You're a liar!'

'Mr Hamilton! Mr Hamilton!'

The pack of animals – this member of it anyway – went through three distinct emotional phases. The first was joy that Bell had been vindicated and Hamilton had been caught.

The second emotion was rage, intensified by Hamilton's lack of remorse, the closed-downness of his body language, his insufferable arrogance. But this emotion slowly died.

The third emotion – and this is the difficult one to admit – was shame. After what seemed like hours of monstering Hamilton and Christine, I walked away: what we had been doing was demeaning, cruel, a blood sport.

The German dramatist Schiller said: 'Revenge is barren: its delight is murder, and its satiety, despair.'

The *Guardian* the next day enjoyed its moment, as was its right. Hamilton had had the law changed so that he could sue the *Guardian*. He had tried to destroy the newspaper's reputation. They had their revenge in black and white: 'A liar and a cheat, official.'

But Hamilton is not just a liar. His tragedy, the hole in the personality of this grotesquely flawed human being, is far greater than that of merely someone who tells lies. I remembered Nietzsche again: 'The visionary lies to himself; the liar only to others.'

Hamilton has a vision of himself that rises far above that of a self-aware liar. No ordinary liar could be capable of such sustained denial, such industrial-strength self-deception.

Hamilton the Visionary did cast a brilliant shadow over many people: the last Prime Minster, who did not sack him when he had the chance; the last but one Prime Minister, who cherished 'our bonny fighter'; the 18,277 voters who put their X next to his name; the Tatton Tories who voted at the Dixon Arms for him to be their candidate; the Hamiltons' familiars – none of them dull-witted – in the media.

Most of the hacks simply served Hamilton by knocking Bell, like the *Daily Telegraph*'s editor, Charles Moore – 'Journalists are at least as despicable as politicians' – and his deranged columnist, Paul Johnson: 'If they vote for Mr Bell, they will be voting for the *Sun* and the *News of the World*.'

Others stood up more directly for Hamilton, like the *Telegraph*'s Janet Daley, who, let us remember, argued that the case against him was 'media self-indulgence . . . the esoterica of newspaper gamesmanship'. And then there was Lynda Lee-Potter. The worst, perhaps, were those who did not address what Hamilton had done or what Bell stood for at all, but sniffed after Bell's private life. What did Nigel Dempster think of Godot's report? I doubt whether he gave it a moment's thought.

And the Third Murderer? *The Daily Mail*'s headline on Godot's verdict on Hamilton was 'THE LIAR WITH A LUST FOR MONEY'. The story was written by Paul Eastham.

Like an inverted pantomime, they had cheered King Rat and booed Dick Whittington. To those of us outside the shadow of the Hamiltons, such devotion was quite mad.

The evidence against Hamilton was overwhelming, corroborated, sustained, coherent, lethal. So how could Hamilton have continued with the fantasy that he would be vindicated? How could Hamilton have conned so many people? How could he have fooled so many: not all of them stupid, none of them bad, none of them mad?

In the days after Godot was published I hit the phone, talking to people who study what goes on inside the human mind. They have rules, which means that it is difficult for them to talk about particular people.

A psychologist was fascinated by Hamilton's personality and discussed him at great length, with the proviso that he remained anonymous. He said: 'He's a very, very insular man who plays everything close to his chest. He behaves like someone who has internal aggressive feelings towards everyone else. He cannot manage normal human relations. He's a very stiff and controlled man. Wherever he looks, he feels there are enemies against whom he has to defend himself. That's a fairly unstable personality. He walks around like a mini-Nietzschean Superman, taking on the entire world. I would suggest that Hamilton is paranoid, that he is deeply unhappy and that he hates himself.

'Then there is the role of his wife. He doesn't see himself as a mummy's boy. He's a big boy. But he has to turn to his wife. She is, in many ways, more of a maternal figure. She seems to adopt a maternal, protective role, rather than that of a lover. He looks like someone who has difficulty coming to terms with his own sexuality.'

The psychologist continued: 'What is so remarkable is that he has not gone into hiding or into shame, unlike Jonathan Aitken,' – another disgraced former Tory MP caught out by the *Guardian* – 'whose reaction to his disgrace has been somewhat more human. Hamilton has relished the opportunity to confront Gordon Downey, the journalists, anyone who speaks ill of him. He thrives on confrontation. It is as if he is orchestrating his own downfall. Somewhere within himself he must carry the

responsibility for what he has done. He is bringing himself down.
I would suggest that Hamilton is a desperately lonely man. He
seems to have self-destructive human relationships. He embraces
not his friends, but his enemies. Perhaps he hates himself. It seems
as if he prefers fear, rage and confrontation. Perhaps he feels inside
a hollow man.'

Ashley Grossman is Professor of Neuro-endocrinology at
Bart's Hospital in London. He saw a comparison between those
who build and reinforce a system of lies and mass suicide cults.
'All of us from time to time tell lies. If the lie is outside the
structure, then we can handle that. But if we construct a house
around that lie, with eaves and guttering and drainpipes, then we
are in trouble. There is a psychological theory that is called
cognitive dissonance, which implies that everything must be
reasonably congruent. So there comes a certain stage where you
start living in that house because there isn't too much else
outside. Then even the most reasonably balanced person will
find it quite difficult to distinguish between truth and non-truth.
They do literally live that lie and it becomes part of their self-
structure. It will be hard then to say that someone is deliberately
lying because, by that stage, the lie becomes self-reinforcing. The
power of the lie is enhanced if there is a *folie à deux*, if two people
are in on the lie together. At its most extreme, the lie can lead to a
mass suicide, like the Heaven's Gate suicides.'

He was referring to the mass suicide in Santa Fe of thirty-nine
members of a cult who, covered in triangular purple shrouds,
took phenobarbitol and alcohol, then pulled plastic bags over
their heads, believing that their souls would be collected by a
UFO hiding behind the Hale-Bopp comet.

Professor Grossman did not say that the Tatton Conservative
Constituency Association went through a similar mental process
to that of the Heaven's Gate cult, which is a pity because it would
have been a great story: 'MASS SUICIDE AT THE DIXON ARMS:
TORIES IN DEATH PACT' would have been a headline to remember.
Had the Tatton Tories known that Hamilton had not even been a

member of the Conservative Party, as he disclosed after the election, then, well. . . .

The Professor went on: 'If you take the case of the suicide cult, it may be that they were all stark raving mad. But it is much more likely that they were just vulnerable individuals, who had built up this self-reinforcing structure that they could no longer see outside. Within the structure it was congruent, it made sense, they understood it, everybody said the same thing. It was the rest of the world that was living the lie. In the same way individuals, especially when there are other people around them, can build themselves into a structure so that it becomes difficult, impossible even, for them to see what is real and what is non-real.'

Dr Tony Cleare is a psychiatrist at King's College School of Medicine. He speculated generally about the power of denial: 'Freud hypothesised that denial was the way in which the consciousness protected itself from horrible truths by keeping them in the unconscious. That's different from lying. A deliberate lie is conscious.'

I raised with him the case of Robert Maxwell, a man similar, in some ways, to Hamilton. A merchant banker once said of Maxwell: 'I've shot that man between the eyes seventeen times before breakfast and he still keeps coming at me.'

Dr Cleare continued: 'If you deny reality to such extreme lengths, you can become very depressed or very violent. It's possible that Maxwell may have committed suicide because he couldn't face external reality.

'People are surprisingly good at realising when people are lying to them: you can tell from body language, the pitch of a voice, verbal clues, that what is said doesn't make sense. We're not bad at detecting when someone tell lies, though people sometimes find it difficult to express their reasoning.'

So that's why Bell got so many votes.

Paul Williams is a psycho-analyst with the British Psycho-Analytical Society. He stressed that he has never met Hamilton and could only speak generally about the kind of behaviour presented by individuals like him. 'From appearances, he seems to be a loner. What is most striking about his behaviour is his seeming appetite for confrontation. His history of destructive attacks, from the Battle of Knutsford Heath to his attack on Sir Gordon Downey, might suggest that he finds it difficult to escape from tension inside himself. It is possible that there could be a relationship between his apparent capacity for attacking others and what would seem to be a self-destructive streak within him.'

Hamilton was a villain, but also a victim too.

He is a hard man to pity. That was why we hacks monstered him so. Learning this   psychological insight, it made me   question my own motives.   Nothing justifies cruelty.   Immediately after Godot, Panda   Bear resigned as chairman of the   Tatton Tories. He said: 'I feel desperately   sorry for Neil and Christine.'

He had been wrong to support Hamilton when he was in power; and we had been right to oppose Hamilton then. But, after the fall, Panda Bear's statement was a more human response than our monstering of him at Number Four Millbank; and a wiser one, too.

But none of this quite explains how Hamilton came to be so convincing, how he came to win the admiration of one Prime Minister and the tacit support of another. Maybe we will never understand that.

Clever, forceful, self-serving, Hamilton symbolised the high noon of Thatcherism. He was elected at the time of Mrs Thatcher's great victory following the Falklands War. To him, then, and his friends like Kelvin Mackenzie, at that time the master of the *Sun*, they could do no wrong. There was no such thing as wrong; they only had to be themselves and enjoy power.

Hamilton became corrupted, utterly.

Enter Democracy.

SELECT BIBLIOGRAPHY

Absalom, R., *A strange alliance. Aspects of escape and survival in Italy 1943–1945* (Florence, 1991)

Auden, W.H., *Selected Poems* (London, 1938)

Baudelaire, Charles, *Selected Poems*, trans. Joanna Richardson (Harmonsworth, 1975)

Beckett, S., *Waiting for Godot* (London, 1955)

Bell, M., *In Harm's Way: Reflections of a War Zone Thug* (London, 1995)

La Difesa della Razza (Rome, 1938)

Dixon, N., *On the Psychology of Military Incompetence* (London, 1976)

Edgley, R., *Reason in Theory and Practice* (London, 1969)

Freud, S., 'Uber Psychoanalyse', (Vienna, 1910). English translation: 'The Origin and Development of Psycho-Analysis' (*American Journal of Psychology*, trans. H.W. Chase)

Leigh, D. and Vulliamy, E., *Sleaze: The Corruption of Parliament*, (London, 1997)

Lichtenberg, G.C., *The Lichtenberg Reader*, trans. Franz Mautner and Henry Hatfield (London, 1959)

Mack Smith, D., 'Anti-British propaganda in fascist Italy', in *Inghilterra e Italia nel '900'* (Florence, 1973)

Nietzsche, F., *A Nietzsche Reader*, trans. R.J. Hollingdale (London, 1977)

Twilight of the Idols, trans. R.J. Hollingdale (London, 1968)

Shakespeare, W., *Macbeth* (London, 1623)

Sweeney, J., *The Life and Evil Times of Nicolae Ceausescu* (London, 1991)

Trading with the Enemy: Britain's Arming of Iraq (London, 1993)

Taylor, S.J., *Stalin's Apologist* (Oxford, 1990)

Vaculik, L., *Edice Petlice* (Prague, 1973). English translation: *A Cup of Coffee with My Interrogator*, trans. George Theiner (London, 1987)

USEFUL ADDRESSES

Lord Byro's poetry is available from:

The Lord Byro Against Scallywag Tories Party
c/o Lord Byro
26 Falcon Grove
New Basford
Nottingham
NG7 7NB